Hallee Crockpotter

and the Chamber of Sacred Ingredients
A Cookbook (and Parody)

by

HALLEE "J.K." BRIDGEMAN
(JUST KIDDING)
A.K.A. "HALLEE THE HOMEMAKER"

Magical Slow Cooker Recipes All Spelled Out!

Parody Cookbook Series book 4

Published by

House of Bread Books™

COPYRIGHT NOTICE

Hallee Crockpotter and the Chamber of Sacred Ingredients by Hallee Bridgeman

Parody Cookbook Series book 4

Original cover art and graphics by Amanda Gail Smith (www.amandagailstudios.com).

PUBLISHED BY:

HOUSE OF BREAD BOOKS™

an imprint of: Olivia Kimbrell Press™*, P.O. Box 470, Fort Knox, KY 40121-0470. The *Olivia Kimbrell Press*™ colophon and open book logo are trademarks of Olivia Kimbrell Press™.

**Olivia Kimbrell Press™ is a publisher offering true to life, meaningful fiction from a Christian worldview intended to uplift the heart and engage the mind.*

Library Cataloging Data

Names: Bridgeman, Hallee (Hallee Bridgeman) 1972-

Title: Hallee Crockpotter; and the Chamber of Sacred Ingredients / Hallee Bridgeman

298 p. 6 in. × 9 in. (15.24 cm × 22.86 cm)

Description: House of Bread Books™ digital eBook edition | House of Bread Books™ Trade paperback edition | Kentucky: House of Bread Books™, 2017.

Summary: It doesn't take magic or a spell to make whole food/real food meals – even when you need to leave it and go! Hallee the Homemaker shares a cauldron full of recipes that will make the slow cooker work even better than if you have a Time Turner on hand!

Identifiers: ISBN-13: 978-1-68190-115-2 (trade) | 978-1-68190-116-9 (POD) | 978-1-68190-114-5 (ebk.) | ePCN: 2018901798

1. slow cooker 2. crockpot 3. whole foods cooking 4. biblical diet 5. real food recipes 6. feeding a family 7. easy economical recipes

---

for *Hallee Crockpotter*

"Traded my Nimbus 2000 for a 6 quart slow cooker!" —

—a homemaker in **ATLANTA JOURNAL**ed

"Transfigured my cooking like a magic wand!" —

—a guy in **WASHINGTON POST**ed on his blog

"Even Muggles can't muddle these recipes!" —

—someone in **NEW YORK** said a few **TIMES**

"This spell book, er, cookbook is a real Keeper!" —

—a reader in **OHIO DEMOCRAT**ically opined

"Fantastic Eats and Where to Find Them!" —

—a lady in **L.A POST**ed

Table of Contents

Foreword

By Hallee the Homemaker

Magic! Sorcery! Spells! Rituals! Wizards, warlocks, witches, necromancers, sorcerers, and sorceresses. From ancient fairy tales to the classical works of William Shakespeare, J. R. R. Tolkien, and C. S. Lewis all the way up to the modern works of J. K. Rowling, it seems that our culture has no lack of magical creatures, spells, and practitioners. There is no escaping the fact that both secular culture and modern Christendom alike are fascinated with that phenomenon commonly referred to as magic.

The topic of magic incites major controversy in and out of Christian circles. Some believe magic is a harmless fictitious convention used to spice up children's books and fairy tales; or a handy duex ex machina required for a speedy conclusion to a clear morality tale. To others, magic is an dark gateway that can lead to evil thoughts or even demon-worship and attempted satanic rituals. The debate can be quite polarizing.

Thou shall not suffer a witch to live. Exodus 22:18

There is a big difference between the witches spoken of in the Bible and the illusionists of today. The magicians in the Bible, by and large, were drug dealers who created powerful mind altering and often toxic potions that led to addiction and very often killed those who ingested them–just as often happens with illegal drugs today. Historians inform us that many were simply charlatans who fooled others into believing they had arcane knowledge of ancient secrets and could tell fortunes. They performed the equivalent of elaborate modern day "confidence" scams by, for example, clandestinely drugging (read: poisoning) their clientele or innocent children into having mysterious "illnesses" which they then "magically" cured–for a price. In the hostile wilderness where capital punishment was the norm, it is logically sound that crimes of this scale would merit the death penalty, is it not?

As Christians who believe in the veracity of the Bible, we should be the first to affirm that there are very real supernatural forces in the world and always have been. Both in fiction and in history, magic has existed since the dawn of the world, as seen in Ancient Mesopotamia, the Greek and Roman Empires, and woven throughout the pages of Scripture. From sources as diverse as the Bible, to classical centuries-old fairy tales, to the modern epic fantasy series' we know today, magic is in no short supply.

So what should we take away from all this? Is magic just harmless good fun? Or is there a demonic dominion that would deceive us into thinking so?

The continual exposure of the modern mind to the pervasive onslaught of secular television, movies, music, books, and video games requires Christians to use wisdom and discernment in choosing exactly what they allow their minds to consume. When it comes to magic, just like many camels we humans swallow to strain a gnat, I personally think the debate is often off-center and off-topic. Instead of debating the magical act itself, or the topic in general, or boycotting an entire industry, I think we should just answer this question – what is the intent?

That, I believe, is the basic yardstick by which we can measure any questionable thing. What is it's intent? If we arrive at the answer to that question, the intent question, then we instantly settle the entire debate. To determine the intent of magic, we can ask three simple questions and they are, what is the source, what sort of deed is occuring, and what is the result?

For example, when our Lord broke the few loaves and fishes and fed the thousands, the source of the "magic" was our Creator, the deed was to assuage hunger among a multitude, and the result was a demonstration of God's limitless power and understanding of our human condition. This was not an evil act. By contrast, when someone is cursed, or killed, or hurt, or injured, or impelled to perform an immoral act – and the result serves a sinful end – that is certainly an evil act.

Three of the most well-known magical series of the past hundred years were written by Christian authors. J.R.R. Tolkien, author of Lord of The Rings, C.S. Lewis, author of the Chronicles of Narnia, and J.K. Rowling, author of Harry Potter, to which this cookbook gives a very definite, though somewhat tongue in cheek, nod. All of these authors claim Christianity and all of them deliberately embrace magic and the use of Biblical allusion in their works. All three works are very powerful tales that vividly illustrate the conflict of good and evil, the inner tension that even good characters face in choosing to behave righteously, and the incredibly seductive power evil can offer. All have central characters that clearly allude to Jesus Christ and His sacrificial work on the cross. Personally, I cannot think this is a coincidence.

Personally, I see the magical tales, and for that matter any other epic stories of self-sacrifice for a greater good that depict starkly Biblical archetypes, as an opportunity for teachable moments. I see them as inroads in a very closed off and secular world that we, as Christians, could travel in order to break bread with tax collectors because, as cool and interesting as the character of Harry Potter is, I know someone much more fascinating. Likewise, as heroic as the wizard Gandalf the Gray is, I personally know a man who was much more heroic and sacrificed everything for love. What an opportunity to introduce someone to the real supernatural world in which we live!

Introduction

By Hallee the Homemaker

One of the most frequent dinnertime complaints moms have is lack of time. I totally get it. It's tough trying to get a balanced, nutritious meal on the dinner table when you only have a limited amount of time in which to make it. That is why whenever I need an easy-to-prepare meal I can be sure the whole family will love, I get out my crock pot. From prep to clean up, it is the biggest time saving appliance I own.

As book deadlines approach, my slow cooker definitely gets a workout. In fact, I own two slow cookers and use them both, sometimes at the same time. A slow cooker is a tool that should be in any well stocked kitchen.

Some of the recipes in this book allow you to toss ingredients in and come back hours later. Some require frequent monitoring and fussing. Some don't even take more than an hour or two until completion. Rest assured, every one of these recipes is wholesome, real food, that will help nourish your family even with the ease of preparation. (Well, maybe not the chocolate mud cake…)

Some time-saving tips:

Love your legumes.

One cup of dried beans usually equals about 2 cups of cooked beans, plus the liquid. I will cook 4 cups of dried beans at a time in my slow cooker, then freeze the 8 cups of cooked beans in quart-sized freezer bags. They do well in the freezer. (Actually, as I type this, I have 4 cups of dried black beans cooking in a slow cooker!)

Having the beans already prepared allows me to have fresh tasting beans that don't have that faint metallic taste I can nearly always detect in canned beans, and also gives me instant access to just about a can's worth of beans right out of my freezer.

Another time-saver:

If you have the ability to have a "prep day", you can pre-prepare several elements of a slow cooker meal, including some of the meat, and freeze them (meat separate from veggies) all together. When it's time to load up the slow cooker, you can just pull everything out of the freezer. Hardly any work at all.

It's nice to have a cooking surface away from the kitchen sometimes, and slow cookers provide that. If it's an element to a big holiday meal, throwing something into the slow cooker and plugging it in outside of the kitchen will allow you to continue to prepare a large meal without the slow cooker getting in your way.

How ever you use your slow cooker, and regardless of your reasons behind it, this cookbook is intended to help your slow cooker become one of your favorite appliances.

You Are What You Eat: INGREDIENTS

While the title and many themes in this book are meant to be fun and a parody, the recipes are absolutely real. I find no greater way to show my love to my friends and family than to provide amazing food created with good ingredients. There are three main principles I follow in cooking:

✓ Eat only substances God created for food. Avoid what is not designed for food.

✓ As much as possible, eat foods as they were created—before they were changed or converted into something humans think might be better.

✓ Avoid food addictions. Let no food or drink become your god.

In keeping with these three principles, nearly everything I cook I make from scratch. While this notion may sound odd to modern readers, cooking with fresh, whole, organically and locally grown food was common and "normal" until as recently as just 25 years ago.

I grind my own wheat to make flour. Every recipe in this book that calls for flour is made with fresh ground flour. I use either soft white wheat berries (for "quick" breads and pastries), or a combination of hard red and hard white wheat berries (for yeast breads). I also grind other grains like kamut wheat, quinua, rye, and corn for corn meal. The whole grain flour or meal that results is not the same as whole wheat flour found in the grocery stores. Store-bought whole wheat flour will not act the same, and store-bought processed "enriched" white flour is incredibly bad for human health. So, experiment with flours and see what works and what doesn't work for you. Make adjustments. It may be that you have to mix whole wheat and white flours to make some recipes work for you.

When purchasing supplies, look for "aluminum free". One of the reasons I use aluminum free is because I don't really want to be consuming the metal. But, another major reason to use it is because it will drastically improve the taste of your end product. Baking powder with aluminum creates a "tinny" taste that some palates pick up on right away.

Whenever I refer to butter, I am talking about actual butter from an actual cow, never substitutes. Butter should be unsalted, real butter. I do not cook with salted butter or any kind of margarine or any kind of "buttery spread".

I do my best to avoid genetically modified foods (GMOs). Topping the list of GMOs are corn, soy, and canola. This is why, when a recipe calls for corn or corn meal, I always recommend using organic ingredients, because in order to be labeled organic in the United States, it also cannot be GMO. I actually grind my own cornmeal from organic popcorn. If you have a grain mill, you can too.

I use extra virgin olive oil almost exclusively in my cooking. At time of print for this cookbook, organic canola oil is incredibly expensive. Generically labeled "vegetable oil" is almost always genetically modified (GMO) corn oil or processed and/or genetically modified soy oil or a combination of the two. Any kind of processed soy ⓘ, even from organic soy bean, is very toxic to men and boys ⓘ and not really recommended for girls and women either!

Probably the thing you'll notice most throughout this cookbook is that I never cook with pork. My family follows a Levitical Diet ⓘ—in that we don't eat foods that are specifically prohibited by the Bible. This means pork and bottom feeders like catfish and all shellfish are out.

The truth is we don't miss pork. Turkey breakfast sausage is a favorite in our home as is beef bacon. Turkey ham is a substitute that works in moderation for ham. And beef bacon is amazing and wonderfully versatile—as well as better tasting than any pork bacon any of us ever tasted.

ⓘ For more information on the world wide web, visit:

www.halleethehomemaker.com/2010/10/tip-saving-money-on-yeast/

www.halleethehomemaker.com/2011/04/the-dirty-dozen/

www.halleethehomemaker.com/levitical-diet/

www.halleethehomemaker.com/2009/09/soy-oh-boy/

www.halleethehomemaker.com/2012/10/milk-it-does-a-body-good/

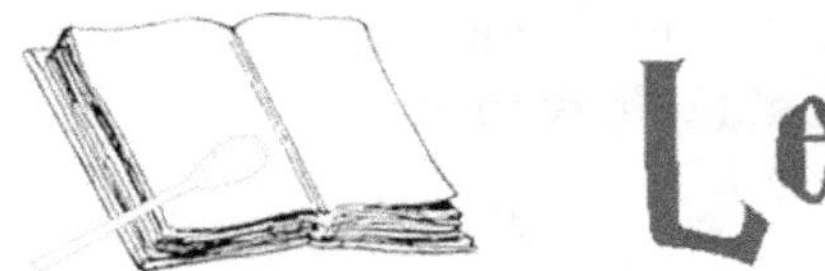

Legend

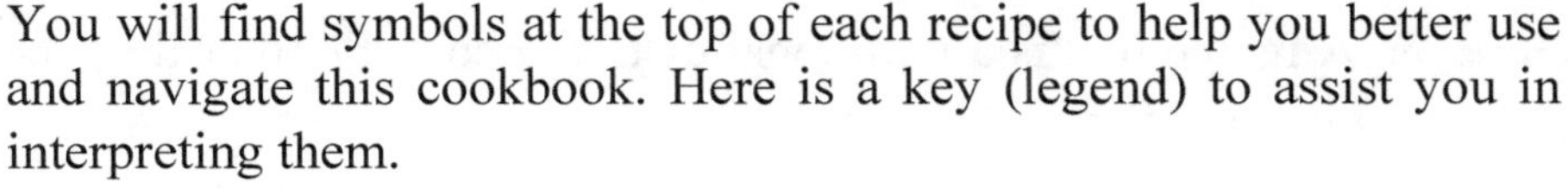

You will find symbols at the top of each recipe to help you better use and navigate this cookbook. Here is a key (legend) to assist you in interpreting them.

Freezes well

Sometimes, it's nice to pre-make something, or make big batches and freeze the excess for later meals.

Quick and Easy

Some nights or mornings, quick and easy is the theme of the meal. These dishes take little preparation and use supplies that don't take a lot of planning or cooking times.

Lent/Daniel Fast/Vegan Friendly

These dishes are 100% real whole food, vegan friendly. No meat products, no meat, no dairy or egg, no processed foods. Suitable for a Daniel Fast, Lent, or incorporating into a vegan menu.

Vegetarian

Not "vegan"—may contain dairy or egg, but no meat.

Kosher Friendly

If you keep Kosher, your kitchen is Kosher, and your ingredients are Kosher, these dishes are Kosher friendly. No dairy mixing with meat, no unclean meats, etc.

Holiday Fare

This dish goes well with a roast turkey, rack of lamb, goose, or a roast beef: traditional holiday meals.

Gluten Free

All ingredients in this recipe are gluten free.

International

A recipe that is a traditional dish in a country other than the United States.

Calls for alcohol

This recipe originally calls for alcohol, usually wine. If you abstain from alcohol even in cooking, you can substitute a 100% pure white or dark grape juice (make sure there is no apple juice in it) along with one teaspoon of distilled vinegar to approximate the same flavor and properties of wine in most recipes. Other substitutes such as non-alcoholic beer are also noted as they apply.

Entrée

This recipe is a full entrée.

Other symbols used in this cookbook:

INFORMATION: More information on the world wide web. When you can find more information about something on the internet, I have put an INFORMATION symbol ⓘ next to it and provided the link address in the notes.

Birds

It Isn't Magic

Poultry is such a versatile meat, but sometimes we get tired of the same dishes over and over again. This section contains some amazing new recipes combining flavorful spices and giving you a new break from the same old.

There's also some old favorites in here. Did you know you can roast a whole chicken in the slow cooker? You can! It's a wonderful way to have a beautiful bird waiting on you at the end of the day. There are chili recipes, stew recipes, and even an ol' Kentucky Hot Brown recipe.

Poultry doesn't have to be plain. Or boring.

You'll discover that most of my recipes are made with chicken thighs. The reason for this is because during the low and slow cooking of a slow cooker, the bone-in, skin-on meat stays moist and full of flavor. You are welcome to substitute chicken breasts, if that's your family's preference. If so, I would still recommend keeping the bone in and skin on during the cooking process so that the meat stays as moist as possible.

Selecting Poultry

When selecting poultry, here are a few things to keep in mind:

—Try to always purchase free range birds from reputable farms that have humane practices with their fowl. You will pay more per pound for your meat, but at least you know it wasn't raised in unsanitary conditions so crowded it can't even move around.

—Try to purchase vegetarian fed birds. Among other things, in the case of chickens at least, this means that it wasn't fed dead chickens.

If it's free range, it likely also ate bugs and such, but its feed would have been vegetarian.

—Try to purchase local fowl. This will ensure the freshest meat available.

The color of the skin of chicken, duck, and turkey varies from white to yellow. This doesn't mean anything about the freshness or quality of the meat.

Handling Poultry

When handling poultry, here are some things to keep in mind:

—Never defrost frozen meat at room temperature. Always defrost either in the refrigerator or in a pan of cold water (changing the water every 30 minutes).

—Never reuse an implement (plate, knife, cutting board, etc.) that has come in contact with raw meat. Always wash with hot, soapy water before reusing.

—Wash your hands constantly when handling raw poultry.

—Always, always, cook poultry until an instant-read thermometer inserted into the thickest part of the meat registers 165° degrees F (75° degrees C). This is important. Even if the thermometer reads the proper degree, if the juices are pink, continue cooking. The juices must run clear before the meat is safe to eat.

Buy the Right Amount

The amount of poultry you need to buy varies based on serving needs:

—Whole chicken will feed 1 to 2 people per pound.

—Bone in skin on parts will feed 2 to 3 people per pound

—Boneless, skinless breasts will feed 3 to 4 people per pound

How to Break Down a Chicken

When I buy chicken, I'll buy a few packages of breasts (on the bone with the skin on), a few packages of wings (whole wings—I break down my own "Buffalo" style), leg-thigh quarters, and the rest that I purchase are whole chickens. It's so much cheaper to break your own chicken down than to pay the price for a "whole cut up chicken". Substantially cheaper. Cheaper like half as much per pound cheaper.

It's very—very—easy to break down a chicken, and the more you do it, the easier it gets. Here's how:

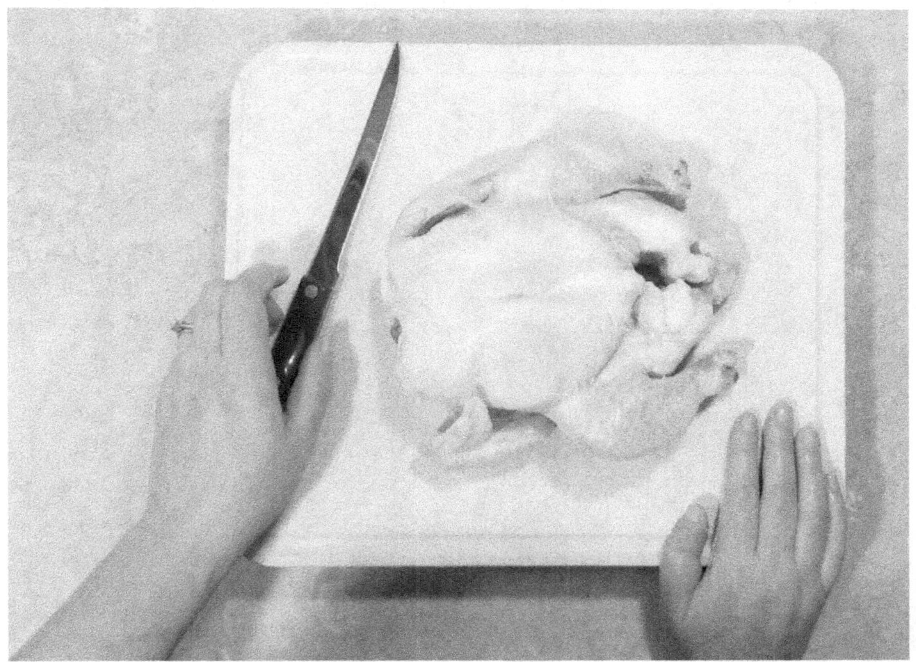

Have a large cutting board, a cleared off area, and a sharp knife.

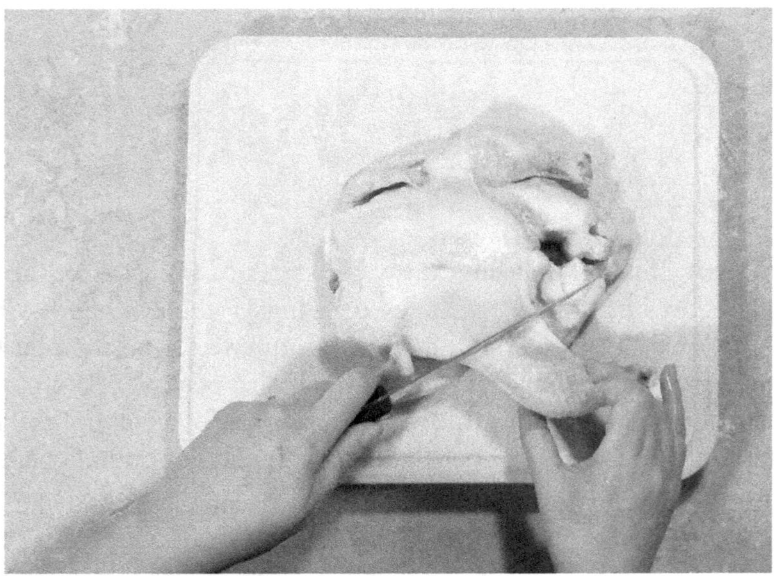

Take your knife and slice through the skin (you should not be slicing meat—it should only be skin here) until you reach the leg joint.

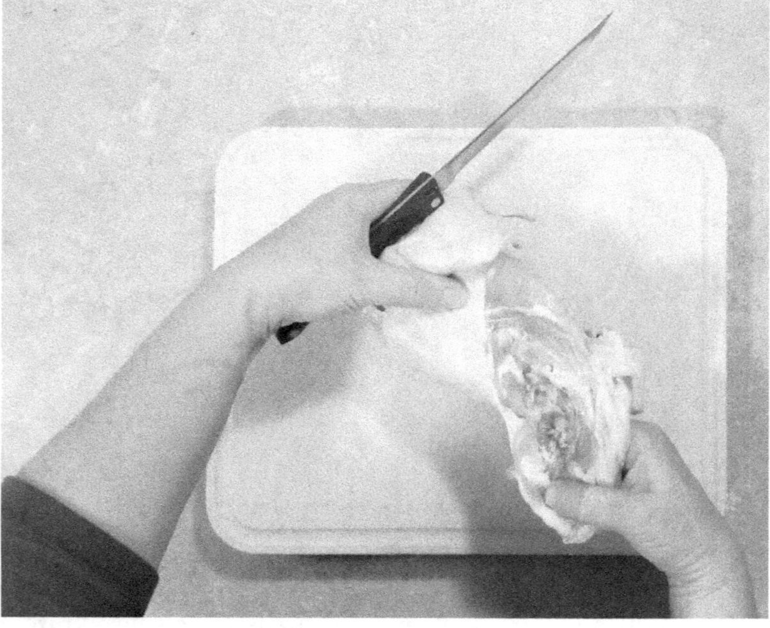

Grip the leg in one hand and the body in the other and bend the leg back until the joint pops out.

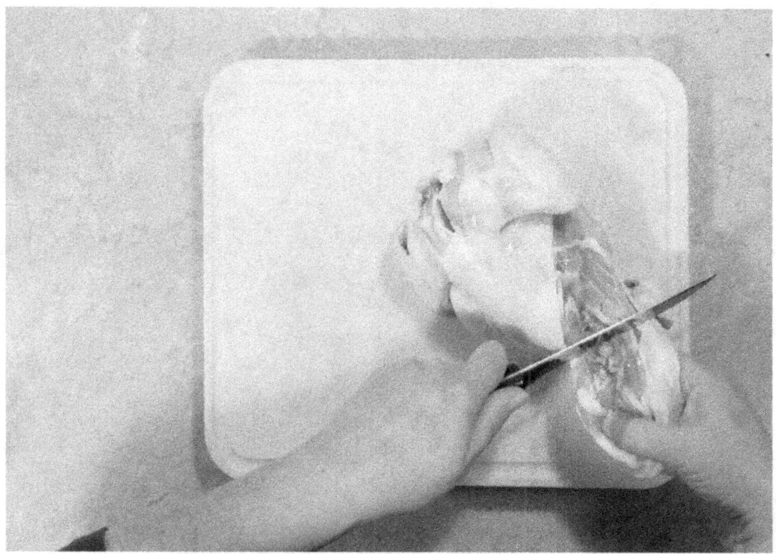

Place the knife between the joint and the bone.

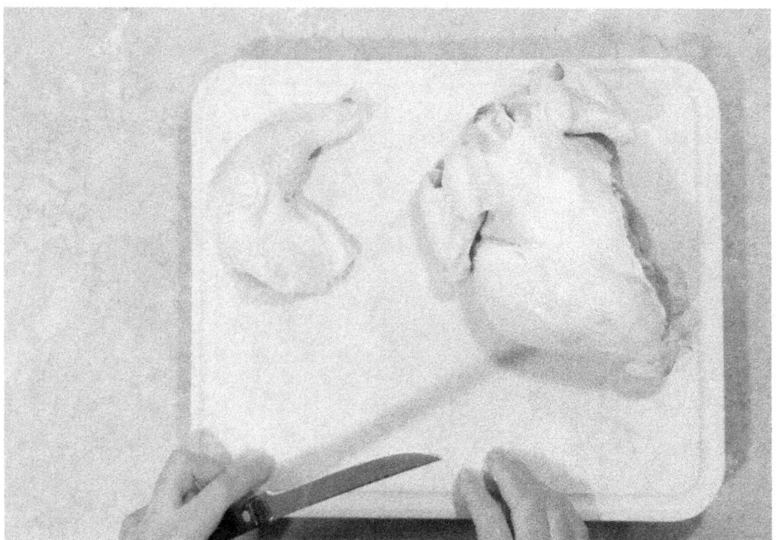

Cut to remove the leg and the thigh.

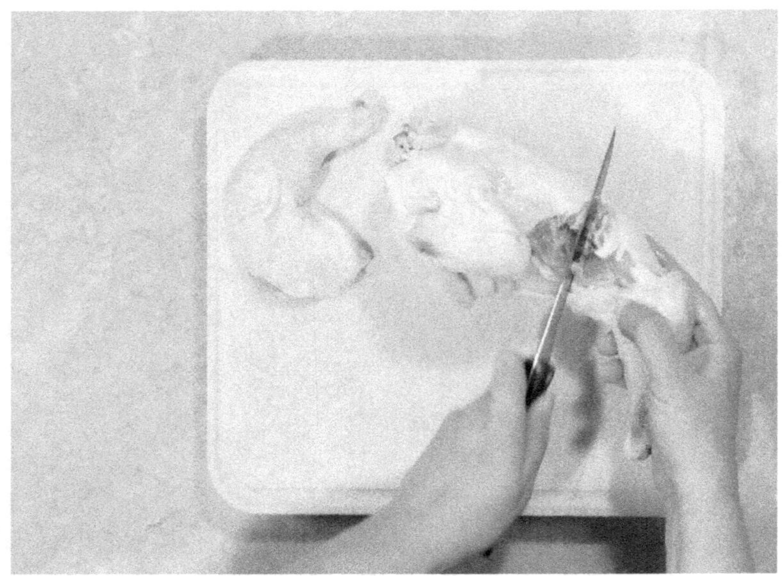

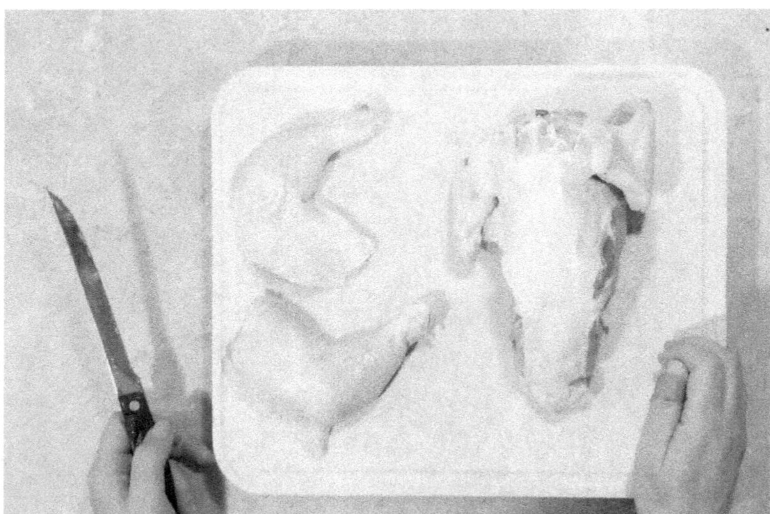

Repeat with the other leg.

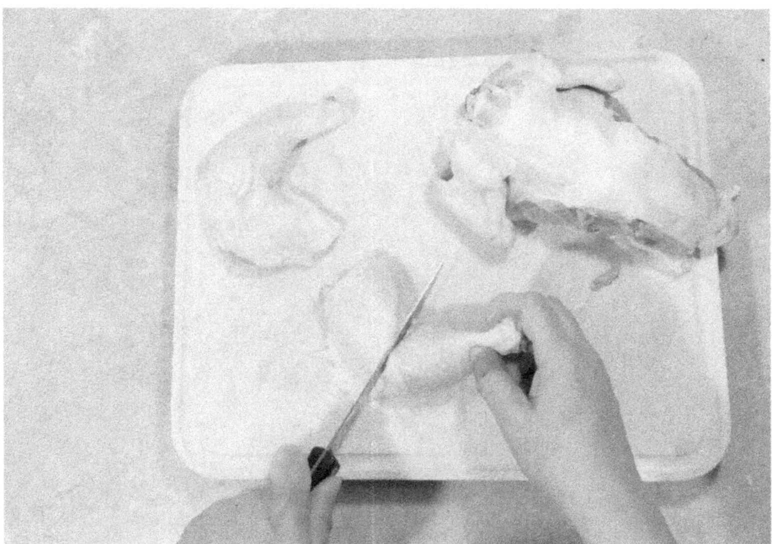

Similar to the instructions above, run your knife blade around the circumference of skin between the drumstick and the joint.

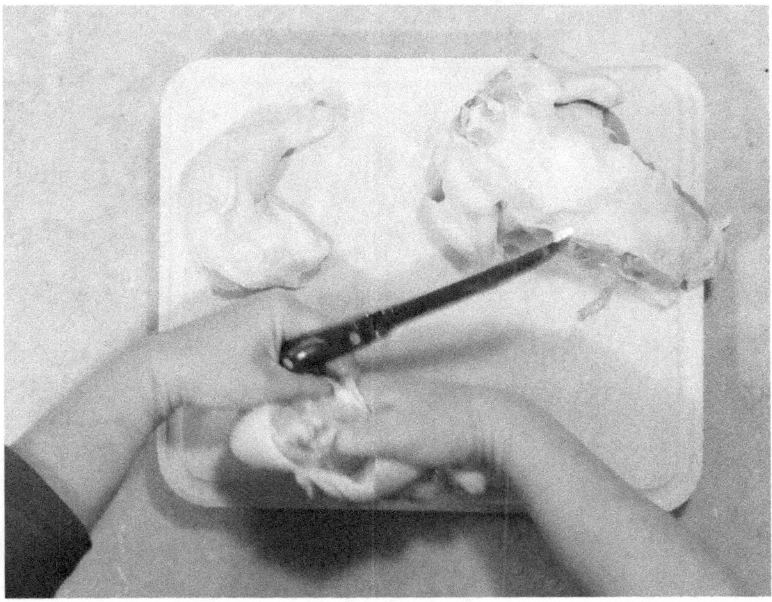

Pop the joint between the drumstick and the thigh.

Use the blade to separate the drumsticks and thighs.

Now you're ready to tackle the wings.

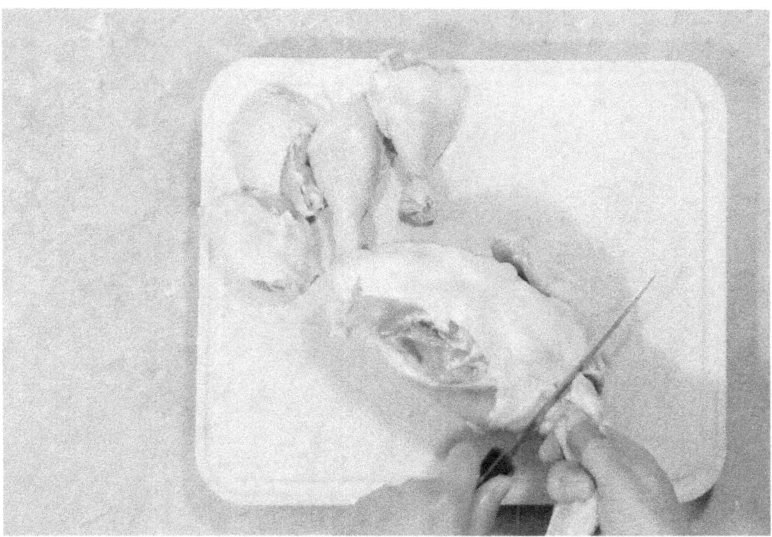

Lift up a wing to reveal the "underarm" of the bird. Similar to the way you removed the thighs and drumsticks, run your knife all around the joint of the wing.

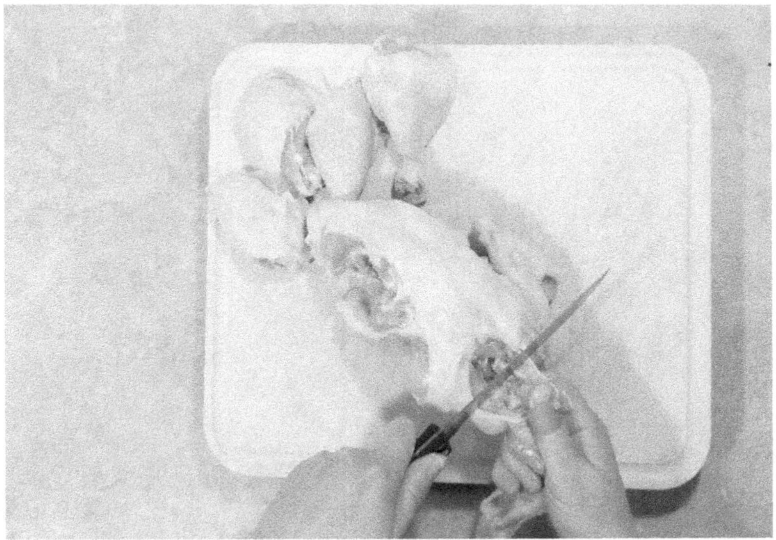

Once you've cut the skin and meat from around the joint, grab the wing firmly in one hand and the bird in the other and bend the wing backward until the joint pops out. Use the knife blade to separate the wings from the bird.

Cut away any remaining skin or meat and the wing is now off of the body.

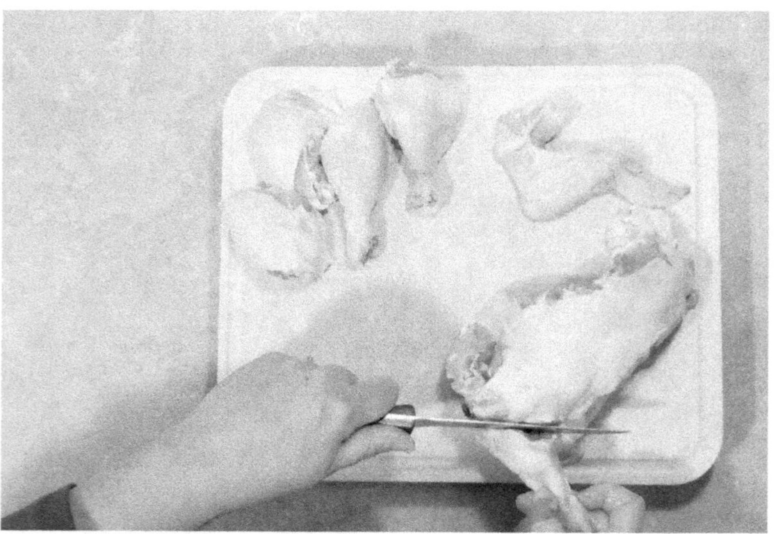

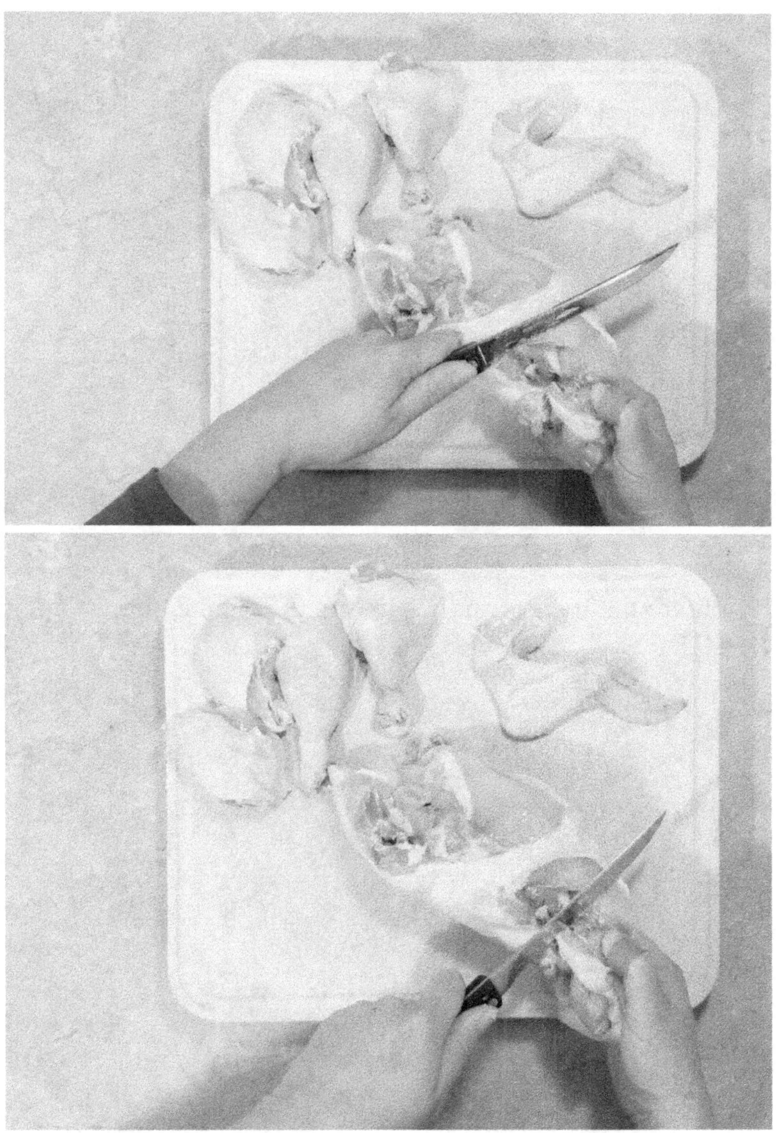

Repeat with the other wing.

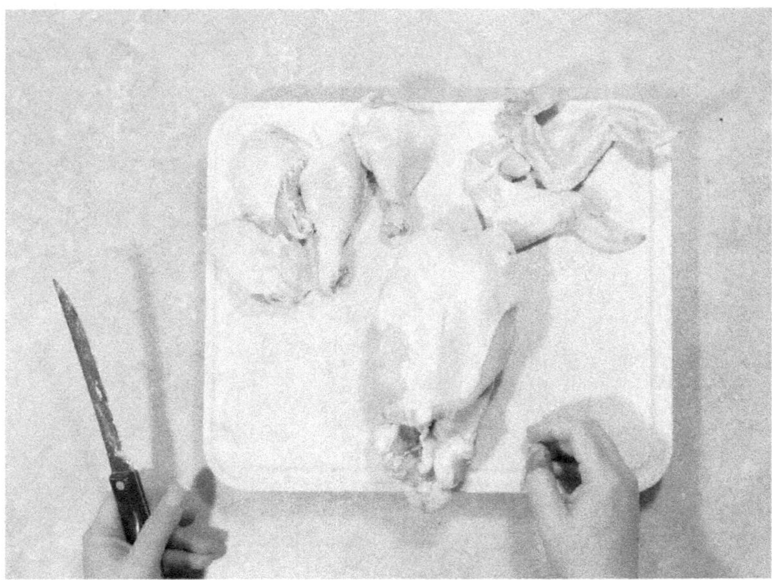

What's left are the breasts and back. Lay the chicken breast up

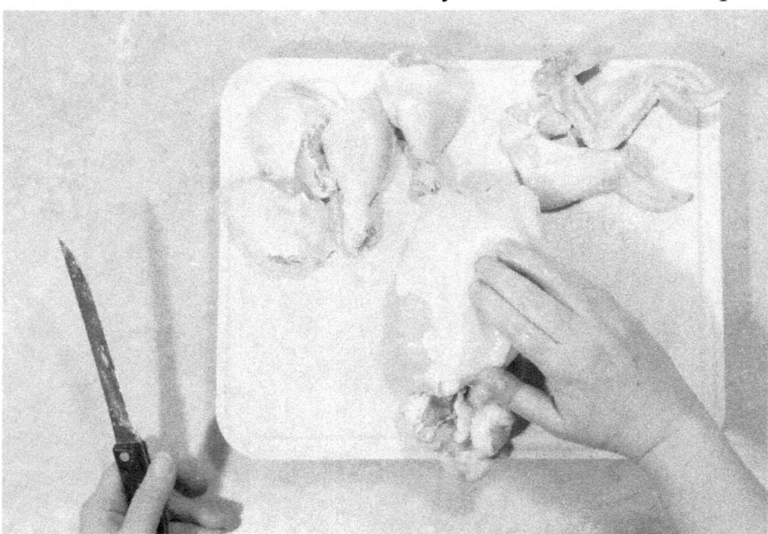

There is a breastbone right in between the two breasts. You can locate it by feel.

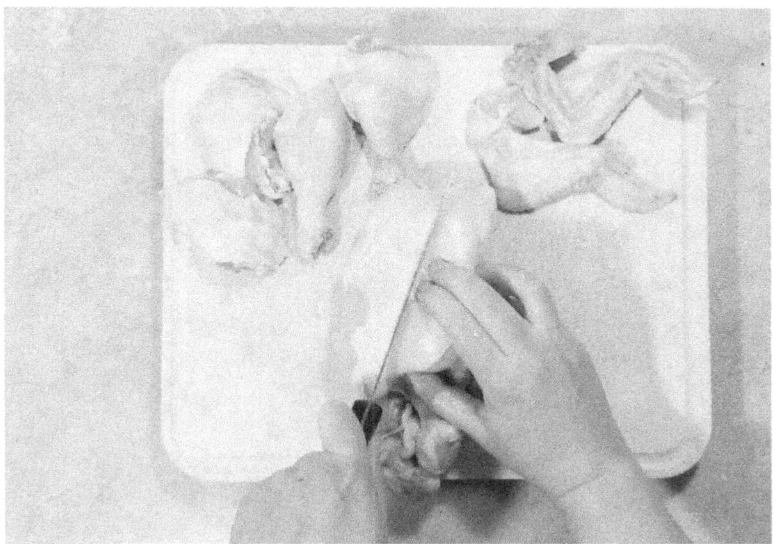

Put your knife against that bone, as close as you can get to it. There is breast meat on it, so the closer you get to that bone, the less meat you lose off of your breast.

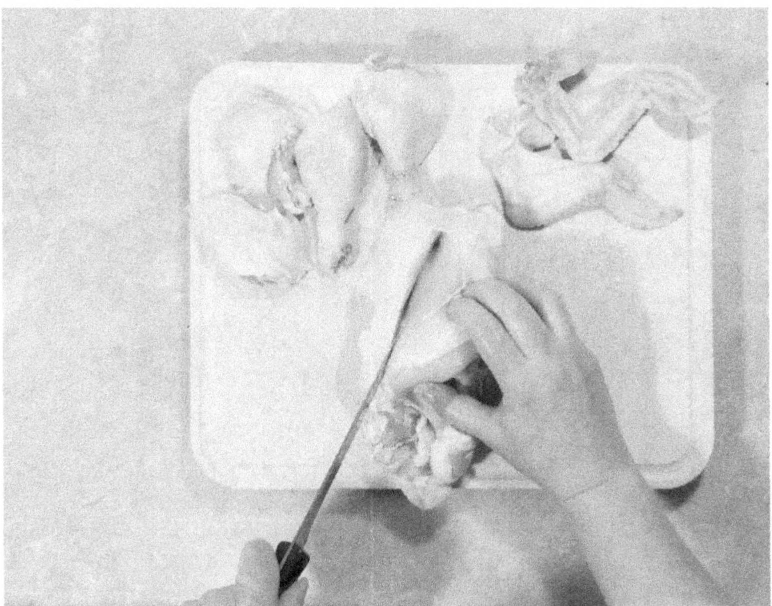

Cut down until your breasts separate in half.

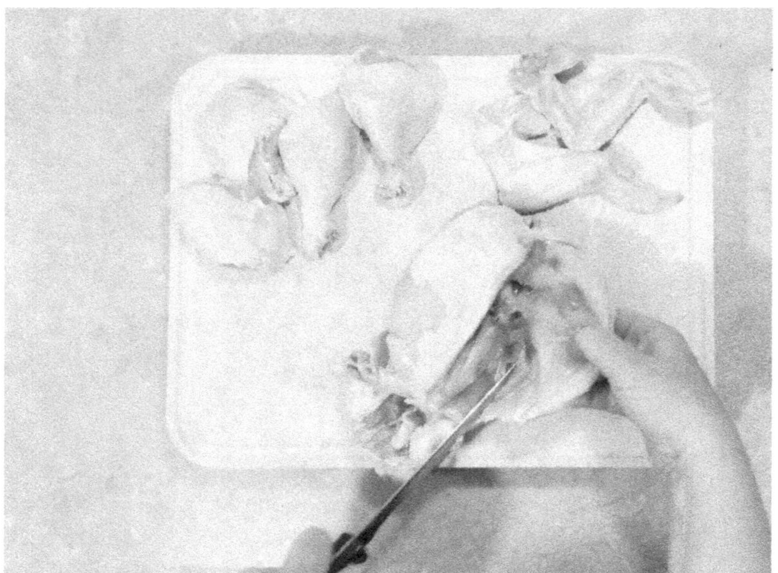

You can see that bone on the piece my hand is touching, and you can see the meat on the other piece. That is what we just cut—what we just separated.

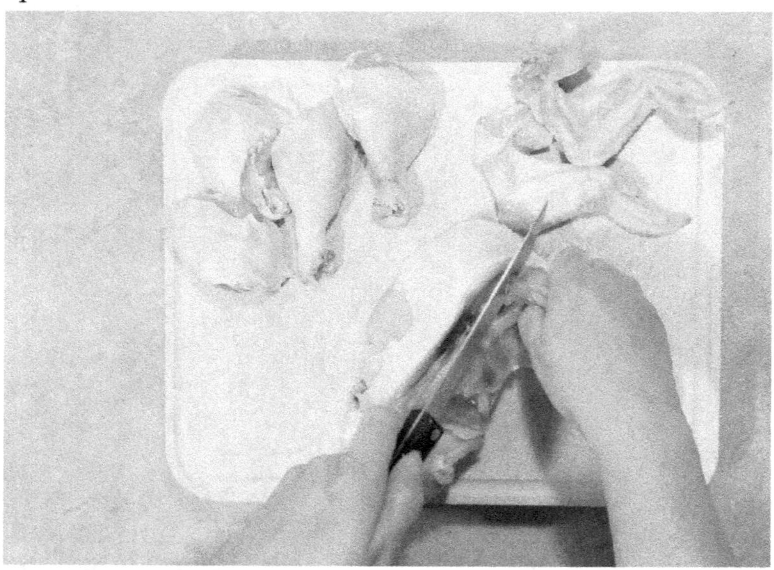

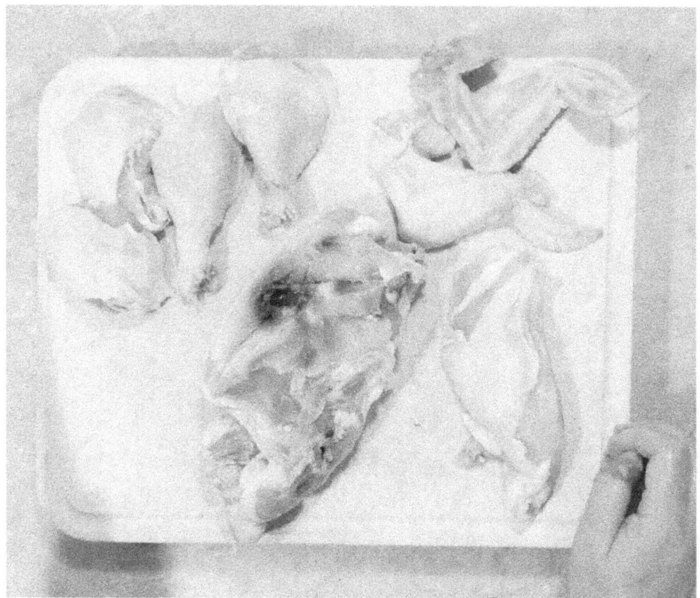

Cut around the bone to remove the breast from the backbone. I keep the breast on the bone if I'm going to bake or boil them.

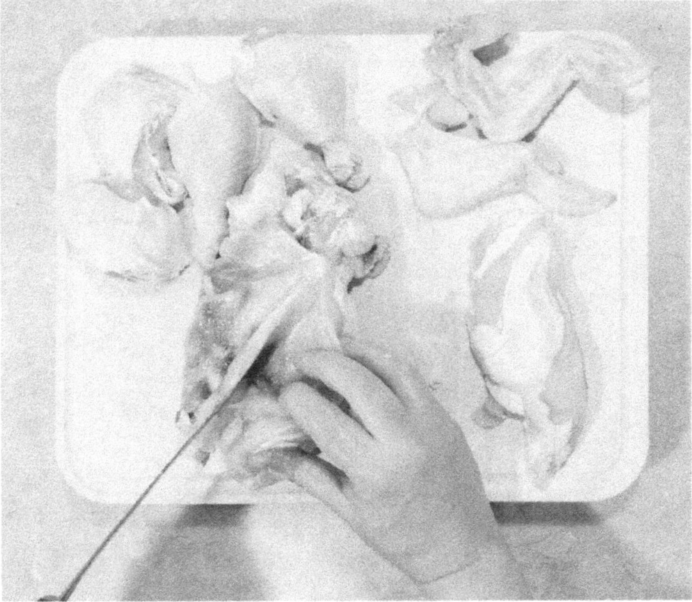

Repeat with the other breast.

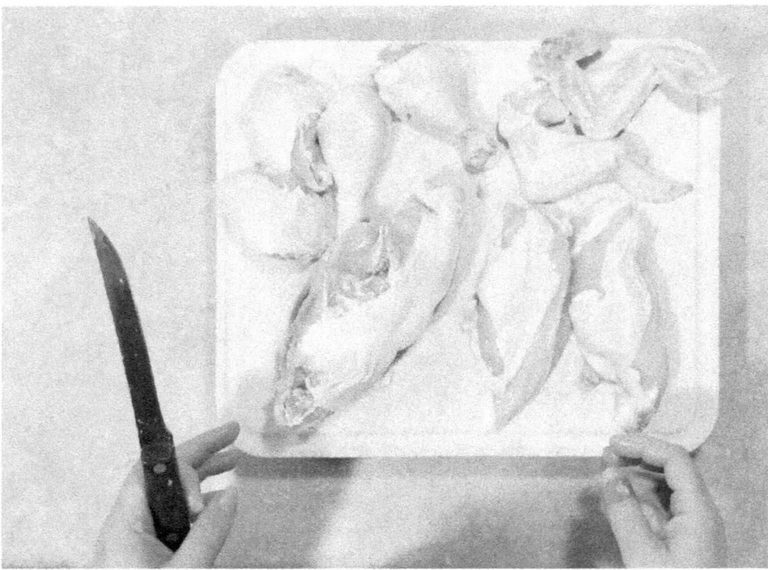

What you have left is the backbone and carcass. Don't discard it. Use this to make a homemade chicken broth.

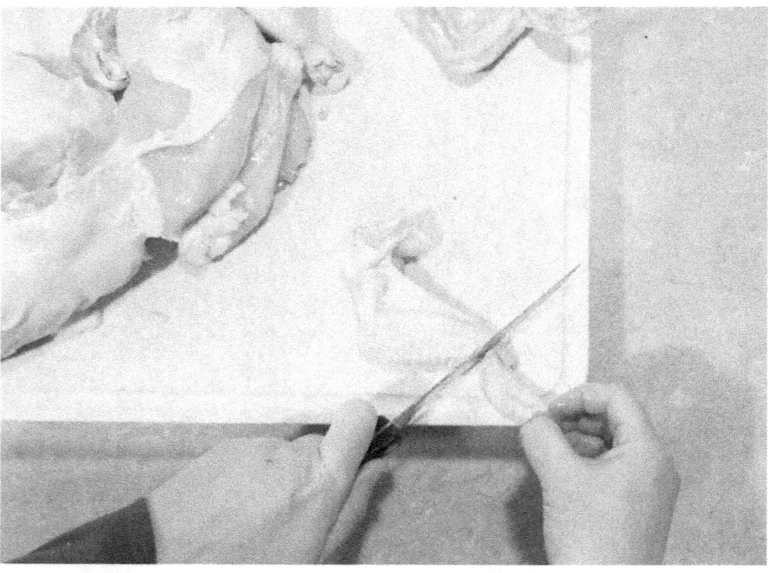

For making stocks or broths, be sure to cut the tips off the wings and toss them in too.

You can get up to 6 pints of broth from one chicken carcass.

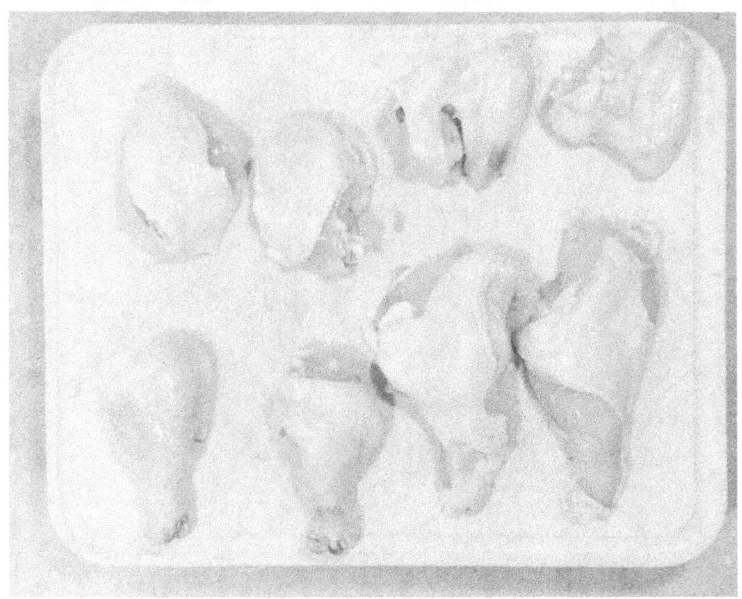

Here is a whole cutup chicken waiting for its transformation into something delicious! If I hadn't stopped to take pictures, I would have had it done in less than 5 minutes.

ⓘ For the latest information about the current Agricultural Marketing Service USDA standards for grading meat and other consumable commodities, visit the official website at:

http://www.ams.usda.gov/AMSv1.0/Grading

ⓘ I have included a recipe for Hallee's Heavenly Homemade Bird Brothⓘ in this cookbook.

Gringotts' Crock Pot Roasted Chicken

Whole Roasted Chicken

It is too easy to roast an entire chicken in the slow cooker.

Seriously.

Season it however you want, set it in the slow cooker breast up, and cook it on low for 6-8 hours. It is that easy. I've even (don't tell anyone) put a frozen bird (one that did not have a giblets bag in the carcass—if it does, don't do this) in the slow cooker, set the temperature to high, and in about 6 hours, had a fully cooked chicken that was falling off of the bones.

Play with different spice blends for seasoning. This cookbook has so many options from which to choose—you could go with sagey-savory, kicking taco flavor, spicy Oriental flavors—it's your choice. Or, you could dump a bottle of barbeque sauce over it and let it get flavored with the tangy sweetness of the sauce.

Nutrition Facts

Serving Size: 6 oz (170g)
Servings Per Container: 8

Amount Per Serving	
Calories 490	Calories from Fat 310
	% Daily Value*
Total Fat 34g	**52%**
Saturated Fat 9g	**45%**
Trans Fat 0g	
Cholesterol 200mg	**67%**
Sodium 160mg	**7%**
Total Carbohydrate 0g	**0%**
Dietary Fiber 0g	**0%**
Sugars 0g	
Protein 43g	
Vitamin A 30% •	Vitamin C 8%
Calcium 4% •	Iron 15%

* Percent Daily Values are based on a 2,000 calorie diet. Your daily values may be higher or lower depending on your calorie needs:

	Calories:	2,000	2,500
Total Fat	Less than	65g	80g
Sat Fat	Less than	20g	25g
Cholesterol	Less than	300mg	300mg
Sodium	Less than	2,400mg	2,400mg
Total Carbohydrate		300g	375g
Dietary Fiber		25g	30g

How ever you cook it, make sure the internal temperature, with the thermometer inserted in the thickest part of the thigh without touching the bone, reads 165° degrees F (75° degrees C) before serving.

Hotter Potter Brown

Hallee's Signature Crock Pot Hot Brown

According to the official history of the world-famous Brown Hotel in Louisville, Kentucky, way back in the 1920's, the hotel drew more than 1,200 guests each and every evening for the dinner dance they hosted. In the wee hours of the morning, the guests would grow tired of dancing and retire to Kentucky's only (at the time) 5-star restaurant for a bite to eat.

Diners rapidly grew bored with the traditional eggs and toast, so Chef Fred K. Schmidt set out to create something new. His unique creation was an open-faced turkey sandwich with sliced Roma tomato and a delicate Mornay sauce and bacon and… the Hot Brown was born!

Nutrition Facts

Serving Size: 1 complete piece (467g)
Servings Per Container: 6

Amount Per Serving	
Calories 650	Calories from Fat 190
	% Daily Value*
Total Fat 21g	**32%**
Saturated Fat 7g	**35%**
Trans Fat 0g	
Cholesterol 190mg	**63%**
Sodium 2410mg	**100%**
Total Carbohydrate 43g	**14%**
Dietary Fiber 4g	**16%**
Sugars 4g	
Protein 70g	

Vitamin A 4%	•	Vitamin C 20%
Calcium 15%	•	Iron 30%

* Percent Daily Values are based on a 2,000 calorie diet. Your daily values may be higher or lower depending on your calorie needs:

	Calories:	2,000	2,500
Total Fat	Less than	65g	80g
Sat Fat	Less than	20g	25g
Cholesterol	Less than	300mg	300mg
Sodium	Less than	2,400mg	2,400mg
Total Carbohydrate		300g	375g
Dietary Fiber		25g	30g

This recipe is what I like to call my Hot Brown in a Crock Pot. The Romano adds that wonderful rich cheesy flavor that is a nod to the Gruyere originally used in Chef Schmidt's now world-famous Mornay sauce. If you wanted to, you could add or substitute in Gruyere or another cheese.

You don't really need to top this recipe with bacon but if you choose to I highly recommend a good smoked beef bacon. The contrast in flavors is seriously amazing and unforgettable.

2 pounds turkey meat (light or dark is fine, just not ground meat)

1/2 cup Pecorino Romano, plus 1 tablespoon for garnish, grated (see NOTES)

3 cups Hallee's Traditional Turkey Gravy ⓘ

1/2 tsp rubbed sage

1/4 tsp parsley

1/2 tsp Hallee's Pre-Made Poultry Rub Recipe 1 ⓘ

1 tsp Worcestershire sauce

28 ounces mashed potatoes (leftover mashed potatoes are fine)

6 slices bread, toasted

2 Roma tomatoes, sliced

1/4 tsp paprika

12 slices of beef or turkey bacon (optional)

3 1/2 to 4 qt slow cooker

kitchen tongs

measuring cups/spoons

good sharp knife

cutting board

6 individual serving plates or wide shallow bowls

You will need to have about 3 servings of mashed potatoes on hand about 10 minutes prior to serving.

Directions

Place turkey in slow cooker. Add 1/2 cup grated Romano cheese. Sprinkle with sage and parsley. Top with Hallee's Traditional Turkey Gravy ⓘ.

Cover and cook on low heat for 8 hours, or high heat for 4 hours.

Using kitchen tongs, remove turkey from cooker; place on cutting board and briefly let cool.

Meanwhile, stir Hallee's Pre-Made Poultry Rub Recipe 1 ⓘ and Worcestershire sauce into gravy in cooker.

If necessary, slice bread. Toast bread.

Once bread is toasted arrange each slice in the center of 6 individual serving plates.

Slice Roma tomatoes.

Cut turkey into 1/4 inch slices.

Place 4 slices of Roma tomatoes on each toast slice in a crisscross with one end of each tomato slice toward the center and one end toward each corner of the toast.

Place 2 slices of turkey on each toast slice.

Top each with 1/4 cup mashed potatoes.

Spoon gravy over potatoes.

Lightly dust with paprika.

Top the entire plate with 2 crisscrossed slices of beef bacon or turkey bacon if you like.

Garnish with grated Pecorino Romano or Parmigiano Reggiano (Parmesan) and fresh parsley.

Yield

Serves 6

Notes

Grated Parmigiano Reggiano (Parmesan) will substitute for the Pecorino Romano for the garnish. You could substitute it for the Romano entirely but will result in a MUCH stronger flavor that may be undesirable. If looking for a substitute, I would recommend a good Gruyere which would also more closely emulate a Mornay sauce.

Serve this dish with a side of cranberry sauce for a holiday flare.

ⓘ I have included two recipes for Hallee's Pre-Made Poultry Rubs in this cookbook. This particular recipe calls for poultry rub number 1 which is sage and marjoram based, but feel free to experiment with your seasonings.

ⓘ I have included the recipe for Hallee's Tantalizing Traditional Turkey Gravy in this cookbook. Find that recipe and many others on my website at:

http://www.halleethehomemaker.com/2010/11/traditional-turkey-gravy/

Charmed White Chicken Chili with Hominy

Wonderful White Chicken Chili with Hominy

Nutrition Facts

Serving Size: (552g)
Servings Per Container: 6

Amount Per Serving	
Calories 380	Calories from Fat 50
	% Daily Value*
Total Fat 5g	**8%**
Saturated Fat 1.5g	**8%**
Trans Fat 0g	
Cholesterol 120mg	**40%**
Sodium 1210mg	**50%**
Total Carbohydrate 41g	**14%**
Dietary Fiber 10g	**40%**
Sugars 5g	
Protein 44g	
Vitamin A 8% •	Vitamin C 30%
Calcium 10% •	Iron 25%

* Percent Daily Values are based on a 2,000 calorie diet. Your daily values may be higher or lower depending on your calorie needs:

	Calories:	2,000	2,500
Total Fat	Less than	65g	80g
Sat Fat	Less than	20g	25g
Cholesterol	Less than	300mg	300mg
Sodium	Less than	2,400mg	2,400mg
Total Carbohydrate		300g	375g
Dietary Fiber		25g	30g

My husband is southern to the core. His parents hailed from Kentucky and South Carolina and his father graduated from the Citadel. He refers to the War Between the States as "The Recent Unpleasantness" and it's only slightly tongue in cheek! In short, he comes from a proud southern family with proud southern roots and he's not just whistling Dixie.

This means that he will never understand certain things like why I voluntarily top my scrambled eggs with Hallee's Homemade Organic Ketchupⓘ and I, meanwhile, will never understand his affinity for things like… hominy.

In fact, the first time I ever even tried hominy I had already passed my thirtieth year. One night when I was not feeling very well my very southern husband whipped up a batch for me—his southern version of Jewish mother chicken soup.

Oh, my. It was really good. Even not feeling so well at the time, it was good.

I thought to myself, "Self, if I could make hominy like this, I could almost understand the appeal." Well, in this recipe, I believe I have found a way.

A savory white chili made with chicken, white beans, and white hominy makes for a tasty change of pace from the usual spicy ground beef and kidney beans. You can use just about any combination of light colored bean you like from old reliable white beans to great northern, white navy, white kidney (cannellini), corona, or lupini.

Any legume is going to be packed with flavor and nutrition. You could even use lighter colored beans like cranberry beans or pink beans, though I'm not sure that would qualify as a "white" chili.

I don't use canned beans. The night before you want to make this recipe, put 3 cups of dried white beans (any kind of white bean will do—from baby limas to navy beans—they're all equally yummy and can be used in this recipe) in the slow cooker and cover them with 2-3 inches of water. Add about 1/2 tsp salt (Kosher or sea salt is best) then cover and cook on low overnight.

The hominy adds body and a fresh, surprisingly crisp island of flavor to every bite, a taste even the most skeptical Yankee will have to confess is pretty yummy.

1 1/4 lbs chicken thighs, skin on and bone in

6 cups cooked and drained white beans (3 15.5 ounce cans drained and rinsed if using cans)

2 cups (15.5 ounce can) white hominy, drained (See NOTES)

1 1/2 cup Hallee's Homemade Cream of Mushroom Soupⓘ

8 cups filtered water

2 1/2 TBS Hallee's Homemade Taco Seasoning Spice Blendⓘ

1/2 cup (4.5 oz can) green chiles, chopped

Sour cream or plain yogurt, if desired, for garnish

Chopped green onions, if desired, for garnish

At least 3 1/2 to 4 qt slow cooker
kitchen tongs
good sharp knife
cutting board
2 forks
measuring cups/spoons

Serves 8

If using dried beans, soak and cook them until tender.

Place chicken thighs in slow cooker. The chicken is placed on the bottom of the cooker where it is hottest because it needs more cooking than the rest of the ingredients. Top with remaining ingredients except yogurt (or sour cream) and onions.

Cover and cook until chicken is no longer pink; on low heat for 8 hours or on high heat for 4 hours.

About 10 to 15 minutes before serving, use kitchen tongs to remove the bird thighs from the slow cooker and place on cutting board. Using 2 forks, remove the skin and discard, then de-bone meat and discard bones.

According to your preference, either cut meat into bite-size cubes or shred meat with 2 forks. For this recipe, I prefer to shred the meat. Either way, return just the meat to slow cooker and mix well.

Before serving, stir gently to break up chicken pieces. Serve topped with plain yogurt or sour cream and sprinkled with chopped green onions.

Serving suggestion: Drizzle a little lime juice and honey (pure, raw, local honey is always best) over a plate of sliced oranges, jicama, and red onion for a unique Mexican-style salad that goes well with this dish.

Serving suggestion: If you want to go all out southern, you serve chili on top of riceⓘ.For information about a tip for preparing perfect brown rice, follow this link:

http://www.halleethehomemaker.com/2009/11/perfect-brown-rice/

Possible substitution: If your family is not fond of hominy, as I once was not, just add another can of your favorite light colored beans.

Possible substitution: Thighs really are the best part of the bird for a slow cooker because they keep their shape, flavor, and moisture; especially when you leave the bone in. If you substitute boneless bird meat, you may want to add it to the top of the slow cooker ingredients as much as 1 to 2 hours after cooking starts so it doesn't overcook. Or you can precook the meat, cube it, and add it 10 or 15 minutes before serving.

Possible substitution: In my experience, turkey works just as well as chicken nearly all of the time.

Ingredient notes:

ⓘ I have included a recipe for Hallee's Homemade Cream of Mushroom Soupⓘ in this cookbook. If you don't have it on hand and have no time to whip up a batch, be sure to use a good organic soup with low or no salt.

I'm not a fan of the packaged seasoning mixes only because they contain ingredients other than the spices. If you have store-bought Taco Seasoning on hand, you can substitute a single 1.25 oz store-bought packet 2 1/2 TBS Hallee's Homemade Taco Seasoning Spice Blendⓘ. But you can easily make your own.

This recipe is also on my website:

http://www.halleethehomemaker.com/2011/09/homemade-taco-seasoning-mix/

To make your own just combine 2 tsp to 1 TBS chili powder (to taste), 2 tsp onion powder, 1 tsp ground cumin, 1 tsp garlic powder (not garlic salt), 1 tsp paprika, 1 tsp ground oregano, and 1 tsp sugar. Optionally, throw in 1/2 tsp Kosher or sea salt. Mix all ingredients well and there you have it. About 1.5 oz of Hallee's Homemade Taco Seasoning Spice Blend®.

Miscellaneous: Since I have been asked many times since writing the intro to this article, I must confirm that, yes, I really do top my scrambled eggs with my very own Hallee's Homemade Organic Ketchup.

Black Forest Blush Sauce with Turkey & Penne

Creamy Blush Sauce with Turkey & Penne

The bird thighs are the best part of the bird for a slow cooker because they keep their shape, flavor, and moisture; especially when you leave the bone in. If you substitute boneless bird meat, you may want to add it to the slow cooker 1 to 2 hours after cooking starts so it doesn't overcook. Or you can precook the meat, cube it, and add it just before serving.

In this recipe, you can easily substitute 8 to 10 chicken thighs (about 2 to 2 1/2 lbs) for the turkey thighs.

Nutrition Facts

Serving Size: (540g)
Servings Per Container: 6

Amount Per Serving	
Calories 880	Calories from Fat 310
	% Daily Value*
Total Fat 34g	**52%**
Saturated Fat 9g	**45%**
Trans Fat 0g	
Cholesterol 260mg	**87%**
Sodium 950mg	**40%**
Total Carbohydrate 74g	**25%**
Dietary Fiber 11g	**44%**
Sugars 12g	
Protein 72g	
Vitamin A 25% •	Vitamin C 30%
Calcium 8% •	Iron 45%

* Percent Daily Values are based on a 2,000 calorie diet. Your daily values may be higher or lower depending on your calorie needs:

	Calories:	2,000	2,500
Total Fat	Less than	65g	80g
Sat Fat	Less than	20g	25g
Cholesterol	Less than	300mg	300mg
Sodium	Less than	2,400mg	2,400mg
Total Carbohydrate		300g	375g
Dietary Fiber		25g	30g

At least 3 1/2 to 5 qt slow cooker

Pot for boiling pasta

measuring cups/spoons

good sharp knife

cutting board

mixing bowl

whisk

4 turkey thighs (about 3 lbs), skin removed

1 quart stewed tomatoes

6 ounce can tomato paste

1 cup filtered water

1 TBS honey (raw, local honey is best)

1 1/2 tsp garlic powder

1 1/2 tsp onion powder

1 tsp salt (Kosher or sea salt is best)

1 tsp oregano

1 tsp basil

1/2 tsp dried sage

1/2 tsp crushed red pepper

1/2 cup half-and-half

1 lb penne pasta

grated Parmigiano Reggiano (Parmesan) cheese

Whisk together tomato paste, water, honey, salt, and spices.

Place turkey in slow cooker. Cover with tomatoes and the tomato paste mixture.

Cover and cook on low heat for 7 to 8 hours or on high heat for 3 1/2 to 4 hours.

When it's almost ready, prepare the pasta according to the package directions.

Using kitchen tongs, remove turkey and place in shallow pan over cooked penne. Cover with aluminum foil to keep warm.

Add half-and-half to cooker and stir. When ready to serve, remove foil and spoon sauce over turkey and pasta.

Sprinkle with grated Parmigiano Reggiano (Parmesan) cheese.

Serves 6

You can use prepared pasta sauce in place of the tomatoes, tomato paste, and spices.

Transfiguration Stew

Chicken Tortellini Vegetable Stew

Cheesy tortellini added near the end of the cooking time means this is a slow cooker meal with a twist.

You can use just about any combination of light colored bean you like from old reliable white kidney (cannellini), to white beans, great northern, white navy, corona, or lupini. Any legume is going to be packed with flavor and nutrition. You could even use lighter colored beans like cranberry beans or pink beans.

Nutrition Facts

Serving Size: (389g)
Servings Per Container: 6

Amount Per Serving	
Calories 700	Calories from Fat 340
	% Daily Value*
Total Fat 37g	**57%**
Saturated Fat 11g	**55%**
Trans Fat 0g	
Cholesterol 100mg	**33%**
Sodium 670mg	**28%**
Total Carbohydrate 61g	**20%**
Dietary Fiber 11g	**44%**
Sugars 4g	
Protein 30g	
Vitamin A 90% •	Vitamin C 8%
Calcium 25% •	Iron 40%

* Percent Daily Values are based on a 2,000 calorie diet. Your daily values may be higher or lower depending on your calorie needs:

	Calories:	2,000	2,500
Total Fat	Less than	65g	80g
Sat Fat	Less than	20g	25g
Cholesterol	Less than	300mg	300mg
Sodium	Less than	2,400mg	2,400mg
Total Carbohydrate		300g	375g
Dietary Fiber		25g	30g

At least 3 1/2 to 4 qt slow cooker

measuring cups/spoons

kitchen tongs

good sharp knife

cutting board

2 forks

If using dried beans, soak overnight, then cook until tender.

1 lbs chicken thighs, bone in and skin on

2 cups cooked (1 can, drained, rinsed) white kidney (cannelloni) beans —OR— 1 cup dried beans, soaked overnight and cooked until tender.

1 3/4 cup (16 oz) Hallee's Heavenly Homemade Bird Brothⓘ

2 cups filtered water

1 package (9 oz) cheese-filled whole grain organic tortellini

2 TBS fresh Parmigiano Reggiano (Parmesan) cheese, grated

1 cup fresh baby spinach leaves, firmly packed

2 medium green onions (2 TBS), sliced

1 tsp dried basil leaves

1 medium bulb fennel, chopped (See NOTES for possible substitution)ⓘ

2 cloves garlic, finely chopped

2 medium carrots (about 3/4 cup), sliced

1/2 tsp salt (Kosher or sea salt is best)

1/4 tsp fresh ground black pepper

In slow cooker, layer chicken, carrots, garlic, fennel, and beans. The chicken is placed on the bottom of the cooker where it is hottest because it needs more cooking than the rest of the ingredients. Sprinkle with salt and pepper. Pour broth and water over top. Stir to combine.

Cover and cook on low heat for 6 to 8 hours or on high heat for 3 to 4 hours.

About 20 minutes before serving, use kitchen tongs or slotted spoon to remove the bird thighs from the slow cooker and place on cutting board. Using 2 forks, remove the skin and discard, then de-bone meat and discard bones.

According to your preference, either cut meat into bite-size cubes or shred meat with 2 forks. For this recipe, I prefer to shred the meat. Either way, return just the meat to slow cooker and mix well.

About 15 minutes before serving, stir tortellini, spinach, onions, and basil into chicken mixture. Increase heat setting to high.

Cover and cook 15 to 20 minutes or until tortellini are tender.

Ladle into bowls to serve. Sprinkle individual servings with freshly grated or shredded Parmigiano Reggiano (Parmesan) cheese.

Serves 6

ⓘ I have included a recipe for Hallee's Heavenly Homemade Bird Brothⓘ in this cookbook. If you don't have stock on hand, be sure to use a good organic stock with low or no salt.

Possible substitution: Thighs really are the best part of the bird for a slow cooker because they keep their shape, flavor, and moisture; especially when you leave the bone in. If you substitute boneless bird meat, you may want to add it to the top of the slow cooker ingredients as much as 1 to 2 hours after cooking starts so it doesn't overcook. Or you can precook the meat, cube it, and add it 10 or 15 minutes before serving.

Possible substitution: In my experience, turkey works just as well as chicken nearly all of the time.

Possible substitution: ⓘYou can use one cup of sliced celery in place of the fennel.

Order of the Phoenix Chicken

Orange Chicken with Green Onions & Walnuts

Hungry for something with an Oriental flavor? Serve this dish over brown rice, or with crunchy noodles. If you have pre-prepared rice, it's a quick fix. Remember—the rice will take 45 minutes to cook so be sure to plan for that.

$^{3}/_{4}$ cup orange marmalade

$^{1}/_{2}$ cup walnut pieces

3 cloves garlic, minced

2 TBS cornstarch

$^{1}/_{4}$ cup teriyaki sauce

4 cups cooked Perfect Brown Riceⓘ

4 green onions (about $^{1}/_{2}$ cup), choppedⓘ

8 chicken thighs (about 2 lbs), bone-in, skin-on

1 $^{1}/_{2}$ cup Hallee's Heavenly Homemade Bird Brothⓘ

6 qt slow cooker for entree

saucepan with lid to cook rice

measuring cups/spoons

good sharp knife/cutting board

kitchen tongs

Mince the garlic

Chopⓘ the onion

Chop the walnuts

Nutrition Facts

Serving Size: (647g)
Servings Per Container: 4

Amount Per Serving	
Calories 1500	Calories from Fat 1010
	% Daily Value*
Total Fat 112g	**172%**
Saturated Fat 29g	**145%**
Trans Fat 0.5g	
Cholesterol 240mg	**80%**
Sodium 1140mg	**48%**
Total Carbohydrate 96g	**32%**
Dietary Fiber 5g	**20%**
Sugars 41g	
Protein 31g	

Vitamin A 10% •	Vitamin C 6%
Calcium 8% •	Iron 15%

* Percent Daily Values are based on a 2,000 calorie diet. Your daily values may be higher or lower depending on your calorie needs:

	Calories:	2,000	2,500
Total Fat	Less than	65g	80g
Sat Fat	Less than	20g	25g
Cholesterol	Less than	300mg	300mg
Sodium	Less than	2,400mg	2,400mg
Total Carbohydrate		300g	375g
Dietary Fiber		25g	30g

About 4 servings

Mix broth, teriyaki sauce, garlic, marmalade, 1/4 cup green onions, and cornstarch in 6 quart slow cooker.

Add chicken and turn with tongs to coat.

Cover and cook until chicken is no longer pink; on low heat for 6 to 8 hours or on high for 3 to 4 hours.

About 45 minutes before the dish is done, make your Perfect Brown Riceⓘ. Chop the remainder of your onions and walnuts. While rice is cooking, use kitchen tongs to remove the bird thighs from the slow cooker and place on cutting board. Using 2 forks, remove the skin and discard, then de-bone meat and discard bones. Place the chicken back into the cooker until ready to serve.

Serve with Perfect Brown Riceⓘ. Sprinkle with walnuts and remaining 1/4 cup green onions before serving.

Really resist the urge to peek and check for check for doneness. Every time the lid on the slow cooker is lifted, heat and steam escapes and 15 to 20 minutes will need to be added to the total cooking time.

ⓘ I have included a recipe for Hallee's Heavenly Homemade Bird Brothⓘ in this cookbook. If you don't have stock on hand, be sure to use a good organic stock with low or no salt.

ⓘ For information about a tip for chopping vegetables, follow this link:

http://www.halleethehomemaker.com/2009/08/tips-chopping-onions/

ⓘ For information about a tip for preparing perfect brown rice, follow this link:

http://www.halleethehomemaker.com/2009/11/perfect-brown-rice/

Sorting Hat Spinach, Chaser Chicken, & Wizard Rice Soup

Spinach, Chicken, & Wild Rice Soup

This is a super healthy and light meal averaging only about 200 calories per serving, low in salt, and just packed with healthy protein and fiber.

If you have healthy homemade broth on hand before getting this recipe in the pot, it is incredibly easy to get started.

This recipe is a real timesaver if you have leftover meat. If you don't have any leftover chicken or turkey to contribute, check the local grocer meat department or freezer case for chopped cooked chicken or stop by the deli counter and pick up a roasted bird that you can cube up and pop in the refrigerator until the main meal is ready to serve.

Nutrition Facts

Serving Size: (107g)
Servings Per Container: 6

Amount Per Serving	
Calories 240	Calories from Fat 45
	% Daily Value*
Total Fat 5g	**8%**
Saturated Fat 1g	**5%**
Trans Fat 0g	
Cholesterol 60mg	**20%**
Sodium 330mg	**14%**
Total Carbohydrate 24g	**8%**
Dietary Fiber 2g	**8%**
Sugars 2g	
Protein 26g	
Vitamin A 25% •	Vitamin C 8%
Calcium 6% •	Iron 10%

* Percent Daily Values are based on a 2,000 calorie diet. Your daily values may be higher or lower depending on your calorie needs:

	Calories:	2,000	2,500
Total Fat	Less than	65g	80g
Sat Fat	Less than	20g	25g
Cholesterol	Less than	300mg	300mg
Sodium	Less than	2,400mg	2,400mg
Total Carbohydrate		300g	375g
Dietary Fiber		25g	30g

Supplies

At least 3 1/2 to 4 qt slow cooker

measuring cups/spoons

good sharp knife

cutting board

ladle

3 cups cooked chicken or turkey, cut into cubes

3 cups pure filtered water

2 cups fresh spinach, shredded

1 $^1/_2$ cup Hallee's Heavenly Homemade Bird Brothⓘ

1 $^1/_2$ cup Hallee's Homemade Cream of Mushroom Soupⓘ

$^2/_3$ cup uncooked wild rice, rinsed and drained

$^1/_2$ tsp dried thyme, crushed

$^1/_4$ tsp fresh ground black pepper

Reserve chicken and spinach until just before serving, then shred the spinach and, if needed, cube the cooked bird meat.

In the slow cooker, combine 3 cups of pure filtered water with 1 $^1/_2$ cup Hallee's Heavenly Homemade Bird Brothⓘ and 1 $^1/_2$ cup Hallee's Homemade Cream of Mushroom Soupⓘ.

Add the wild rice, thyme, and pepper.

Cover and cook on low heat for 7 to 8 hours or on high heat for 3 $^1/_2$ to 4 hours.

Just before serving, stir in the cooked chicken or turkey and the shredded spinach.

Serves about 6

Notes

ⓘ I have included a recipe for Hallee's Heavenly Homemade Bird Brothⓘ in this cookbook. If you don't have stock on hand, be sure to use a good organic stock with low or no salt.

ⓘ I have also included a recipe for Hallee's Homemade Cream of Mushroom Soupⓘ in this cookbook. If you don't have it on hand and have no time to whip up a batch, be sure to use a good organic soup with low or no salt.

Riddikulus Noodle Soup

Chicken & Ramen Noodle Soup

Feeding little mouths? The kids will have an easier time with shelled peas instead of snap peas. You can easily substitute $^{1}/_{4}$ cup (4 oz) of fresh or frozen sweet peas for the sugar snap peas in this recipe. If you use frozen, you may need to cook the soup for about 10 to 15 minutes longer.

My kids LOVE soup with noodles in it—especially Ramen soup. I've used homemade noodles, refrigerated packaged noodles, and the dried noodles from the packs. Whatever your preference, this is a great flavor and a fun soup.

Nutrition Facts

Serving Size: (378g)
Servings Per Container: 6

Amount Per Serving	
Calories 740	Calories from Fat 600
	% Daily Value*
Total Fat 67g	**103%**
Saturated Fat 18g	**90%**
Trans Fat 0g	
Cholesterol 160mg	**53%**
Sodium 1130mg	**47%**
Total Carbohydrate 15g	**5%**
Dietary Fiber 1g	**4%**
Sugars 4g	
Protein 18g	
Vitamin A 10% •	Vitamin C 10%
Calcium 4% •	Iron 10%

* Percent Daily Values are based on a 2,000 calorie diet. Your daily values may be higher or lower depending on your calorie needs:

	Calories:	2,000	2,500
Total Fat	Less than	65g	80g
Sat Fat	Less than	20g	25g
Cholesterol	Less than	300mg	300mg
Sodium	Less than	2,400mg	2,400mg
Total Carbohydrate		300g	375g
Dietary Fiber		25g	30g

6 oz (2 pkg.) Ramen noodles

1 medium stalk celery, choppedⓘ

2 green onions, choppedⓘ

1 cup sugar snap peas

8 oz can bamboo shoots, drained

8 oz can water chestnuts, drained

2 cups (16 oz) fresh carrots, cut to about 2 inches and cut in half lengthwise

$^{1}/_{4}$ cup (4 oz) Hallee's Homemade Oriental Seasoningⓘ

4 cups (32 oz) Hallee's Heavenly Homemade Bird Brothⓘ

6 to 8 chicken thighs (about 1 $^{1}/_{2}$ to 2 lbs), bone in and skin on

At least 3 ½ to 4 qt slow cooker

good sharp knife/cutting board

shallow pan or serving platter and 2 forks

measuring cups/spoons

kitchen tongs

ladle

Toss the unopened “flavor packet” that came with the Ramen noodles into the waste bin.

Slice the carrots

Chopⓘ the celery and onion

Drain the water chestnuts and bamboo shoots

In the slow cooker, layer the chicken thighs, carrots, celery, bamboo shoots, water chestnuts. Pour in Hallee’s Heavenly Homemade Bird Brothⓘ and Hallee’s Homemade Oriental Seasoning.

Cover and cook on low heat for 6 to 8 hours or on high heat for 3 to 4 hours.

About 10 to 15 minutes before serving, use kitchen tongs to remove the bird thighs from the slow cooker and place on cutting board. Using 2 forks, remove the skin and discard, then de-bone meat and discard bones.

According to your preference, either cut meat into bite-size cubes or shred meat with 2 forks. Either way, return just the meat to slow cooker and mix well.

Coarsely break Ramen noodles into soup. Stir in sugar snap peas.

Cover and cook until the noodles are tender, about an additional 10 to 15 minutes.

Just before serving, stir in onions.

If desired, add Kosher salt and fresh ground black pepper to taste.

Serves 6 to 8

ⓘ I have included a super easy recipe for Hallee's Homemade Oriental Seasoning in this cookbook. Avoid using the seasoning packet that comes with Ramen noodles which are loaded with salt and unhealthy chemicals like MSG.

ⓘ I have also included a recipe for Hallee's Heavenly Homemade Bird Brothⓘ in this cookbook. If you don't have stock on hand, be sure to use a good organic stock with low or no salt.

ⓘ For information about a tip for chopping vegetables, follow this link:

http://www.halleethehomemaker.com/2009/08/tips-chopping-onions/

Try this! Serve this Asian inspired soup Japanese Steak House style. Use chopsticks to eat the chicken, noodles, and vegetables, then use pretty Japanese soup spoons to swallow every drop of broth.

Minerva's Chicken Sandwiches

Tuscan-Style Chicken Sandwiches

Focaccia is a flat, round Italian bread with a dense texture that slices perfectly for sandwiches. Look for focaccia in the grocery store's bakery or deli, stop by an Italian bakery, or make your own wonderful fresh bread for this recipe. There are several recipes you can use in my bread cookbook *The Walking Bread; the Bread Will Rise!*

Nutrition Facts

Serving Size: (235g)
Servings Per Container: 6

Amount Per Serving	
Calories 740	Calories from Fat 550
	% Daily Value*
Total Fat 61g	**94%**
Saturated Fat 14g	**70%**
Trans Fat 0g	
Cholesterol 105mg	**35%**
Sodium 840mg	**35%**
Total Carbohydrate 32g	**11%**
Dietary Fiber 2g	**8%**
Sugars 3g	
Protein 17g	
Vitamin A 20% •	Vitamin C 45%
Calcium 4% •	Iron 15%

* Percent Daily Values are based on a 2,000 calorie diet. Your daily values may be higher or lower depending on your calorie needs:

	Calories:	2,000	2,500
Total Fat	Less than	65g	80g
Sat Fat	Less than	20g	25g
Cholesterol	Less than	300mg	300mg
Sodium	Less than	2,400mg	2,400mg
Total Carbohydrate		300g	375g
Dietary Fiber		25g	30g

3 TBS basil pesto

2 garlic cloves, minced

1/4 cup mayonnaise

1 fresh ripe tomato, cut into 6 slices

1/2 tsp Kosher salt (or sea salt)

1 (10-inch) focaccia (Italian flat) bread

1 1/4 lbs (about 6) chicken thighs, bone in and skin on

1/2 cup roasted red bell pepper, cut into bite-sized strips

Preparation

Slice the tomato and red bell pepper.

Mince the garlic.

If needed, whip up a batch of mayonnaise

Supplies

At least 3 1/2 to 4 qt slow cooker
good sharp knife/cutting board
measuring cups/spoons
shallow pan or serving platter and 2 forks
kitchen tongs
slotted spoon
mixing bowl

Yield

Makes 6 sandwiches

Directions

Place the chicken thighs into the slow cooker. Sprinkle with garlic, roasted pepper strips, and Kosher salt.

Cover and cook on low heat for 6 to 7 hours or on high heat for 3 to 3 $^{1}/_{2}$ hours.

About 10 to 15 minutes before serving, use kitchen tongs to remove the bird thighs from the slow cooker and place on cutting board. Using 2 forks, remove the skin and discard, then de-bone meat and discard bones.

According to your preference, either cut meat into bite-size cubes or shred meat with 2 forks. Either way, return just the meat to slow cooker.

In a small bowl, combine mayonnaise and pesto. Blend well.

Cut focaccia into 6 wedges. Split each wedge in half. Spread cut sides with mayonnaise/pesto mixture.

With a slotted spoon, place about $^{1}/_{3}$ cup of chicken mixture onto the bottom half of each focaccia wedge.

Top each with tomato slice and serve open faced or cover with the top half of the focaccia.

Notes

Here's a great tip! Freeze any remaining pesto to use on pasta or crostini, or to add a flavor boost to sauces, soups, eggs, or rice. Drop the pesto in 1 to 2 TBS portions onto a waxed paper lined cookie sheet. Freeze until firm. Transfer the frozen pesto portions to a food storage freezer bag. Remove only what you need when you need it and return the resealed bag to the freezer as you go.

Leprechaun's Chicken with Tarragon & Leeks

Chicken with Tarragon & Leeks

This is a simple, hearty dish with clean flavors and nice color. I love serving it mid-week when I need something to break the monotony of the easy fall-back of tomato based soups and casseroles dishes. It's a full meal—add a nice salad and you have a beautiful plate.

$^{1}/_{3}$ cup heavy cream

1 TBS chopped fresh tarragon

1 10-ounce package frozen peas

1 $^{1}/_{2}$ lbs (about 16) baby new potatoes

1 tsp salt (Kosher or sea salt is best)

3 leeks, white and light green parts, rinsed well, halved lengthwise, then sliced into 1 $^{1}/_{2}$ inch pieces

1 $^{1}/_{2}$ lbs (about 8 small) chicken thighs, bone in and skin on

1 cup dry white wine① (see NOTES for possible substitute)

4 to 6 quart slow cooker

kitchen tongs

good sharp knife

cutting board

2 forks

measuring cups/spoons

Scrub the potatoes, but leave the skin on.

Prepare and slice the leeks. (Note: in the base where the green meets the white, you'll need to clean with attention—dirt is often caught there.)

Place the potatoes on the bottom of slow cooker and place the chicken thighs on top. The chicken is placed near the bottom of the cooker where it is hottest because it needs more cooking than most of the rest of the ingredients.

Add the leeks, wine, and salt.

Cover and cook until the chicken and potatoes are tender; on low for 6 to 7 hours or on high for 3 to 4 hours.

About 10 to 15 minutes before serving, use kitchen tongs to remove the bird thighs from the slow cooker and place on cutting board. Using 2 forks, remove the skin and discard, then de-bone meat and discard bones.

Nutrition Facts

Serving Size: (548g)
Servings Per Container: 4

Amount Per Serving	
Calories 1040	Calories from Fat 720
	% Daily Value*
Total Fat 80g	**123%**
Saturated Fat 23g	**115%**
Trans Fat 0g	
Cholesterol 190mg	**63%**
Sodium 490mg	**20%**
Total Carbohydrate 49g	**16%**
Dietary Fiber 7g	**28%**
Sugars 9g	
Protein 24g	
Vitamin A 60% •	Vitamin C 60%
Calcium 8% •	Iron 25%

* Percent Daily Values are based on a 2,000 calorie diet. Your daily values may be higher or lower depending on your calorie needs:

	Calories:	2,000	2,500
Total Fat	Less than	65g	80g
Sat Fat	Less than	20g	25g
Cholesterol	Less than	300mg	300mg
Sodium	Less than	2,400mg	2,400mg
Total Carbohydrate		300g	375g
Dietary Fiber		25g	30g

According to your preference, slice meat into long strips, cut meat into bite-size cubes, or shred meat with 2 forks. For this recipe, my personal preference is to shred the meat. Transfer the chicken to plates.

Transfer all but 4 of the potatoes from the slow cooker to plates. Using a fork or potato masher, smash the remaining potatoes into the cooking liquid to thicken.

Add the peas and cream and cook just until heated through; on high for about 3 to 5 minutes. Spoon over the chicken and sprinkle with the tarragon.

Serves 4

Possible substitution: Thighs really are the best part of the bird for a slow cooker because they keep their shape, flavor, and moisture; especially when you leave the bone in. If you substitute boneless bird meat, you may want to add it to the top of the slow cooker ingredients as much as 1 to 2 hours after cooking starts so it doesn't overcook. Or you can precook the meat, cube it, and add it 10 or 15 minutes before serving.

Possible substitution: In my experience, turkey works just as well as chicken nearly all of the time.

ⓘ If you abstain from alcohol even in cooking, you can substitute a 100% pure grape juice (ensure there is no apple juice in it) and one teaspoon of distilled vinegar to approximate the same flavor and properties while cooking.

Mandragora Stew

Greek Chicken Stew

This is a hearty stew with the surprising flavors of cinnamon and lemon. You can serve it over rice or simply with a side salad.

$^1/_2$ cup filtered water (optional)

extra virgin olive oil or unsalted butter

1 tsp ground cinnamon

$^1/_2$ tsp dried oregano leaves

$^1/_4$ cup chopped parsley

$^1/_3$ cup tomato paste

2 tsp grated lemon peel zest

2 cloves garlic, finely chopped

$^1/_2$ tsp salt (Kosher or sea salt is best)

$^1/_2$ tsp fresh ground black pepper

1 lbs (1 bag frozen) small whole onions

3 $^1/_2$ cups fresh (or 2 cans 25-ounce cans) tomatoes, diced

2 cups carrots, halved lengthwise and cut to 1 inch (baby-cut carrots cut lengthwise also work)

3 lbs (about 6) chicken thighs, bone-in and skin on

Nutrition Facts

Serving Size: (415g)
Servings Per Container: 6

Amount Per Serving	
Calories 1070	Calories from Fat 910
	% Daily Value*
Total Fat 101g	**155%**
Saturated Fat 28g	**140%**
Trans Fat 0.5g	
Cholesterol 240mg	**80%**
Sodium 330mg	**14%**
Total Carbohydrate 18g	**6%**
Dietary Fiber 4g	**16%**
Sugars 9g	
Protein 24g	

Vitamin A 25%	•	Vitamin C 40%
Calcium 6%	•	Iron 15%

* Percent Daily Values are based on a 2,000 calorie diet. Your daily values may be higher or lower depending on your calorie needs:

	Calories:	2,000	2,500
Total Fat	Less than	65g	80g
Sat Fat	Less than	20g	25g
Cholesterol	Less than	300mg	300mg
Sodium	Less than	2,400mg	2,400mg
Total Carbohydrate		300g	375g
Dietary Fiber		25g	30g

4 to 6 quart slow cooker

kitchen tongs

good sharp knife

cutting board

2 forks

measuring cups/spoons

Cut carrots

Chop garlic

Dice tomatoes

Zest lemon

Lightly grease the inside of the slow cooker with either extra virgin olive oil or unsalted butter according to personal taste.

Place chicken thighs in slow cooker. Top with carrots and onions. The chicken is placed near the bottom of the cooker where it is hottest because it needs more cooking than most of the rest of the ingredients.

Sprinkle with cinnamon, salt, pepper and garlic; top with tomatoes. If needed, add up to $^{1}/_{2}$ cup filtered water.

Cover and cook until vegetables are tender and chicken pulls apart easily with a fork; on low heat for 7 to 9 hours or on high heat for 3 $^{1}/_{2}$ to 4 hours.

Remove chicken to cutting board with kitchen tongs or slotted spoon. Using 2 forks, remove the skin and discard, then de-bone meat and discard bones.

According to your preference, slice meat into long strips, cut meat into bite-size cubes, or shred meat with 2 forks. For this recipe, my personal preference is to shred the meat. Cover to keep warm.

Stir tomato paste, lemon peel zest, and oregano into liquid in slow cooker. Cover and cook until thickened and hot; about 15 minutes longer.

Stir chicken into mixture in slow cooker, breaking up larger pieces as needed.

To serve, spoon stew in shallow bowls, and top with parsley.

Serves 6

ⓘ Serve this stew with a fresh, hot, homemade batch of Granny Everman's Yeast Rolls

http://www.halleethehomemaker.com/2009/08/granny-everman's-yeast-rolls/

Try this tip: For added flavor, try adding roasted garlic or Hallee's Inviting Italian Seasoningⓘ.

Possible substitution: In my experience, turkey works just as well as chicken nearly all of the time. Either turkey thighs or chicken thighs work equally well in this recipe.

Possible substitution: Thighs really are the best part of the bird for a slow cooker because they keep their shape, flavor, and moisture; especially when you leave the bone in. If you substitute boneless bird meat, you may want to add it to the top of the slow cooker ingredients as much as 1 to 2 hours after cooking starts so it doesn't overcook. Or you can precook the meat, cube it, and add it 10 or 15 minutes before serving.

Sneakoscope Chicken & Bertie Bott's Every Flavour Bean Soup

Southwestern Chicken & White Bean Soup

"White chili" is a favorite in our household, and this is a good substitute for the creamy, spicy bird-based chili. It has great flavor and a nice kick. Serve this with your favorite corn bread, or top it with strips of tortilla.

1 lbs Skinless, boneless chicken breasts, cut into 1-inch cubes

1 1/2 cup (14 oz) Hallee's Heavenly Homemade Bird Broth ⓘ

1 TBS extra virgin olive oil

16 oz (1 can) small white beans, rinsed and drained (or 1 cup dried beans, soaked overnight and cooked until tender)

1 large onion (about 1 cup), chopped ⓘ

1 cup frozen whole kernel corn

1 cup chunky salsa ⓘ

3 cloves garlic, minced

2 tsp ground cumin

At least 3 1/2 to 4 qt slow cooker

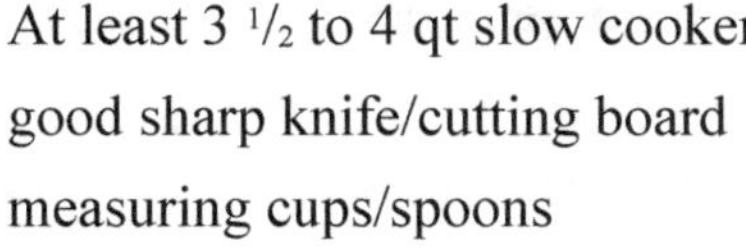

good sharp knife/cutting board

measuring cups/spoons

Serves 6

Nutrition Facts

Serving Size: (415g)
Servings Per Container: 6

Amount Per Serving	
Calories 250	Calories from Fat 45
	% Daily Value*
Total Fat 5g	**8%**
Saturated Fat 1g	**5%**
Trans Fat 0.5g	
Cholesterol 50mg	**17%**
Sodium 540mg	**23%**
Total Carbohydrate 29g	**10%**
Dietary Fiber 6g	**24%**
Sugars 4g	
Protein 24g	
Vitamin A 6% •	Vitamin C 8%
Calcium 8% •	Iron 20%

* Percent Daily Values are based on a 2,000 calorie diet. Your daily values may be higher or lower depending on your calorie needs:

	Calories:	2,000	2,500
Total Fat	Less than	65g	80g
Sat Fat	Less than	20g	25g
Cholesterol	Less than	300mg	300mg
Sodium	Less than	2,400mg	2,400mg
Total Carbohydrate		300g	375g
Dietary Fiber		25g	30g

Chopⓘ the onion

If using dried beans, soak overnight then cook until tender.

Mix broth, salsa, garlic, cumin, beans, corn, and onion in slow cooker.

Heat oil in skillet over medium-high heat. Add chicken and cook until browned, stirring often. When done, top slow cooker contents with chicken.

Cover and cook until chicken is no longer pink; on low heat for 6 to 8 hours or on high heat for 3 to 4 hours.

ⓘ I have included a recipe for Hallee's Heavenly Homemade Bird Brothⓘ in this cookbook. If you don't have stock on hand, be sure to use a good organic stock with low or no salt.

ⓘ For information about a tip for chopping vegetables, follow this link:

http://www.halleethehomemaker.com/2009/08/tips-chopping-onions/

ⓘ For a good recipe to make your own homemade fresh salsa, follow this link:

http://www.halleethehomemaker.com/2009/09/spicy-tomato-jalapeno-salsa/

Bludger Buffalo Chili

Buffalo Chicken Chili

Buffalo style chicken wings are a favorite treat for all of my kids. Any time I find a recipe with a buffalo flavor, I try it out on them. This one was a real winner. You honestly can't beat a soup based in chicken and black beans—add the buffalo style sauce and you have a delicious, zangy, hearty soup to warm you on the coldest of nights.

FOR THE ENTRÉE

2 $^{1}/_{2}$ lb chicken thighs, skin on and bone in

1 cup Hallee's Heavenly Homemade Bird Brothⓘ

1 can (28 oz) organic diced tomatoes, undrained

1 can (15 oz) black beans, drained, rinsed (or 1 cup dried beans, soaked overnight and cooked until tender)

1 large onion (about 1 cup), choppedⓘ

2 medium carrots (about 1 cup), choppedⓘ

2 medium stalks celery, sliced (about 1 cup)

2 tsp chili powder

$^{1}/_{2}$ tsp Kosher salt (or sea salt)

extra virgin olive oil or unsalted butter according to personal taste

FOR THE TOPPING:

Crumbled blue cheese, if desired

FOR THE BUFFALO WING SAUCE:

4 TBS bottled hot pepper sauce (use your personal favorite)

3 TBS unsalted butter, melted

1 TBS paprika

$^{1}/_{2}$ tsp ground cayenne pepper

$^{1}/_{4}$ tsp fresh ground black pepper

Nutrition Facts

Serving Size: (555g)
Servings Per Container: 6

Amount Per Serving	
Calories 1030	Calories from Fat 810
	% Daily Value*
Total Fat 90g	**138%**
Saturated Fat 27g	**135%**
Trans Fat 0.5g	
Cholesterol 215mg	**72%**
Sodium 1240mg	**52%**
Total Carbohydrate 30g	**10%**
Dietary Fiber 9g	**36%**
Sugars 7g	
Protein 26g	
Vitamin A 120% •	Vitamin C 30%
Calcium 15% •	Iron 20%

* Percent Daily Values are based on a 2,000 calorie diet. Your daily values may be higher or lower depending on your calorie needs:

	Calories:	2,000	2,500
Total Fat	Less than	65g	80g
Sat Fat	Less than	20g	25g
Cholesterol	Less than	300mg	300mg
Sodium	Less than	2,400mg	2,400mg
Total Carbohydrate		300g	375g
Dietary Fiber		25g	30g

5 to 6 qt slow cooker

measuring cups/spoons

good sharp knife

cutting board

mixing bowl

whisk

If using dried beans, soak the beans overnight then cook until tender. Chop the onion, carrots, and celery.

FOR THE ENTRÉE

Lightly grease the inside of the slow cooker with either extra virgin olive oil or unsalted butter according to personal taste. Place chicken things in bottom of the cooker.

Add all of the ingredients except homemade buffalo wing sauce and blue cheese.

Cover and cook on low heat for 6 to 8 hours or on high heat for 3 to 4 hours.

Remove chicken to cutting board with kitchen tongs or slotted spoon. Using 2 forks, remove the skin and discard, then de-bone meat and discard bones.

According to your preference, slice meat into long strips, cut meat into bite-size cubes, or shred meat with 2 forks. Return the meat to the cooker and stir.

FOR THE BUFFALO WING SAUCE:

Sometime before the entree finishes cooking, make a batch of homemade buffalo wing sauce. In a small mixing bowl, whisk together 3 TBS melted unsalted butter and 4 TBS of your favorite bottled hot pepper sauce. When well combined, whisk in 1 TBS paprika, 1/2 tsp ground cayenne pepper, and 1/4 tsp fresh ground black pepper. This makes about 1/4 cup of homemade buffalo wing sauce. Reserve in an airtight container in the refrigerator if needed.

Stir in homemade buffalo wing sauce. Cover and cook on high for about 10 more minutes.

Uncover and serve, sprinkled with blue cheese.

Serves 6

ⓘ I have included a recipe for Hallee's Heavenly Homemade Bird Brothⓘ in this cookbook. If you don't have stock on hand, be sure to use a good organic stock with low or no salt.

ⓘ For information about a tip for chopping vegetables, follow this link:

http://www.halleethehomemaker.com/2009/08/tips-chopping-onions/

Bertie's Turkey Chili

Red & White Turkey Chili

Shoepeg corn was a pre-Civil-War term for a corn with small, peg-shaped kernels. They're sweeter than your standard corn. They add a nice crisp sweetness to this zesty chili. I love topping this dish with sliced avocado and crispy tortilla strips.

2 lb turkey thighs, skin removed

3 1/2 cup Hallee's Heavenly Homemade Bird Brothⓘ

2 TBS flour (I use fresh ground soft white wheat)

1/4 cup filtered water

16 oz (1 can) white shoepeg corn

15.5 oz (1 can) great northern beans, drained (or 1 cup dried beans, soaked overnight and cooked until tender)

15 oz (1 can) dark red kidney beans, drained (or 1 cup dried beans, soaked overnight and cooked until tender)

9 oz (2 cans 4.5 oz each) chopped green chiles, undrained

1 medium onion (about 1/2 cup), choppedⓘ

1 clove garlic, finely chopped

2 tsp ground cumin

2 tsp chili powder

1/8 tsp ground cayenne pepper

Salt (Kosher or sea salt is best) to taste

1 lime, cut into wedges, if desired

extra virgin olive oil or unsalted butter

Supplies

4 to 5 quart slow cooker
measuring cups/spoons
good sharp knife
cutting board

Preparation

If using dried beans, soak the beans overnight then cook until tender. Dice the onion and chop the garlic.

Directions

Lightly grease the inside of the slow cooker with either extra virgin olive oil or unsalted butter according to personal taste.

Mix all ingredients except turkey, corn, flour, water and lime in cooker. Place turkey on top of everything in the cooker.

Cover and cook on low heat for 8 to 10 hours or on high heat for 3 $^{1}/_{2}$ to 4 hours.

About 10 to 15 minutes before serving, use kitchen tongs to remove the bird thighs from the slow cooker and place on cutting board. Using 2 forks, remove the skin and discard, then de-bone meat and discard bones.

Nutrition Facts

Serving Size: (552g)
Servings Per Container: 6

Amount Per Serving	
Calories 380	Calories from Fat 50
	% Daily Value*
Total Fat 5g	**8%**
Saturated Fat 1.5g	**8%**
Trans Fat 0g	
Cholesterol 120mg	**40%**
Sodium 1210mg	**50%**
Total Carbohydrate 41g	**14%**
Dietary Fiber 10g	**40%**
Sugars 5g	
Protein 44g	
Vitamin A 8% •	Vitamin C 30%
Calcium 10% •	Iron 25%

* Percent Daily Values are based on a 2,000 calorie diet. Your daily values may be higher or lower depending on your calorie needs:

	Calories:	2,000	2,500
Total Fat	Less than	65g	80g
Sat Fat	Less than	20g	25g
Cholesterol	Less than	300mg	300mg
Sodium	Less than	2,400mg	2,400mg
Total Carbohydrate		300g	375g
Dietary Fiber		25g	30g

According to your preference, either cut meat into bite-size cubes or shred meat with 2 forks. Either way, return just the meat to slow cooker and mix well.

Add turkey meat and corn to cooker.

In small bowl, mix flour and water; whisking to ensure there are no clumps. Stir into turkey mixture. If needed, increase to high heat.

Cover and cook and additional 20 to 30 minutes or until thoroughly heated and slightly thickened.

Serves 6

ⓘ I have included a recipe for Hallee's Heavenly Homemade Bird Brothⓘ in this cookbook. If you don't have stock on hand, be sure to use a good organic stock with low or no salt.

ⓘ For information about a tip for chopping vegetables, follow this link:

http://www.halleethehomemaker.com/2009/08/tips-chopping-onions/

Hagrid's Herbed Turkey Breast

Hallee's Herbed Turkey Breast

Your entire house will smell like Thanksgiving then entire time this turkey breast is cooking. Your family will feel like they're getting a mid-week feast when you serve it. You can keep it simple and serve it with a salad and a fresh veggie, or you can go all out and pile the plates with mashed potatoes and stuffing. This should serve your entire family with some leftovers to make sandwiches the next day. I personally prefer a bone-in turkey breast, but that may end up being too big for your slow cooker. Boneless is a fine substitute.

1 $^{1}/_{2}$ cup Hallee's Homemade Cream of Mushroom Soupⓘ

1 TBS Hallee's Pre-Made Poultry Rub Recipe 1ⓘ

1 TBS chopped fresh parsley

$^{1}/_{2}$ cup filtered water

4 $^{1}/_{2}$ to 5 lbs turkey breast

At least 3 $^{1}/_{2}$ to 6 qt slow cooker

measuring cups/spoons

good sharp knife/cutting board

mixing bowl

whisk

Nutrition Facts

Serving Size: (439g)
Servings Per Container: 8

Amount Per Serving	
Calories 550	Calories from Fat 160
	% Daily Value*
Total Fat 17g	**26%**
Saturated Fat 9g	**45%**
Trans Fat 0g	
Cholesterol 265mg	**88%**
Sodium 730mg	**30%**
Total Carbohydrate 5g	**2%**
Dietary Fiber 0g	**0%**
Sugars 3g	
Protein 88g	
Vitamin A 15% •	Vitamin C 4%
Calcium 10% •	Iron 15%

* Percent Daily Values are based on a 2,000 calorie diet. Your daily values may be higher or lower depending on your calorie needs:

	Calories:	2,000	2,500
Total Fat	Less than	65g	80g
Sat Fat	Less than	20g	25g
Cholesterol	Less than	300mg	300mg
Sodium	Less than	2,400mg	2,400mg
Total Carbohydrate		300g	375g
Dietary Fiber		25g	30g

If using homemade cream of mushroom soup, prepare the soup.

Mix soup and water in slow cooker. Rinse turkey with cold water and pat dry. Rub turkey with poultry seasoning and place in cooker. Sprinkle with parsley.

Cover and on low heat for 6 to 8 hours or on high heat for 4 1/2 to 5 hours. Insert meat thermometer into thickest part of the meat without touching the bone to check for doneness. Cook until temperature reads 165° degrees F (75° degrees C).

Let stand for 10 minutes before slicing.

Serves 8

ⓘ I have included a recipe for Hallee's Homemade Cream of Mushroom Soupⓘ in this cookbook. If you don't have it on hand and have no time to whip up a batch, be sure to use a good organic soup with low or no salt.

ⓘ I have included two recipes for poultry rubsⓘ in this cookbook. This particular recipe calls for poultry rub number 1 which is sage and marjoram based, but feel free to experiment with your seasonings.

Norbert's Tropical Turkey

Saucy Tropical Turkey

I enjoy going away from savory poultry dishes to saucy and almost sweet. This dish has so many amazing flavors that give it a tropical feel. It's wonderful to take to a potluck, or to serve next to rice at a luau themed party.

In this recipe, you can easily substitute 8 to 10 chicken thighs (about 2 to 2 1/2 lbs) for the turkey thighs.

Nutrition Facts

Serving Size: (391g)
Servings Per Container: 6

Amount Per Serving	
Calories 410	Calories from Fat 110
	% Daily Value*
Total Fat 13g	**20%**
Saturated Fat 3g	**15%**
Trans Fat 0g	
Cholesterol 150mg	**50%**
Sodium 830mg	**35%**
Total Carbohydrate 37g	**12%**
Dietary Fiber 2g	**8%**
Sugars 26g	
Protein 38g	
Vitamin A 20% •	Vitamin C 90%
Calcium 4% •	Iron 15%

* Percent Daily Values are based on a 2,000 calorie diet. Your daily values may be higher or lower depending on your calorie needs:

	Calories:	2,000	2,500
Total Fat	Less than	65g	80g
Sat Fat	Less than	20g	25g
Cholesterol	Less than	300mg	300mg
Sodium	Less than	2,400mg	2,400mg
Total Carbohydrate		300g	375g
Dietary Fiber		25g	30g

3 to 4 turkey thighs (about 2 1/2 lbs), skin removed

2 TBS extra virgin olive oil

1 small onion, halved and sliced

1/2 cup apricot preserves

1 red bell pepper, cubed

1 tsp grated lemon peel (zest)

1 tsp ground fresh ginger

1/4 cup filtered water

2 TBS cornstarch

Hot cooked rice or noodles

20 oz (1 can) pineapple chunks, drained

3 TBS gluten-free soy sauce (Tamari or fermented soy sauce strongly preferred)

At least 3 ½ to 6 qt slow cooker

measuring cups/spoons

good sharp knife

cutting board

mixing bowl

Jar with lid or blender bottle (something to mix cornstarch and water)

Slice onion.

Cube red bell pepper.

Zest lemon peel and ginger.

Rinse turkey and pat dry.

Heat oil in skillet. Brown turkey on all sides.

Place onion in slow cooker. Transfer turkey to slow cooker and top with pineapple and bell pepper.

In small bowl, combine preserves, soy sauce, lemon zest, and ginger. Mix well. Spoon over turkey.

Cover and cook on low heat for 6 to 7 hours or on high heat for 3 to 3 ½ hours.

Insert meat thermometer into thickest part of the meat without touching the bone to check for doneness. Cook until temperature reads 165° degrees F (75° degrees C).

Using kitchen tongs, remove turkey from slow cooker and place in shallow pan. Cover with aluminum foil to keep warm. (NOTE: Turkey will continue to cook.)

Blend water and cornstarch until smooth. A sports cup or a jar with a blender ball works well for this. Once blended, stir into the slow cooker.

Cook on high heat for 10 to 15 minutes or until sauce is slightly thickened. Adjust seasonings, if desired.

Using kitchen tongs, return turkey to slow cooker. Cook until hot.

Serve with rice or noodles.

Yield

Serves 6

Notes

This recipe is delicious, hearty, and filling when served over rice yet still light and healthy.

Malfoy's Chicken Rice Soup

Slow-Simmered Chicken Rice Soup

Chicken and rice soup is one of those comfort foods for me. It reminds me of lunch on cold Sundays after church. The wild rice gives it a nice nutty flavor and texture. Serve with a crusty French bread and a garden salad.

1 lbs skinless, boneless chicken breasts, cut into cubes

5 $^1/_4$ cup (about 42 oz) Hallee's Heavenly Homemade Bird Broth ⓘ

$^1/_2$ cup uncooked regular long-grain white rice

2 stalks celery (about 1 cup) , coarsely chopped ⓘ

1 medium onion ($^1/_2$ cup), chopped ⓘ

$^1/_2$ cup uncooked wild rice

3 carrots, sliced

1 TBS extra virgin olive oil

2 tsp dried thyme leaves, crushed

$^1/_4$ tsp crushed red pepper

(optional) sour cream

(optional) green onions, chopped ⓘ

Nutrition Facts

Serving Size: (379g)
Servings Per Container: About 6

Amount Per Serving	
Calories 190	Calories from Fat 40
	% Daily Value*
Total Fat 4.5g	**7%**
Saturated Fat 1g	**5%**
Trans Fat 0.5g	
Cholesterol 50mg	**17%**
Sodium 650mg	**27%**
Total Carbohydrate 16g	**5%**
Dietary Fiber 2g	**8%**
Sugars 4g	
Protein 20g	
Vitamin A 110% •	Vitamin C 8%
Calcium 4% •	Iron 6%

* Percent Daily Values are based on a 2,000 calorie diet. Your daily values may be higher or lower depending on your calorie needs:

	Calories:	2,000	2,500
Total Fat	Less than	65g	80g
Sat Fat	Less than	20g	25g
Cholesterol	Less than	300mg	300mg
Sodium	Less than	2,400mg	2,400mg
Total Carbohydrate		300g	375g
Dietary Fiber		25g	30g

Dice the onion.

Chop the celery.

Dice the carrots.

Supplies

At least 3 1/2 qt slow cooker
measuring cups/spoons
good sharp knife
cutting board

Directions

Mix wild rice and oil in slow cooker. Cover and cook on high for 15 minutes.

Add broth, thyme, red pepper, celery, onion, and chicken to cooker.

Cover and cook until chicken is no longer pink; on low heat for 6 to 8 hours or on high heat for 3 to 4 hours.

Serve with sour cream and green onion if desired.

Yield

Serves 6

Notes

ⓘ I have included a recipe for Hallee's Heavenly Homemade Bird Brothⓘ in this cookbook. If you don't have stock on hand, be sure to use a good organic stock with low or no salt.

ⓘ For information about a tip for chopping vegetables, follow this link:

http://www.halleethehomemaker.com/2009/08/tips-chopping-onions/

Fowl Tempered Chili

Chicken Enchilada Chili

This is definitely one of my favorite chili flavors—combining the spicy kick of enchiladas with the beans and meat in a chili. This is wonderful served with plain yogurt, sliced avocado, crispy tortilla strips on top. Your whole house will smell amazing the entire time this is cooking.

At least 3 1/2 to 4 qt slow cooker
kitchen tongs
good sharp knife
cutting board
2 forks
measuring cups/spoons
Small saucepan
Blender

1 1/4 lbs chicken thighs, bone in and skin on

2 cups dried pinto beans soaked overnight and cooked until tender (or 2 15-ounce cans pinto beans)

1 medium yellow bell pepper (1/2 cup), choppedⓘ

1 medium green bell pepper (1/2 cup), choppedⓘ

1 medium onion (1/2 cup), choppedⓘ

2 cloves garlic, minced

2 14.5 ounces diced tomatoes

FOR THE ENCHILADA SAUCE:

1/4 cup chili powder

2 TBS extra virgin olive oil

1 14.5 ounces can diced tomatoes

2 cloves garlic, chopped

2 tsp honey

1/2 tsp salt (Kosher or sea salt is best)

1/2 tsp dried oregano

1/4 tsp ground cumin

1/3 cup plain yogurt (or sour cream)

2 TBS chopped fresh cilantro

Nutrition Facts

Serving Size: (507g)
Servings Per Container: 6

Amount Per Serving	
Calories 420	Calories from Fat 100
	% Daily Value*
Total Fat 11g	**17%**
Saturated Fat 2.5g	**13%**
Trans Fat 0g	
Cholesterol 90mg	**30%**
Sodium 1120mg	**47%**
Total Carbohydrate 50g	**17%**
Dietary Fiber 16g	**64%**
Sugars 10g	
Protein 33g	
Vitamin A 50% •	Vitamin C 160%
Calcium 20% •	Iron 30%

* Percent Daily Values are based on a 2,000 calorie diet. Your daily values may be higher or lower depending on your calorie needs:

	Calories:	2,000	2,500
Total Fat	Less than	65g	80g
Sat Fat	Less than	20g	25g
Cholesterol	Less than	300mg	300mg
Sodium	Less than	2,400mg	2,400mg
Total Carbohydrate		300g	375g
Dietary Fiber		25g	30g

Make the enchilada sauce:

Heat oil in small saucepan over medium heat. Add chili powder. Reduce heat to medium-low, and cook for 4 minutes.

Place undrained tomatoes in blender. Add the chili powder/oil mixture, garlic, honey, and salt. Blend until smooth. Stir in the oregano and cumin. Return to saucepan and bring to a boil. Reduce heat to a simmer and cook for 10 minutes. May be stored in tightly covered container in the refrigerator for up to 2 weeks.

If using dried beans, soak overnight then cook until tender.

Dice onion, and peppers. Mince garlic.

Grease slow cooker with olive oil or unsalted butter. Place chicken in slow cooker. Cover with onions, peppers, garlic, tomatoes, pinto beans, and enchilada sauce.

Cover and cook on Low heat setting 6 to 8 hours.

About 10 to 15 minutes before serving, use kitchen tongs or

slotted spoon to remove the bird thighs from the slow cooker and place on cutting board. Using 2 forks, remove the skin and discard, then de-bone meat and discard bones. According to your preference, either cut meat into bite-size cubes or shred meat with 2 forks. For this recipe, I prefer to cut meat into bite-size cubes. Either way, return just the meat to slow cooker and mix well.

Cover and cook another 10 to 15 minutes.

Stir mixture to break up chicken.

Ladle into serving bowls. Top each serving with plain yogurt (or sour cream) and cilantro.

Serves 6

Possible substitution: Thighs really are the best part of the bird for a slow cooker because they keep their shape, flavor, and moisture; especially when you leave the bone in. If you substitute boneless bird meat, you may want to add it to the top of the slow cooker ingredients as much as 1 to 2 hours after cooking starts so it doesn't overcook. Or you can precook the meat, cube it, and add it 10 or 15 minutes before serving.

Possible substitution: In my experience, turkey works just as well as chicken nearly all of the time.

Possible substitution: Regular stewed tomatoes, along with some chopped onion and a dash of garlic powder or finely chopped fresh garlic, can be used in place of the flavored stewed tomatoes.

Tip: Lifting the lid of your slow cooker can add up to 20 minutes of cooking time. Instead, spin the lid to clear it of condensation so you can check the food.

Whomping Willow Nachos

Shredded Chicken Nachos

This recipe is the perfect occasion to get out your festive, brightly colored serve ware. Arrange garnishes in attractive serving bowls in advance; cover and refrigerate them for up to six hours.

The bird thighs are the best part of the bird for a slow cooker because they keep their shape, flavor, and moisture; especially when you leave the bone in. If you substitute boneless bird meat, you may want to add it to the slow cooker 1 to 2 hours after cooking starts so it doesn't overcook.

Or you can precook the meat, cube it, and add it 30 minutes or so before serving. You can even prepare the chicken in advance and keep it warm on low setting for up to two hours before serving. It freezes well in a tightly covered container, ready to pull out and heat up whenever you're ready for it.

If you are in a big hurry and don't have time to prepare your own pinto beans, tomatoes, or chilis, I have included the standard sizes for store-bought cans. Be sure to always choose organic when given a choice. The extra flavor is often worth the extra penny and you avoid consuming GMOs and pesticides.

Nutrition Facts

Serving Size: (507g)
Servings Per Container: 6

Amount Per Serving	
Calories 340	Calories from Fat 60
	% Daily Value*
Total Fat 7g	**11%**
Saturated Fat 2g	**10%**
Trans Fat 0g	
Cholesterol 140mg	**47%**
Sodium 870mg	**36%**
Total Carbohydrate 30g	**10%**
Dietary Fiber 10g	**40%**
Sugars 7g	
Protein 37g	
Vitamin A 25% •	Vitamin C 70%
Calcium 10% •	Iron 25%

* Percent Daily Values are based on a 2,000 calorie diet. Your daily values may be higher or lower depending on your calorie needs:

	Calories:	2,000	2,500
Total Fat	Less than	65g	80g
Sat Fat	Less than	20g	25g
Cholesterol	Less than	300mg	300mg
Sodium	Less than	2,400mg	2,400mg
Total Carbohydrate		300g	375g
Dietary Fiber		25g	30g

NACHOS:

8 to 10 (about 2 lbs) chicken thighs, skin on and bone in

2 1/2 TBS Hallee's Homemade Taco Seasoning Spice Blendⓘ

1 3/4 cup (15 oz can) pinto beans, drained

1 3/4 cup (14.5 oz can) diced tomatoes, undrained

1/2 cup (4.5 oz can) green chiles, chopped

1 small onion (about 1/2 cup) onion, chopped

1 small green pepper (about 1/2 cup) chopped

2 TBS lime juice

organic restaurant style tortilla chips

TOPPINGS:

4 oz (1 cup) shredded Colby-Monterey Jack cheese

3/4 cup sour cream

3/4 cup chunky salsaⓘ

1/4 cup sliced green onions

1/4 cup sliced ripe olives

2 TBS chopped fresh cilantro

1 lime, cut into 12 wedges

At least 3 1/2 to 4 qt slow cooker

good sharp knife/cutting board

shallow pan or serving platter and 2 forks

measuring cups/spoons

kitchen tongs

ladle

If using dried beans, prepare pinto beans by soaking them overnight then cooking until tender.

Place chicken thighs in slow cooker. Sprinkle with taco seasoning blend. Top with beans, tomatoes, chiles, and lime juice.

Cover and cook until chicken is no longer pink; on low heat for 6 to 8 hours or on high heat for 3 to 4 hours.

About 10 to 15 minutes before serving, use kitchen tongs to remove the bird thighs from the slow cooker and place on cutting board. Using 2 forks, remove the skin and discard, then de-bone meat and discard bones.

According to your preference, either cut meat into bite-size cubes or shred meat with 2 forks. Either way, return just the meat to slow cooker and mix well.

Mash the beans in the slow cooker.

Just before serving, place all the toppings ingredients in individual serving bowls or dishes with serving spoons or forks as appropriate.

To serve, have guests place chips on serving plates. Spoon about 1/2 cup of chicken mixture onto the chips. Top nachos with desired toppings.

Chicken mixture can be held on low setting for continuous returns for second helpings for up to 2 hours.

About 12 servings

Notes

I'm not a fan of the packaged seasoning mixes only because they contain ingredients other than the spices. If you have store-bought Taco Seasoning on hand, you can substitute a single 1.25 oz store-bought packet for 2 1/2 TBS Hallee's Homemade Taco Seasoning Spice Blendⓘ. But you can easily make your own Homemade Taco Seasoning Spice Blend. This recipe is included in the back of this cookbook and is also on my website including full nutritional information:

http://www.halleethehomemaker.com/2011/09/homemade-taco-seasoning-mix/

To make your own just combine 2 tsp to 1 TBS chili powder (to taste), 2 tsp onion powder, 1 tsp ground cumin, 1 tsp garlic powder (not garlic salt), 1 tsp paprika, 1 tsp ground oregano, and 1 tsp sugar. Optionally, throw in 1/2 tsp Kosher or sea salt. Mix all ingredients well and there you have it. About 1.5 oz of Hallee's Homemade Taco Seasoning Spice Blendⓘ.

ⓘ For a good recipe to make your own homemade fresh salsa, follow this link:

http://www.halleethehomemaker.com/2009/09/spicy-tomato-jalapeno-salsa/

Red Meats

It's No Illusion.

Red meat is so versatile in the way that you can use it. Whole roasts, ground, cubed, sliced thin—you really have no limit in how you can cook it in the slow cooker.

Many traditional oven dishes, like lasagna, meatballs, enchiladas—even pizza—can be prepared ahead of time and set to cook in a slow cooker. You can come home at the end of a busy day to a meal already made for you.

One of the great things about cooking in a slow cooker is that, with the low and slow method of cooking, almost any cut of meat will be tender by the time it's finished cooking. Whole roasts will actually fall apart. Cubed meat will be fork-tender. So if you're wanting red meat but your pocketbook isn't really a fan, buying a cheaper cut to use in a slow cooker dish is the perfect answer.

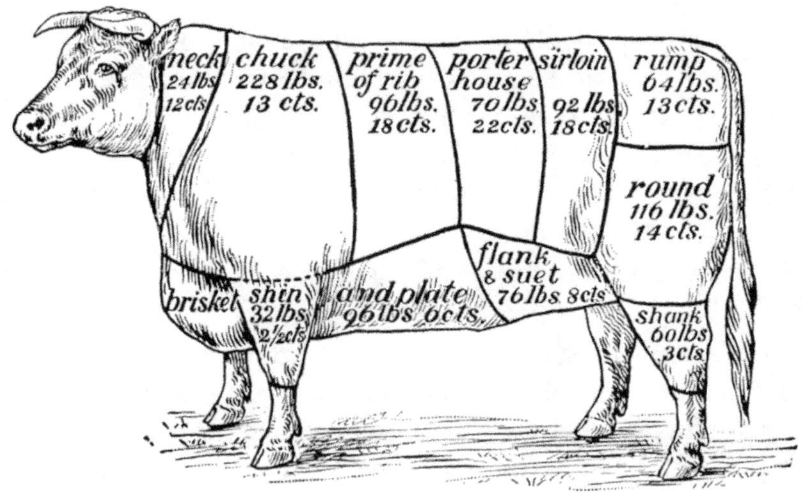

Kinds, Cuts, & Grades of Red Meats

Red meats commonly include cuts of beef just like you can purchase at your corner grocer as well as lamb and goat in specialty butcher shops. Red meat also includes traditional game meats such as bison and venison. There are different cuts and grades of red meat and some are going to cook better than others in certain recipes.

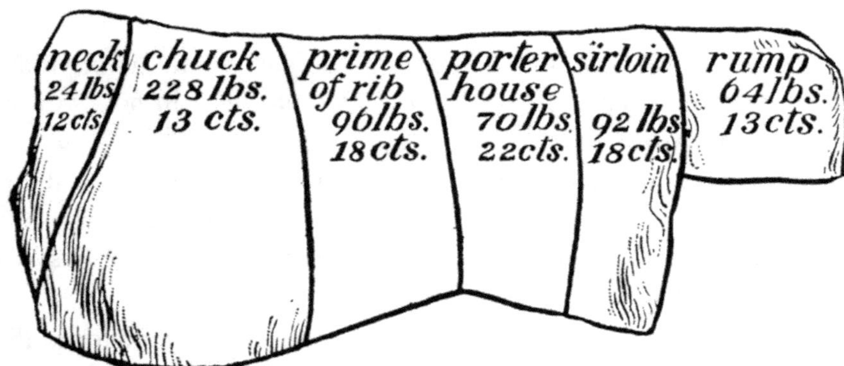

The "best" cuts come from the "top" of—or "high" on—the animal which is where we get the ironic expression "living high on the hog" for instance. Top sirloin, for instance, means that the cut came from the upper rear part of the animal as opposed to bottom sirloin, which is properly called the flank or suet cut. The top cuts are the best roasts and thickest most juicy and delicious steaks.

When buying high cuts such as ribeye, sirloin, prime, or rump, look for meat that has some fat marbling around the edges. Expect it to be pricey. Try to keep in mind that it is going to taste absolutely amazing. Even though it feels like a high price to pay for a meal, it will ultimately cost you less than a dinner out for 1 at any 5-star chop-house.

Keep in mind, too, that a single pound of beef can easily feed 2-4 adults.

In the United States, cuts can be voluntarily graded by the Department of Agriculture according to USDA standards. USDA meat grading is voluntary and the meat packing plants have to pay for grading so that cost is passed along to the consumers. The eight possible USDA grades for beef from best to worst are Prime, Choice, Select, Standard, Commercial, Utility, Cutter, and Canner while chicken, turkey, duck, and other inspected game birds like geese and pigeon can be graded with the letter system graded from A to F.

The "low cuts" come from "where the sun doesn't shine" on the animal. They are perfect for use in a slow cooker because they will become tender in the low and slow cooking method.

ⓘ For the latest information about the current Agricultural Marketing Service USDA standards for grading meat and other consumable commodities, visit the official website at:

http://www.ams.usda.gov/AMSv1.0/Grading

The vast majority of widely available graded beef in groceries across these United States is graded Standard. While Standard cuts are very good, when purchasing USDA graded beef, try to purchase at least Select and expect to pay more for Choice and far more for Prime cuts (which are usually reserved for 5-star restaurants). There is no significance to USDA Grade A beef anymore than USDA Choice chicken, so read labeling carefully to avoid clever marketing.

Oftentimes, you can obtain very high quality meat equal to or better than USDA graded cuts at a reduced cost when you purchase from a local butcher, preferably one who either raises the animals himself or sources cuts from local sustainable farms. The animal should be at least partially grass-fed and humanely butchered.

Firebolt Barbecued Beef Brisket

Smoky Barbecued Beef Brisket

Serve this tomato rich beef with a side of coleslaw and fresh fruit for dessert. It is unforgettable.

1 fresh beef brisket (2-to-3 lbs)

1/4 cup honey (pure, raw, local honey is always best) or brown sugar

1/2 cup Hallee's Homemade Organic Ketchupⓘ

1/3 cup filtered water

1/2 cup bottled hot pepper chili sauce

3 TBS flour

2 TBS Worcestershire sauce

2 TBS distilled vinegar

1 1/2 tsp liquid smoke

1 tsp chili powder

1/2 tsp garlic powder

1/2 tsp dry mustard

1/4 tsp celery seeds

1/8 tsp fresh ground black pepper

Nutrition Facts

Serving Size: (235g)
Servings Per Container: 8

Amount Per Serving	
Calories 350	Calories from Fat 120
	% Daily Value*
Total Fat 13g	**20%**
Saturated Fat 4.5g	**23%**
Trans Fat 0g	
Cholesterol 105mg	**35%**
Sodium 590mg	**25%**
Total Carbohydrate 20g	**7%**
Dietary Fiber 1g	**4%**
Sugars 14g	
Protein 36g	
Vitamin A 8% •	Vitamin C 6%
Calcium 2% •	Iron 20%

* Percent Daily Values are based on a 2,000 calorie diet. Your daily values may be higher or lower depending on your calorie needs:

	Calories:	2,000	2,500
Total Fat	Less than	65g	80g
Sat Fat	Less than	20g	25g
Cholesterol	Less than	300mg	300mg
Sodium	Less than	2,400mg	2,400mg
Total Carbohydrate		300g	375g
Dietary Fiber		25g	30g

Trim any fat from the meat.

Cut meat into large portions that it will fit into slow cooker

At least 3 1/2 to 4 qt slow cooker
good sharp knife and cutting board
small and medium mixing bowls
measuring cups/spoons
medium saucepan
shallow pan
aluminum foil

In small mixing bowl, combine chili powder, garlic powder, celery seed, and fresh ground black pepper. DO NOT USE SALT. Sprinkle evenly over all sides of meat. Rub in with your fingers. Put meat into slow cooker.

In medium mixing bowl, combine ketchup, hot sauce, honey, vinegar, Worcestershire sauce, liquid smoke, and dry mustard. When well mixed, pour over meat.

Cover and cook on low heat for 8 to 10 hours or on high for 4 to 6 hours. Remove meat from slow cooker, reserving juices, and place in shallow pan then cover with foil to keep warm.

Skim fat from cooking juices. Measure 2 1/2 cups of the juices and set aside. In medium saucepan, stir the water into the flour. Slowly stir in reserved juices. Cook and stir over medium heat until thickened and bubbly. Cook and stir for 1 to 2 minutes more.

Thinly slice meat across the grain and fan on platter or individual plates. Drizzle with sauce or serve sauce on the side.

6 to 8 servings

Notes

If you have a smoker, you can make your own liquid smoke. Using no accelerates, starters, or chemicals at all, get your smoker going with your favorite wood chips. Empty a tray of ice cubes into a pie pan and placing it inside the smoker. The smoke will condense on the ice. Once the ice melts, heat the liquid in a saucepan to reduce by about a third and concentrate the flavors.

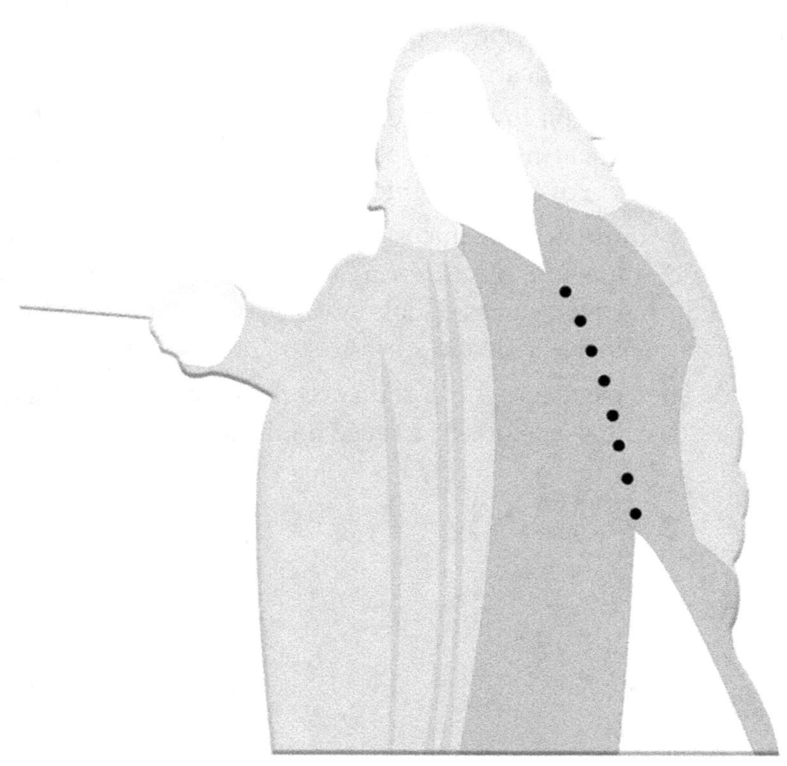

Butterbeer Barbecued Beef Sandwiches

Root Beer Barbecued Beef Sandwiches

Better than any "pulled pork" sandwich you have ever tried. Use organic "root beer" which has no HFCS and is made from actual roots like sassafras so it's really tasty. This recipe is truly a favorite of my friends and family. Every time I've taken it to a potluck, it's been consumed so that there isn't even any juices left in the pan! Enjoy—something about the root beer really makes the beef delicious.

1 4-lb boneless beef rump roast, trimmed of fat

2 TBS + 1 cup organic root beer (I use organic root beer, because it's made from actual roots and uses real sugar or cane juice instead of high fructose corn syrup)

2 TBS extra virgin olive oil

Kosher or sea salt to taste

fresh ground black pepper to taste

16 whole wheat hamburger buns

2 cups Kelly's Organic Barbecue Sauceⓘ

16 sandwiches

Nutrition Facts

Serving Size: (156g)
Servings Per Container: 16

Amount Per Serving	
Calories 300	Calories from Fat 50
	% Daily Value*
Total Fat 6g	**9%**
Saturated Fat 1g	**5%**
Trans Fat 0g	
Cholesterol 0mg	**0%**
Sodium 1000mg	**42%**
Total Carbohydrate 57g	**19%**
Dietary Fiber 1g	**4%**
Sugars 22g	
Protein 9g	

Vitamin A 10% •	Vitamin C 6%
Calcium 6% •	Iron 10%

* Percent Daily Values are based on a 2,000 calorie diet. Your daily values may be higher or lower depending on your calorie needs:

	Calories:	2,000	2,500
Total Fat	Less than	65g	80g
Sat Fat	Less than	20g	25g
Cholesterol	Less than	300mg	300mg
Sodium	Less than	2,400mg	2,400mg
Total Carbohydrate		300g	375g
Dietary Fiber		25g	30g

At least 3 1/2 to 4 qt slow cooker
good sharp knife and cutting board
measuring cups/spoons
large iron skillet
saucepan
shallow pan
aluminum foil
forks
mixing bowl
whisk

Trim any fat off of the roast.

Salt and pepper both sides then rub it in with your fingertips.

Preheat slow cooker.

Heat oil in the skillet over medium-high heat until hot. Add the roast. Sear on each side for 1 minute. Cook until nicely browned on all sides. Immediately place the beef in a preheated slow cooker.

Add 2 TBS root beer to the skillet. Cook and stir with a whisk, scraping up all of the yummy brown bits from the seared roast. Pour into mixing bowl and add 1 1/2 cups of barbecue sauce and the remaining root beer. Pour over beef in slow cooker.

Cover and cook on low heat for 10 to 11 hours or on high for 5 to 5 1/2 hours.

About 20 minutes before serving, remove beef from slow cooker and place in shallow pan. Loosely cover with foil to keep warm.

Pour juices from slow cooker into saucepan. Cook over medium-high heat for about 15 minutes, stirring regularly, until juices are thickened and reduced to about 3 cups.

Meanwhile, shred beef with 2 forks. Return to slow cooker.

Stir remaining $^{1}/_{2}$ cup barbecue sauce into reduced juices in pan. Pour sauce over beef. Add salt and pepper to taste. Mix well.

Spoon about $^{1}/_{2}$ cup beef mixture onto each bun.

This is a perfect dish to take to any gathering. Try serving with your favorite hot sauce.

The only way to make this dish even better would be to start with a batch of your very own Hallee's Homemade Organic Ketchup and Kelly's Organic Barbecue Sauceⓘ. I cannot even explain how the flavors explode with incredible depth when these homemade items, and not store-bought factory substitutes, form the base. I have included recipes for these in this cookbook and strongly encourage you to try them out. You might just thank me later.

Crookshanks Cheese Steak

Philly Cheese Steak Sandwiches

Once America's capital, Philadelphia was the site of the very first Continental Congress and is the present-day home of the Liberty Bell as well as the nation's first and longest serving US Mint. America's first hospital, first children's hospital, first medical school, and first cancer center were all born in Philadelphia. The very first department store is still operating on the corner of Broad and Chestnut Streets. The world's first computer, the ENIAC, booted up in America's fifth largest city and shortly developed its first "bug," an actual moth that caused a short circuit.

Nutrition Facts

Serving Size: (275g)
Servings Per Container: 4

Amount Per Serving	
Calories 220	Calories from Fat 80
	% Daily Value*
Total Fat 8g	**12%**
Saturated Fat 3.5g	**18%**
Trans Fat 0g	
Cholesterol 80mg	**27%**
Sodium 400mg	**17%**
Total Carbohydrate 8g	**3%**
Dietary Fiber 2g	**8%**
Sugars 3g	
Protein 27g	

Vitamin A 4%	•	Vitamin C 60%
Calcium 4%	•	Iron 15%

* Percent Daily Values are based on a 2,000 calorie diet. Your daily values may be higher or lower depending on your calorie needs:

	Calories:	2,000	2,500
Total Fat	Less than	65g	80g
Sat Fat	Less than	20g	25g
Cholesterol	Less than	300mg	300mg
Sodium	Less than	2,400mg	2,400mg
Total Carbohydrate		300g	375g
Dietary Fiber		25g	30g

Sports and the arts are important to natives. Who could forget the Rocky films or non-fictional hall of fame boxing legends who call the city of brotherly love their home including "Philadelphia" Jack O'Brien, Joey Giardello, Sonny Liston, and Joe Frazier to name a few. Did you know the Philadelphia Eagles defeated Cincinnati in Temple Stadium way back in 1934 in the world's first ever professional football game? The city hosted America's first play in 1767, a commitment to the arts and performing arts that is manifest today in more than 100 theater companies, more than 2000 outdoor wall murals, a full symphony orchestra, and the largest public collections of paintings and statues in America all lovingly cared for and maintained in more than 100 museums.

The city of Philadelphia can claim so many achievements for our nation and the world from such diverse areas of culture as politics, medicine, sports, the arts, and science that it is almost funny to think that most people only associate "Philly" with a sandwich.

But, hey, it's a great sandwich.

Traditionally served with a single Kosher dill pickle spear on the side of a griddle toasted hoagie roll, it is equally good on a French bread bun or Kaiser roll. Since the meat is cut into very fine 1 1/4 inch strips, you need not use top cuts. In fact, you can marinate thin cut flank steak or bottom sirloin strips and it is just as tasty if not better.

The onion and bell pepper with the beef and melted cheese are simply delicious. Enjoyed with a crisp Kosher dill, it is truly a great achievement in a sandwich and should rank among any of Philadelphia's 150 plus fine dining establishments.

1 lb boneless beef round steak (1 inch thick), fat trimmed, cut into 1 1/4 inch strips

1 TBS unsalted butter, melted

2 medium onions, sliced

1 tsp garlic powder

1 tsp fresh ground black pepper

1/2 tsp salt (Kosher or sea salt is best)

1 large green bell pepper, cut into rings

1/4 cup Hallee's Savory Stocky Crock Pot Beef Brothⓘ

4 crusty French bread sandwich rolls, split (or Hoagie buns or Kaiser rolls)

4 (1-oz.) slices provolone cheese, halved

Kosher dill pickles or spears for garnish

mayonnaiseⓘ to taste (completely optional)

Supplies

at least 3 ½ to 4 quart slow cooker

griddle or skillet to toast buns

medium mixing bowls

basting brush

slotted spoon

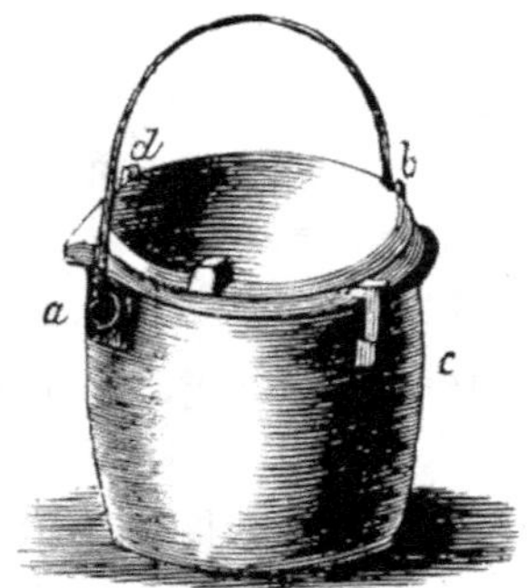

Preparation

Slice onions

Cut bell pepper

Directions

In medium bowl, combine melted butter and onions. Mix well to thoroughly coat.

Sprinkle beef with garlic-pepper blend and salt.

In slow cooker, layer all of the beef, all of the bell pepper, and half of the onions in as many layers as you like until the ingredients are used up. Top with remaining half of onions.

Pour beef broth slowly over mixture in slow cooker.

Cover; cook on low heat for 6 to 8 hours or on high heat for 3 to 4 hours.

About 15 to 20 minutes before serving, either slice fresh garlic (preferred) or reserve some garlic powder (not garlic salt). Cut your buns in half. Try to leave a "hinge" down one side.

Place open bun halves, cut side up, on ungreased cookie sheet and lightly coat cut sides with butter (using basting brush if desired to achieve very light coating). Place in oven and broil 2 to 3 inches from heat toasting buns only until just firm—no more than about 30 seconds to 1 minute—then remove from oven. While still toasty hot, either rub with fresh garlic (preferred) or lightly dust with garlic powder. Let stand a few minutes.

About 10 minutes before serving, use slotted spoon and place beef mixture on bottom halves of buns.

Top each with 2 slices of cheese. Place in oven and broil 2 to 3 inches from heat until cheese is melted and top halves of buns are well toasted—about 2 to 5 minutes depending on your oven and altitude.

(If you are like my husband, at this stage of sandwich making, you will now slather mayonnaise on the top half.)

Place top halves over cheese and serve with a Kosher dill pickle and—in the south at least—mayonnaise on the side.

Serves 4

Possible substitutions:

Mozzarella cheese can easily be used instead of the provolone.

If you don't have French bread buns, use hoagie buns or try or Kaiser rolls instead.

Notes on Ingredients:

ⓘ I have included a recipe for Hallee's Savory Stocky Crock Pot Beef Brothⓘ in this cookbook. If you don't have stock on hand, be sure to use a good organic stock with low or no salt.

ⓘ If you want to make your own French breadⓘ, it is super easy. Check out my recipe either in "The Walking Bread: The Bread Shall Rise" cookbook or at this link:

http://www.halleethehomemaker.com/2009/08/french-bread/

ⓘ If you want to make your own mayonnaise, it is equally easy. Check out my recipe at this link:

http://www.halleethehomemaker.com/2009/09/mayonnaise/

Miscellaneous:

In the last quarter century or so, one negative has besmirched this American icon. In Philadelphia, when ordering an authentic Philly Steak from Geno's or Pat's, you can now order it "wit'" meaning "with" Cheez Whiz® instead of provolone. That means instead of actual cheese you can select (and I quote) "a thick processed cheese sauce—or spread—sold by Kraft Foods®" which doesn't actually contain *cheese*.

While native Philadelphians might stare in abject horror when southerners like my husband personalize an authentic Philly since my husband prefers his Philly Steak with mayonnaiseⓘ (snort!), I am equally certain he could fairly ask if they knew just what they were eating their sandwich "wit'" in return.

Cheez Whiz® comes in jars and doesn't actually contain any dairy, so it would never come about naturally, like when adding an acid to milk. Rather it was (and I quote again) "developed by a team of food scientists." I should stop there but I just can't. Cheez Whiz® can be used to get out difficult stains, is a good substitute for axle grease in an emergency, and just one tiny little single serving (carefully defined as just 2 itsy-bitsy level tablespoons by the manufacturer—a division of Philip Morris which also produces such healthy products as Marlboro cigarettes) contains 90 calories and 25% of the daily recommended dose of salt. In short, making your Philly steak "wit'" that utter junk, I mean Cheez Whiz®, is not something I consider "wise" so maybe stick "wit'" real provolone.

Cenatur's Corned Beef & Cabbage

Corned Beef & Cabbage

You don't have to wait for Saint Patrick's Day to roll around for an excuse to make this simple corned beef and cabbage recipe. If I had my way, we would whip this recipe up at least once a month. Leftovers make outstanding sandwiches for the next-day lunch boxes, or you can cube up the corned beef and fry it with some potatoes, creating the favorite corned beef hash for breakfast!

1 (4 to 5 pound) corned beef, rinsed

1 medium head of cabbage, cut into 2-inch wedges

6 red potatoes, halved

4 carrots, cut into 1/2 inch chunks

1 medium onion, cut into 1/2 inch chunks

2 cups Hallee's Savory Stocky Crock Pot Beef Broth ⓘ

8 oz beer (see NOTES for possible substitute) ⓘ

3 large bay leaves

1 TBS stone ground mustard

1 tsp black peppercorns

At least 3 1/2 to 4 qt slow cooker

measuring cups/spoons

good sharp knife/cutting board

Preparation

Trim any fat from the meat.

If needed cut meat into large portions that it will fit into slow cooker

Directions

Place onions, carrots, and potatoes in the bottom of a large slow cooker pot.

Rinse the corned beef and lay it over the vegetables. Add in bay leaves, peppercorns, and stone ground mustard (if using the spice packet from the corned beef, use that instead of the spices listed in the recipe).

Pour beer and beef broth over everything. Make sure liquid covers most of the corned beef. If not, add filtered water or more stock until the beef is covered.

Cover and cook on low for 8 hours or on high for about 5.

Add the cabbage to the slow cooker and cook until cabbage is just tender (about 30 minutes).

Plate beef and veggies.

Slice beef against the grain and serve with extra mustard.

Nutrition Facts

Serving Size: (1215g)
Servings Per Container: 8

Amount Per Serving	
Calories 1130	Calories from Fat 390
	% Daily Value*
Total Fat 44g	**68%**
Saturated Fat 14g	**70%**
Trans Fat 1.5g	
Cholesterol 155mg	**52%**
Sodium 3830mg	**160%**
Total Carbohydrate 127g	**42%**
Dietary Fiber 15g	**60%**
Sugars 14g	
Protein 57g	
Vitamin A 100% •	Vitamin C 290%
Calcium 15% •	Iron 60%

* Percent Daily Values are based on a 2,000 calorie diet. Your daily values may be higher or lower depending on your calorie needs:

	Calories:	2,000	2,500
Total Fat	Less than	65g	80g
Sat Fat	Less than	20g	25g
Cholesterol	Less than	300mg	300mg
Sodium	Less than	2,400mg	2,400mg
Total Carbohydrate		300g	375g
Dietary Fiber		25g	30g

Yield

Serves 8

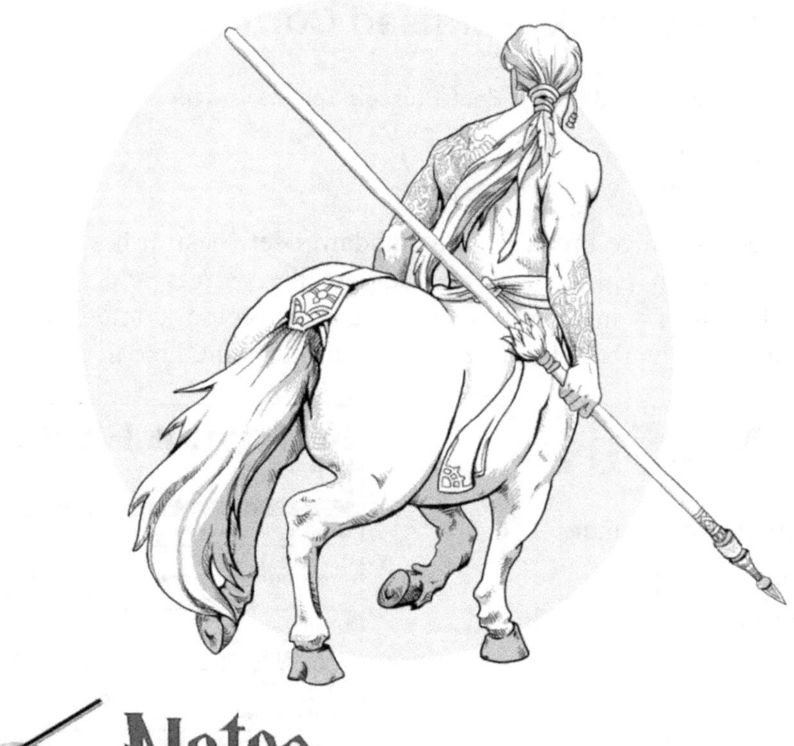

ⓘ If you abstain from alcohol even in cooking, you can substitute a nonalcoholic beer to approximate the same flavor and properties while cooking. In this recipe, you could simply substitute filtered water, as well, though it would not have the same flavor, obviously.

ⓘ I have included a recipe for Hallee's Savory Stocky Crock Pot Beef Brothⓘ in this cookbook. If you don't have stock on hand, be sure to use a good organic stock with low or no salt.

You can buy corned beef at the grocery store that has a seasoning packet in it. If you use the packet, don't include the mustard, bay leaves, or peppercorn in this recipe.

Basilisk's Best Ale-Braised Corned Beef

Ale-Braised Corned Beef, Brussels Sprouts, & Carrots

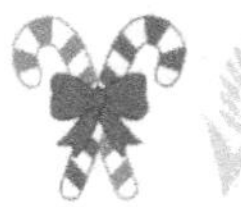   

Corned beef is a nice break from a standard beef roast. It has a richer flavor, and when paired with vegetables like carrots and Brussels sprouts, becomes a meal in a single pot. This recipe, combining the sour cream and the fresh tarragon, is such a full-bodied meal.

5 to 6 quart slow cooker

measuring cups/spoons

good sharp knife

cutting board

3 large bay leaves

2 TBS whole-grain mustard

1 TBS stone ground mustard

1 tsp black peppercorns

3/4 pound Brussels sprouts

1/2 cup sour cream

1 TBS chopped fresh tarragon

12 oz bottle alcoholic or nonalcoholic amber ale (no appreciable taste difference)

3 lbs uncooked corned beef brisket (with spice packet, if included)

1 pound carrots, peeled and cut into 3-inch lengths

Nutrition Facts

Serving Size: (444g)
Servings Per Container: 6

Amount Per Serving	
Calories 580	Calories from Fat 350
	% Daily Value*
Total Fat 38g	**58%**
Saturated Fat 13g	**65%**
Trans Fat 1g	
Cholesterol 130mg	**43%**
Sodium 2880mg	**120%**
Total Carbohydrate 17g	**6%**
Dietary Fiber 5g	**20%**
Sugars 5g	
Protein 37g	
Vitamin A 260% •	Vitamin C 190%
Calcium 10% •	Iron 30%

* Percent Daily Values are based on a 2,000 calorie diet. Your daily values may be higher or lower depending on your calorie needs:

	Calories:	2,000	2,500
Total Fat	Less than	65g	80g
Sat Fat	Less than	20g	25g
Cholesterol	Less than	300mg	300mg
Sodium	Less than	2,400mg	2,400mg
Total Carbohydrate		300g	375g
Dietary Fiber		25g	30g

Preparation

Trim any fat from the meat.

Slice the carrots.

Clean and trim the Brussels sprouts.

Yield

Serves 6

Directions

Place the beef in the bottom of the slow cooker. Sprinkle with the spice packet (if included) or the peppercorns, bay leaves, and mustard. Add the carrots and cover with the ale. Cook, covered, until the beef is tender, on low heat for 7 to 8 hours or on high heat for 4 to 5 hours.

Ten minutes before serving, thinly slice the Brussels sprouts. (This is easiest to do in a food processor with the slicing blade.)

Transfer the beef from the slow cooker to a cutting board; set slow cooker to high heat if necessary. Add the Brussels sprouts to the carrots and liquid in the slow cooker. Cook, covered, until the Brussels sprouts are tender, 4 to 6 minutes.

Meanwhile, in a small bowl, combine the sour cream, mustard, and tarragon.

Slice the beef. Serve with the vegetables and sour cream sauce.

Notes

Here's a Tip: Corned beef brisket is sold in the supermarket meat case uncooked, which is different from the cooked corned beef you find at the deli counter. The uncooked brisket often comes with a packet of spices. Those without the spice packet have already been cured. You can either add the spice packet to this recipe, if your brisket came with one, or you can add 2 TBS of your own Montreal Steak Seasoningⓘ.

Bloggart Bratwurst with Slitherin Sauerkraut & Potatoes

Beef Bratwurst with Sauerkraut

Bratwurst and sauerkraut are two of my favorite combinations. This recipe is a treat for me. I serve it with a dark rye bread and stone ground mustard—the perfect meal!

1 1/2 lbs all beef bratwurst links

1/4 cup dry white wine (see NOTES for possible substitute)ⓘ

1/2 cup Hallee's Savory Stocky Crock Pot Beef Brothⓘ

1 1/2 lbs red new potatoes (about 18), halved if large

1/4 cup chopped fresh flat-leaf parsley

2 cups Kosher sauerkraut, drained

1 small onion, thinly sliced

1 tsp caraway seeds

1/2 tsp Kosher salt (or sea salt)

1/4 tsp fresh ground black pepper

4 to 6 quart slow cooker

measuring cups/spoons

good sharp knife

cutting board

Nutrition Facts

Serving Size: (247g)
Servings Per Container: 8

Amount Per Serving	
Calories 370	Calories from Fat 240
	% Daily Value*
Total Fat 27g	**42%**
Saturated Fat 13g	**65%**
Trans Fat 0g	
Cholesterol 65mg	**22%**
Sodium 490mg	**20%**
Total Carbohydrate 17g	**6%**
Dietary Fiber 3g	**12%**
Sugars 2g	
Protein 14g	
Vitamin A 4% •	Vitamin C 25%
Calcium 4% •	Iron 10%

* Percent Daily Values are based on a 2,000 calorie diet. Your daily values may be higher or lower depending on your calorie needs:

	Calories:	2,000	2,500
Total Fat	Less than	65g	80g
Sat Fat	Less than	20g	25g
Cholesterol	Less than	300mg	300mg
Sodium	Less than	2,400mg	2,400mg
Total Carbohydrate		300g	375g
Dietary Fiber		25g	30g

Halve the potatoes, if necessary.

Chop parsley

In slow cooker, mix together the potatoes, sauerkraut, onion, broth, wine, caraway seeds, salt, and tsp pepper. Nestle the bratwurst in the vegetables.

Cover and cook until the potatoes are tender, on low for 6 to 8 hours or on high for 4 to 5 hours.

Sprinkle the bratwurst, potatoes, and sauerkraut with the parsley

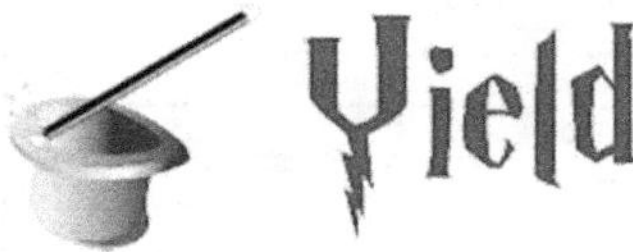

Serves 8

ⓘ I have included a recipe for Hallee's Savory Stocky Crock Pot Beef Brothⓘ in this cookbook. If you don't have stock on hand, be sure to use a good organic stock with low or no salt.

ⓘ If you abstain from alcohol even in cooking, you can substitute a 100% pure grape juice (ensure there is no apple juice in it) and one teaspoon of distilled vinegar to approximate the same flavor and properties while cooking.

Prefect Perfect Pot Roast

Weekday Pot Roast

The preparation time for this recipe is no more than 15 minutes and it can cook overnight or while you are at work for an amazing, melt in your mouth, tender and juicy comfort food you won't soon forget.

My husband's office has monthly potlucks, and I always send him with a slow cooker full of this pot roast and vegetables. He's never returned home with any food left over.

This is also a perfect "Company's Coming" kind of meal. You can get everything prepared and cooking in the slow cooker, and have hours left before your company arrives.

Nutrition Facts

Serving Size: (422g)
Servings Per Container: 8

Amount Per Serving	
Calories 430	Calories from Fat 140
	% Daily Value*
Total Fat 15g	**23%**
Saturated Fat 6g	**30%**
Trans Fat 0.5g	
Cholesterol 120mg	**40%**
Sodium 630mg	**26%**
Total Carbohydrate 32g	**11%**
Dietary Fiber 3g	**12%**
Sugars 4g	
Protein 42g	

Vitamin A 60% •	Vitamin C 15%
Calcium 8% •	Iron 30%

* Percent Daily Values are based on a 2,000 calorie diet. Your daily values may be higher or lower depending on your calorie needs:

	Calories:	2,000	2,500
Total Fat	Less than	65g	80g
Sat Fat	Less than	20g	25g
Cholesterol	Less than	300mg	300mg
Sodium	Less than	2,400mg	2,400mg
Total Carbohydrate		300g	375g
Dietary Fiber		25g	30g

at least 3 1/2 to 4 qt slow cooker
shallow pan/aluminum foil
good sharp knife/cutting board
heavy kitchen tongs
large iron skillet or frying pan to brown the roast
measuring cups/spoons
whisk

FOR THE ROAST:

2 to 2 1/2 pound boneless beef bottom round or chuck roast, trimmed of fat

4 medium potatoes (about 1 lbs), each cut into wedges

3 cups fresh or frozen carrots (baby carrots will work)

4 to 6 stalks (about 2 cups) fresh celery, chopped

2 medium onion (about 3/4 cup), thickly sliced

6 ounces baby bella mushrooms

1 TBS extra virgin olive oil

2 tsp dried basil leaves, crushed

1 TBS Montreal Steak Seasoning Rubⓘ

FOR THE GRAVY:

1/2 cup flour (I use fresh ground soft white wheat)

2 cups Hallee's Savory Stocky Crock Pot Beef Brothⓘ

dash salt (Kosher or sea salt is best) to taste

Dash fresh ground pepper to taste

Chop the celery and carrots. The resultant pieces should fit comfortably inside a table spoon.

Cut the potatoes into wedges then slice the wedges to spoon sized pieces.

Brown the Roast:

Sprinkle all sides of the roast with Montreal Steak Seasoning Rub. Rub it in with your fingertips until you have a good even coating and you've filled in the nooks and crannies.

Heat the extra virgin olive oil in iron skillet over medium-high heat. Add roast and cook, turning with heavy kitchen tongs. Do not puncture the roast. Cook about 1 to 2 minutes on each side or until nicely browned.

Remove roast to shallow pan and cover with aluminum foil to keep warm.

Make the Gravy:

Put the flour and the beef broth into a jar, cover, and shake until smooth.

Using the whisk, whisk the flour mixture into the drippings in the pan. Bring to a boil. Boil and whisk 2 minutes.

Salt and pepper to taste.

Make the Roast:

Place the potatoes, carrots, celery, and onion in the crock pot. Sprinkle with basil.

Top with the browned roast.

If the roast has released any juices into the shallow pan, whisk them into the gravy. Pour the gravy over the roast and vegetables.

Cover and cook until the roast is fork tender; on low heat for 6 to 8 hours or on high for 4 to 6 hours.

Remove roast from cooker and let stand 10 minutes. Serve roast with vegetables and gravy.

Yield

This roast will serve 6 to 8 and translates well into all kinds of delicious leftovers

Notes

ⓘ I have included a recipe for Hallee's Savory Stocky Crock Pot Beef Brothⓘ in this cookbook. If you don't have stock on hand, be sure to use a good organic stock with low or no salt.

Increasing the vegetables and using a larger roast with a 6 quart slow cooker is a great idea for large family gatherings.

It's somewhat important to use homemade Montreal Steak Seasoning Rubⓘ in this recipe. Store-bought versions nearly always contain salt. Using salt with your red meat rub will change the flavor, texture, and end result. You may still enjoy it when all is said and done, but I promise you and your family will like the intense, meaty flavors of a salt-free rub much more. I challenge you to try it and then feel free to add salt when the dish is done.

Sorcerer's Lasagna

Slow-Cooked Lasagna

Pasta can overcook in a slow cooker. For perfect results, watch your cook time carefully and use no-boil lasagna noodles.

This is not a "traditional" lasagna—it uses alfredo sauce instead of ricotta cheese, and is cooked in the slow cooker instead of the oven. However, it is the perfect weekday meal for your family, and gives a break from the go-to spaghetti.

1 lbs lean ground beef

1 TBS extra virgin olive oil

3 1/4 cup Hallee's Homemade Spaghetti Sauceⓘ

2 cups Awesome Alfredo sauceⓘ

8 oz (1 can) no-salt-added tomato sauce

9 oz (1/2 pkg.) no-boil lasagna noodles (about 8)

3 cups (12 oz) shredded mozzarella cheese

1/4 cup grated Parmigiano Reggiano (Parmesan) cheese

at least 4 to 5 qt slow cooker

large iron skillet or frying pan to brown the ground beef

measuring cups/spoons

good sharp knife/cutting board

Prepare pasta sauce, if necessary

Heat oil in skillet over medium heat. Brown ground beef in skillet until thoroughly cooked, stirring frequently. Drain. Reduce heat and reserve.

Lightly grease the inside of the slow cooker with either extra virgin olive oil or unsalted butter according to personal taste. Spread 3/4 cup of tomato pasta sauce in the bottom of the slow cooker. Stir the remaining tomato pasta sauce into the ground beef.

Nutrition Facts

Serving Size: (293g)
Servings Per Container: 8

Amount Per Serving	
Calories 580	Calories from Fat 320
	% Daily Value*
Total Fat 36g	**55%**
Saturated Fat 19g	**95%**
Trans Fat 1g	
Cholesterol 115mg	**38%**
Sodium 970mg	**40%**
Total Carbohydrate 36g	**12%**
Dietary Fiber 6g	**24%**
Sugars 10g	
Protein 34g	
Vitamin A 35% •	Vitamin C 15%
Calcium 50% •	Iron 20%

* Percent Daily Values are based on a 2,000 calorie diet. Your daily values may be higher or lower depending on your calorie needs:

	Calories:	2,000	2,500
Total Fat	Less than	65g	80g
Sat Fat	Less than	20g	25g
Cholesterol	Less than	300mg	300mg
Sodium	Less than	2,400mg	2,400mg
Total Carbohydrate		300g	375g
Dietary Fiber		25g	30g

Layer 3 lasagna noodles over sauce in slow cooker, breaking noodles as needed to make them fit well. Top with 1/3 of the Alfredo pasta sauce, spreading evenly. Sprinkle with 1 cup of mozzarella cheese, spreading evenly. Top with 1/3 of the beef mixture, spreading evenly.

Repeat layering twice, using 2 lasagna noodles in the final layer. Sprinkle grated Parmigiano Reggiano (Parmesan) cheese over top.

Cover and cook on low heat for 3 1/2 to 4 1/2 hours.

Cut into wedges and serve.

Serves 8

Try this tip! Substitute some or all of the mozzarella with shredded odds and ends of cheeses you may have in your dairy drawer to put it to good use. Or try a shredded Italian 3 or 5 cheese blend.

ⓘ You can use a 26-ounce jar of pasta sauce if you prefer not to make your own. I would only use organic pasta sauce and be careful of the amount of sugar in the jar.

ⓘ I have included a recipe for homemade Awesome Alfredo sauceⓘ in this cookbook. You can use a 15-ounce jar of alfredo sauce if you prefer not to make your own

Cast a Spell Cuban Braised Beef

Slow Cooker Cuban Braised Beef & Peppers

The spices in this recipe turn a simple flank steak into a kicking party in the mouth. Enjoy the flare of cilantro and peppers in this beef and rice dish.

1 1/2 lbs flank steak, cut crosswise into thirds

28 oz diced tomatoes, drained

2 red bell peppers, sliced 1/2 inch thick

1 onion, cut into 8 wedges

2 tsp dried oregano

1 tsp ground cumin

1 1/2 tsp salt (Kosher or sea salt is best)

1/4 tsp fresh ground black pepper

1/2 cup Hallee's Savory Stocky Crock Pot Beef Brothⓘ

1 cup cooked Perfect Brown Riceⓘ

1 avocado, sliced

1/4 cup fresh cilantro leaves

5 to 6 qt slow cooker

Skillet

Tongs

Measuring cups/spoons

Slice the pepper.

Cut the onion

Slice the avocado.

Chop the cilantro.

In slow cooker, combine the bell peppers, tomatoes, onion, cumin, oregano, salt, and pepper.

Heat extra virgin olive oil in skillet over medium-high heat until hot. Add the red meat. Sear on every side for 30 seconds to 1 minute until nicely browned on all sides. Turn with tongs, avoiding puncturing the meat.

Immediately nestle the steak among the vegetables in the slow cooker.

Whisk 1/2 cup Hallee's Savory Stocky Crock Pot Beef Broth ⓘ into skillet. Whisk to scrape all the bits of caramelized meat from the skillet into the broth to make a flavorful sauce. Add to the slow cooker.

Cook, covered, until the meat is tender and pulls apart easily, on low heat for 7 to 8 hours or on high heat for 4 to 5 hours.

Forty-five minutes before serving, cook the rice.

Using two forks, shred the beef and mix it into the cooking liquid. Serve with the rice and top with the avocado and cilantro.

Nutrition Facts

Serving Size: (397g)
Servings Per Container: 6

Amount Per Serving	
Calories 300	Calories from Fat 100
	% Daily Value*
Total Fat 11g	**17%**
Saturated Fat 3.5g	**18%**
Trans Fat 0g	
Cholesterol 80mg	**27%**
Sodium 920mg	**38%**
Total Carbohydrate 22g	**7%**
Dietary Fiber 6g	**24%**
Sugars 7g	
Protein 28g	
Vitamin A 45% •	Vitamin C 150%
Calcium 10% •	Iron 20%

* Percent Daily Values are based on a 2,000 calorie diet. Your daily values may be higher or lower depending on your calorie needs:

	Calories:	2,000	2,500
Total Fat	Less than	65g	80g
Sat Fat	Less than	20g	25g
Cholesterol	Less than	300mg	300mg
Sodium	Less than	2,400mg	2,400mg
Total Carbohydrate		300g	375g
Dietary Fiber		25g	30g

Serves 6

ⓘ I have included a recipe for Hallee's Savory Stocky Crock Pot Beef Brothⓘ in this cookbook. If you don't have a good broth on hand, be sure to use a good organic broth with low or no salt.

ⓘ For information about a tip for preparing perfect brown rice, follow this link:

http://www.halleethehomemaker.com/2009/11/perfect-brown-rice/

Beater's Beef & Barley Stew

Beef & Barley Stew

Barley is an ancient grain best known for its use in Scotch Broth, beer, and whiskey. Don't hold that against this wonderful whole grain. It is one of my favorite adds to soup.

This recipe calls for pearl barley, which you can find at nearly any grocery store. Pearl barley has had the husk and bran removed before being steamed and polished.

Natural food stores and co-ops stock barley in many forms, including in rolled form similar to oatmeal. If you are familiar with cooking with barley, feel free to experiment with different varieties to create rich textures.

1 lb. Boneless beef round steak ($^1/_2$ inch thick), trimmed of fat, cut to $^3/_4$ inch pieces

1 cup plus 1 $^1/_2$ cup Hallee's Savory Stocky Beef Brothⓘ, divided

$^1/_2$ cup uncooked regular pearl barley

2 cups fresh or frozen cut green beans

2 medium carrots (1 cup), shredded

$^1/_2$ tsp dried thyme leaves

6 ounces white mushrooms, sliced

2 green onions, chopped

1 TBS unsalted butter

1 TBS flour (I use fresh ground soft white wheat)

$^1/_4$ tsp fresh ground black pepper

Salt to taste

Nutrition Facts

Serving Size: (352g)
Servings Per Container: 5

Amount Per Serving	
Calories 290	Calories from Fat 70
	% Daily Value*
Total Fat 7g	**11%**
Saturated Fat 3g	**15%**
Trans Fat 0g	
Cholesterol 65mg	**22%**
Sodium 470mg	**20%**
Total Carbohydrate 28g	**9%**
Dietary Fiber 6g	**24%**
Sugars 4g	
Protein 26g	
Vitamin A 90% •	Vitamin C 15%
Calcium 6% •	Iron 20%

* Percent Daily Values are based on a 2,000 calorie diet. Your daily values may be higher or lower depending on your calorie needs:

	Calories:	2,000	2,500
Total Fat	Less than	65g	80g
Sat Fat	Less than	20g	25g
Cholesterol	Less than	300mg	300mg
Sodium	Less than	2,400mg	2,400mg
Total Carbohydrate		300g	375g
Dietary Fiber		25g	30g

5 to 6 qt slow cooker
Skillet
Tongs
Measuring cups/spoons
Sharp knife/cutting board

Shred the carrots.
Slice the mushrooms
Chop the onions

Heat extra virgin olive oil in skillet over medium-high heat until hot. Add the beef. Sear on every side for 30 seconds to 1 minute until nicely browned on all sides. Turn with kitchen tongs, trying not to puncture the meat.

Place beef in the slow cooker.

Immediately add butter to skillet. Sauté mushrooms and green onions in butter and remaining oil for 5 minutes over medium heat. Whisk in beef broth. Whisk to scrape the bits of caramelized meat from the skillet into the broth to make a flavorful sauce. Whisk in flour until smooth to make a flavorful gravy. Increase heat. Heat to boiling. Reduce heat and simmer for 5 minutes.

Pour the entire contents of the skillet into the slow cooker. Add remaining ingredients.

Cover and cook on low heat for 8 to 10 hours or on high heat for 4 to 5 hours.

Yield

About 5 servings

Notes

For easier prep, you can use cubed beef stew meat. However, it is often much less expensive pound for pound to purchase a small inexpensive chuck or rump roast and cube it yourself.

ⓘ I have included a recipe for Hallee's Savory Stocky Crock Pot Beef Brothⓘ in this cookbook. If you don't have a good broth on hand, be sure to use a good organic broth with low or no salt.

Expectopatronum Enchilada Dinner

Layered Enchilada Dinner

I have a child who could drink enchilada sauce if I put it in a cup for him, so this is absolutely one of his favorite meals. The tangy sauce combined with the corn tortillas really gives a savory flavor to this hearty dish.

1 lbs lean ground beef

1 tsp extra virgin olive oil

1 1/2 cup Hallee's Homemade Cream of Mushroom Soupⓘ

1 1/2 cup prepared Enticing Enchilada sauceⓘ

4.5 oz (1 can) green chiles, choppedⓘ

1 small onion (about 1/3 cup), choppedⓘ

1 garlic clove, minced

10 (6-inch) corn tortillas

12 oz. (3 cups) shredded Monterey Jack

fresh cilantro, choppedⓘ

At least 3 1/2 to 4 qt slow cooker

Skillet / wooden spoon

measuring cups/spoons

good sharp knife

cutting board

Preparation

Chop the onion.

Mince the garlic.

Shred the cheese

Directions

Heat extra virgin olive oil in skillet over medium heat. Brown ground beef, onion, and garlic in skillet, stirring frequently, until thoroughly cooked. Drain. Stir in soup and chiles. Reduce heat and reserve.

Lightly grease the inside of the slow cooker with either extra virgin olive oil or unsalted butter according to personal taste. Spread 1/4 cup of enchilada sauce in the bottom of the slow cooker.

Place 4 corn tortillas over sauce, overlapping and breaking them in half as needed to make an even layer and make them fit well. Top with 1/3 of the beef mixture, spreading evenly. Drizzle with 1/4 cup of the enchilada sauce. Sprinkle with 1 cup of the cheese, spreading evenly.

Repeat layering twice, using 3 corn tortillas and 1/2 of the remaining beef mixture, enchilada sauce, and cheese in each layer.

Cover and cook on low heat for 4 1/2 to 5 1/2 hours.

Let stand about 5 minutes before serving. If desired sprinkle individual servings with fresh cilantro and serve.

Nutrition Facts

Serving Size: (404g)
Servings Per Container: 6

Amount Per Serving	
Calories 720	Calories from Fat 430
	% Daily Value*
Total Fat 48g	**74%**
Saturated Fat 24g	**120%**
Trans Fat 1.5g	
Cholesterol 135mg	**45%**
Sodium 990mg	**41%**
Total Carbohydrate 39g	**13%**
Dietary Fiber 5g	**20%**
Sugars 9g	
Protein 37g	

Vitamin A 30%	•	Vitamin C 20%
Calcium 70%	•	Iron 20%

* Percent Daily Values are based on a 2,000 calorie diet. Your daily values may be higher or lower depending on your calorie needs:

	Calories:	2,000	2,500
Total Fat	Less than	65g	80g
Sat Fat	Less than	20g	25g
Cholesterol	Less than	300mg	300mg
Sodium	Less than	2,400mg	2,400mg
Total Carbohydrate		300g	375g
Dietary Fiber		25g	30g

6 servings

Try topping this with a dollop of plain organic yogurt instead of sour cream for a flavor explosion.

Substitute 12 oz. (3 cups) shredded pepper Jack cheese for the Monterey Jack cheese if you want to add some kick.

If you like green chiles, try doubling the amount in this recipe!

ⓘ You can used canned cream of mushroom soup or jarred enchilada sauce in replacement of homemade in this recipe.

McGonagall'S Presto Pizza Casserole

Slow Cooker Pizza Casserole

This dish will please any meat-lover in your family! Loaded with ground beef, sausage, pepperoni, then covered in cheese, it's the perfect comfort-food casserole. Serve with a loaf of crusty French bread and a garden salad for a terrific meal.

1 1/2 lbs ground beef,

1 lb Italian turkey sausage

1 clove garlic, minced

1/2 cup onion, finely chopped ⓘ

2 packages (3 oz each) sliced turkey pepperoni

1 jar (26 oz) organic pasta sauce (or 3 1/4 cup Hallee's Homemade Spaghetti Sauce ⓘ)

1 lbs corkscrew pasta, cooked and drained

2 cups (8 oz) shredded mozzarella cheese

2 cups freshly grated Parmigiano Reggiano (Parmesan) cheese

2 cans (4 oz each) mushroom stems and pieces, drained

1/2 cup green bell pepper, finely chopped ⓘ

Nutrition Facts

Serving Size: (407g)
Servings Per Container: 8

Amount Per Serving	
Calories 640	Calories from Fat 180
	% Daily Value*
Total Fat 20g	**31%**
Saturated Fat 8g	**40%**
Trans Fat 0g	
Cholesterol 125mg	**42%**
Sodium 1990mg	**83%**
Total Carbohydrate 58g	**19%**
Dietary Fiber 11g	**44%**
Sugars 12g	
Protein 57g	
Vitamin A 20% •	Vitamin C 50%
Calcium 50% •	Iron 60%

* Percent Daily Values are based on a 2,000 calorie diet. Your daily values may be higher or lower depending on your calorie needs:

	Calories:	2,000	2,500
Total Fat	Less than	65g	80g
Sat Fat	Less than	20g	25g
Cholesterol	Less than	300mg	300mg
Sodium	Less than	2,400mg	2,400mg
Total Carbohydrate		300g	375g
Dietary Fiber		25g	30g

At least 3 ½ to 4 qt slow cooker

measuring cups/spoons

good sharp knife/cutting board

skillet

slotted spoon

wooden spoon

Remove the sausage from its casings, if necessary.

Prepare the spaghetti sauce, if necessary

Shred the cheeses

Chop the onion and bell pepper.

Mince the garlic.

In a skillet over medium heat, brown the hamburger meat and the sausage. Drain.

Combine all ingredients in the slow cooker and mix well.

Cover and cook on low heat for 4 hours or on high heat for 2 hours.

About 8 servings

ⓘ If you would like to make your own pasta sauce, with or without meat, you can look up Hallee's Homemade Spaghetti Sauceⓘ on the web at this link:

www.halleethehomemaker.com/2009/09/italian-turkey-sausage-spaghetti-sauce/

ⓘ For information about a tip for chopping vegetables, follow this link:

http://www.halleethehomemaker.com/2009/08/tips-chopping-onions/

Marauder's Map Stew

Meatball Stew

Meatball stews are a staple in almost any cuisine. This one has a bit of a Persian flare to it with the cinnamon and cloves. The meatballs, combined with veggies and a homemade gravy make a thick, rich, hearty stew for your hungriest family member.

FOR THE MEATBALLS

1 3/4 lbs lean grass-fed beef, ground
1 farm fresh eggs
1 medium onion, finely diced
1 cup bread crumbs
2 garlic cloves, minced
1 TBS chopped fresh parsley
1/2 tsp yellow mustard
1/2 tsp salt (Kosher or sea salt is best)
1/2 tsp fresh ground black pepper
1/4 tsp dried oregano
1/4 tsp ground cinnamon
1/4 tsp ground cloves
extra virgin olive oil to grease pan

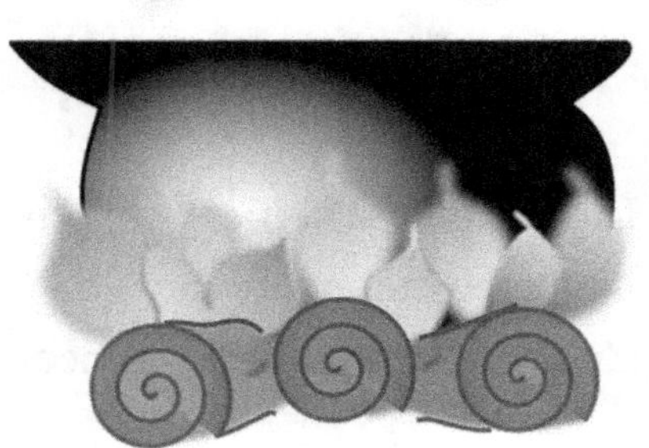

FOR THE STEW

2 cups carrots, cut to about 2 inches and cut in half lengthwise
1 lbs small red potatoes (2 ½ to 3 inch), quartered
6 oz fresh mushrooms, sliced
1 small onion, cut into thin wedges
1 cup Hallee's Revitalizing Roast Beef Gravy ⓘ
1 ¾ cup (14.5 oz can, drained) fresh tomatoes, diced
fresh ground black pepper, if desired

large bowl
measuring cups/spoons
sheet pan
food processor or blender
fine mesh strainer
cast iron skillet
at least 3 ½ to 4 qt slow cooker
kitchen tongs
good sharp knife
cutting board
measuring cups/spoons

Nutrition Facts

Serving Size: (285g)
Servings Per Container: 8

Amount Per Serving	
Calories 260	Calories from Fat 60
	% Daily Value*
Total Fat 6g	**9%**
Saturated Fat 2.5g	**13%**
Trans Fat 0g	
Cholesterol 75mg	**25%**
Sodium 440mg	**18%**
Total Carbohydrate 28g	**9%**
Dietary Fiber 4g	**16%**
Sugars 5g	
Protein 23g	

Vitamin A 110% • Vitamin C 20%
Calcium 6% • Iron 20%

* Percent Daily Values are based on a 2,000 calorie diet. Your daily values may be higher or lower depending on your calorie needs:

	Calories:	2,000	2,500
Total Fat	Less than	65g	80g
Sat Fat	Less than	20g	25g
Cholesterol	Less than	300mg	300mg
Sodium	Less than	2,400mg	2,400mg
Total Carbohydrate		300g	375g
Dietary Fiber		25g	30g

Lightly grease skillet with olive oil.
Grate the onion.
Crush garlic and finely mince.

FOR THE MEATBALLS

In large bowl, combine eggs, onion, bread crumbs, garlic, parsley, mustard, salt, pepper, oregano, cinnamon, and cloves. With damp hands, shape beef mixture into 1-inch balls.

In a skillet, heat extra virgin olive oil over medium high heat. In batches, sear the meatballs on every side turning with kitchen tongs about every 30 seconds. They need not be cooked all the way through as they will finish cooking in the slow cooker. Sear the meatballs until just golden brown on every side.

As batches of meatballs are browned, place into a colander set over shallow bowl or saucepan to preserve drippings.

Reserve all the drippings to make Hallee's Revitalizing Roast Beef Gravyⓘ.

Follow the instructions in Hallee's Revitalizing Roast Beef Gravyⓘ (recipe included in this cookbook) to make your gravy.

FOR THE STEW

In slow cooker, layer all ingredients in this order: carrots, potatoes, mushrooms, onion, meatballs, Hallee's Revitalizing Roast Beef Gravyⓘ, tomatoes, and pepper.

TIP: In this recipe, it is important to place ingredients in the cooker in the order listed. Longer cooking vegetables are on the bottom where they cook more quickly. Already cooked or faster cooking ingredients are layered on top.

Cover and cook on low heat 8 to 10 hours or on high heat for 4 $^{1}/_{2}$ to 5 hours.

Before serving, gently stir stew.

Serves 8

ⓘ I have included a recipe for Hallee's Revitalizing Roast Beef Gravyⓘ in this cookbook.

Possible substitution: Plain or Italian-style meatballs can take the place of the Swedish meatballs. For Italian style-meatballs add 1/8 tsp of crushed red pepper flakes, 1 tsp Hallee's Inviting Italian Seasoningⓘ mix, and 1/2 cup of water to beef mixture prior to making meatballs.

This recipe can easily be doubled and made in a 6-quart slow cooker.

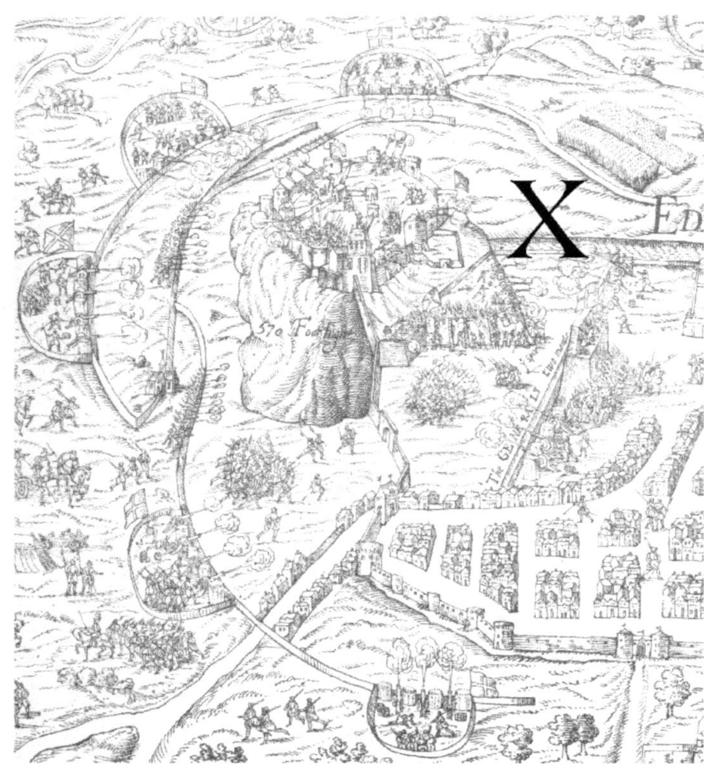

Mirror of Erisad Meatball & Gravy Sandwiches

Meatball & Gravy Sandwiches

This is a great recipe if you're looking for something to feed a crowd—in my case, it was a crowd of hungry teenagers! Homemade Swedish style meatballs floating in a sea of gravy and onions—the perfect combination to put inside hoagie rolls.

FOR THE SWEDISH STYLE MEATBALLS:

3 $^{1}/_{2}$ lbs (24 oz) lean grass-fed beef, ground
2 farm fresh eggs
2 medium onion, finely diced
2 cup bread crumbs
4 garlic cloves, minced
2 TBS chopped fresh parsley
2 tsp yellow mustard
1 tsp salt (Kosher or sea salt is best)
1 tsp fresh ground black pepper
$^{1}/_{2}$ tsp dried oregano
$^{1}/_{2}$ tsp ground cinnamon
$^{1}/_{2}$ tsp ground cloves
extra virgin olive oil to grease pan

FOR THE SANDWICHES:

Swedish style meatballs (see above)

8 French bread buns (or hoagie buns), split (7 to 8 inch long)

3 cups Hallee's Revitalizing Roast Beef Gravyⓘ

2 medium onions, sliced

1 tsp ground nutmeg (See NOTES)

at least 3 ½ to 4 qt slow cooker

measuring cups/spoons

large bowl

fine mesh strainer

cast iron skillet

kitchen tongs

good sharp knife/cutting board

Nutrition Facts

Serving Size: (479g)
Servings Per Container: 8

Amount Per Serving	
Calories 640	Calories from Fat 150
	% Daily Value*
Total Fat 16g	**25%**
Saturated Fat 6g	**30%**
Trans Fat 0.5g	
Cholesterol 170mg	**57%**
Sodium 1290mg	**54%**
Total Carbohydrate 64g	**21%**
Dietary Fiber 4g	**16%**
Sugars 9g	
Protein 57g	
Vitamin A 4% •	Vitamin C 10%
Calcium 15% •	Iron 45%

* Percent Daily Values are based on a 2,000 calorie diet. Your daily values may be higher or lower depending on your calorie needs:

	Calories:	2,000	2,500
Total Fat	Less than	65g	80g
Sat Fat	Less than	20g	25g
Cholesterol	Less than	300mg	300mg
Sodium	Less than	2,400mg	2,400mg
Total Carbohydrate		300g	375g
Dietary Fiber		25g	30g

Lightly grease skillet with olive oil.

Grate the onion.

Crush garlic and finely mince.

FOR THE MEATBALLS

In large bowl, combine eggs, onion, bread crumbs, garlic, parsley, mustard, salt, pepper, oregano, cinnamon, and cloves. With damp hands, shape beef mixture into 1-inch balls.

In a skillet, heat extra virgin olive oil over medium high heat. In batches, sear the meatballs on every side turning with kitchen tongs about every 30 seconds. They need not be cooked all the way through as they will finish cooking in the slow cooker. Sear the meatballs until just golden brown on every side.

As batches of meatballs are browned, place into a colander set over shallow bowl or saucepan to preserve drippings.

Reserve all the drippings to add to the ingredients needed to make Hallee's Revitalizing Roast Beef Gravyⓘ.

Follow the instructions in Hallee's Revitalizing Roast Beef Gravyⓘ recipe included in this cookbook to make your gravy.

FOR THE SANDWICHES

Place onions in slow cooker. Add meatballs and top with gravy.

Cover and cook on low heat 8 to 10 hours or on high heat for 4 $^1/_2$ to 5 hours.

Stir nutmeg (See NOTES) into meatball mixture.

Cut French bread buns (or hoagie buns) horizontally almost in half leaving a "hinge" on one side.

Place 6 meatballs in each bun. Top with gravy.

Serves 8

ⓘ I have included a recipe for Hallee's Revitalizing Roast Beef Gravyⓘ in this cookbook.

Possible substitution: Plain or Italian-style meatballs can take the place of the Swedish meatballs. Omit the nutmeg.

This recipe can easily be doubled and made in a 6-quart slow cooker.

Snape's Spiced Braised Beef with Sweet Potatoes

Spiced Braised Beef with Sweet Potatoes

The cinnamon and cumin in this dish, combined with the flavors of the garbanzo beans and couscous, give it a very Middle Eastern flare. This is a hearty stew perfect for a cold winter day. It would also do well in any potluck environment.

1 1/2 lbs beef chuck, cut into 1 1/2 to 2 inch chunks

1 TBS extra virgin olive oil

1/2 cup of the Hallee's Savory Stocky Crock Pot Beef Brothⓘ (or filtered water)

2 sweet potatoes (about 1 pound), cut into 1/2 inch-thick half-moons

1 28-ounce can whole peeled tomatoes

1 large red onion, cut into wedges

1/2 cup dried apricots

2 tsp ground cumin

2 tsp ground ginger

1/2 tsp ground cinnamon

1/2 tsp cayenne

3/4 tsp salt (Kosher or sea salt is best)

1 10-ounce box couscous (1 1/2 cups)

1 15-ounce can chickpeas, rinsed

2 cups baby spinach (1 1/2 ounces)

1/4 cup roasted almonds, chopped

4 to 6 qt slow cooker

Skillet / tongs

measuring cups/spoons

good sharp knife/cutting board

whisk

Nutrition Facts

Serving Size: (454g)
Servings Per Container: 6

Amount Per Serving	
Calories 600	Calories from Fat 160
	% Daily Value*
Total Fat 18g	**28%**
Saturated Fat 5g	**25%**
Trans Fat 0g	
Cholesterol 95mg	**32%**
Sodium 750mg	**31%**
Total Carbohydrate 69g	**23%**
Dietary Fiber 10g	**40%**
Sugars 14g	
Protein 43g	

Vitamin A 160% •	Vitamin C 30%
Calcium 15% •	Iron 35%

* Percent Daily Values are based on a 2,000 calorie diet. Your daily values may be higher or lower depending on your calorie needs:

	Calories:	2,000	2,500
Total Fat	Less than	65g	80g
Sat Fat	Less than	20g	25g
Cholesterol	Less than	300mg	300mg
Sodium	Less than	2,400mg	2,400mg
Total Carbohydrate		300g	375g
Dietary Fiber		25g	30g

Peel and cut the sweet potatoes.

Slice the onion into wedges.

Roughly chop the dried apricots.

Cut beef into 1-2-inch chunks, trimming fat as needed.

Heat the olive oil in skillet over medium-high heat until hot. Add the meat. Sear on every side for 30 seconds to 1 minute until nicely browned on all sides. Turn with kitchen tongs. Do not puncture the meat.

Whisk the Hallee's Savory Stocky Crock Pot Beef Broth ⓘ (or filtered water) into skillet. Whisk to scrape all the bits of caramelized meat from the skillet into the broth to make a flavorful sauce. Add to the slow cooker.

In slow cooker, combine the beef, potatoes, tomatoes (and their juices), onion, apricots, cumin, ginger, cinnamon, cayenne, salt, and 1/2 cup water.

Cook, covered, until the meat is tender, on high for 4 to 5 hours, or on low for 7 to 8 hours.

About 30 minutes before serving, the chickpeas and the spinach.

Ten minutes before serving, prepare the couscous according to the package directions.

Serve with the couscous and sprinkle with the almonds.

Serves 6

Quick Tip: ***Beef***

Don't be tempted to substitute lean beef in this recipe. Fattier cuts are best for slow braises since they stay moist through hours of cooking.

ⓘ I have included a recipe for Hallee's Savory Stocky Crock Pot Beef Brothⓘ in this cookbook. If you don't have stock on hand, be sure to use a good organic stock with low or no salt.

Golden Snitch Beef

Beef with Apples & Sweet Potatoes

This is such a simple roast with few ingredients, but the sweetness of the apples and sweet potatoes combined with the beefy savoriness of the roast makes what should be simple become something extraordinary. You'll make this and won't look at other roast beef recipes the same again.

2 lbs boneless beef chuck shoulder roast, cubed

1 TBS extra virgin olive oil

1/2 cup Hallee's Savory Stocky Crock Pot Beef Broth

3 medium sweet potatoes, peeled and diced

2 small onions, sliced

2 apples, cored and sliced

2 TBS cold water

1 TBS cornstarch

2 cloves garlic, minced

1 tsp dried thyme leaves, divided

1/4 tsp ground cinnamon

1 tsp Kosher or sea salt

3/4 tsp black pepper, divided

Nutrition Facts

Serving Size: (322g)
Servings Per Container: 6

Amount Per Serving	
Calories 400	Calories from Fat 150
	% Daily Value*
Total Fat 17g	**26%**
Saturated Fat 6g	**30%**
Trans Fat 0.5g	
Cholesterol 125mg	**42%**
Sodium 490mg	**20%**
Total Carbohydrate 23g	**8%**
Dietary Fiber 3g	**12%**
Sugars 10g	
Protein 41g	
Vitamin A 120% •	Vitamin C 10%
Calcium 6% •	Iron 25%

* Percent Daily Values are based on a 2,000 calorie diet. Your daily values may be higher or lower depending on your calorie needs:

	Calories:	2,000	2,500
Total Fat	Less than	65g	80g
Sat Fat	Less than	20g	25g
Cholesterol	Less than	300mg	300mg
Sodium	Less than	2,400mg	2,400mg
Total Carbohydrate		300g	375g
Dietary Fiber		25g	30g

At least 3 1/2 to 4 qt slow cooker

measuring cups/spoons

good sharp knife/cutting board

slotted spoon

wooden spoon

Using a good sharp knife, trim fat from beef and cube into 2 inch pieces.

Peel and dice the sweet potato in 1-inch chunks

Slice the onion

Peel, core, and slice the apples in 1-inch chunks

Heat olive oil in skillet over medium-high heat until hot. Add the meat. Sear on every side for 30 seconds to 1 minute until nicely browned on all sides. Turn with kitchen tongs. Do not puncture the meat.

Whisk the Hallee's Savory Stocky Crock Pot Beef Broth ⓘ (or filtered water) into skillet. Use the whisk to scrape all the bits of caramelized meat from the skillet into the broth to make a flavorful sauce. Add to the slow cooker.

Place beef, sweet potatoes, onions, apples, garlic, salt, 1/2 tsp thyme, and 1/2 tsp pepper in slow cooker.

Cover and cook on low heat for 8 to 9 hours or on high heat for 4 to 5 hours.

Set slow cooker to low heat if necessary. Transfer beef, sweet potatoes, and apples to platter and cover with aluminum foil to keep warm. Let liquid stand in slow cooker for 5 minutes and allow fat to rise. Skim off fat.

Combine water, cornstarch, remaining 1/2 tsp thyme, 1/4 tsp pepper, cinnamon, and water. Mix until cornstarch is fully incorporated into the water (otherwise, it will clump).

Cook 15 minutes on low heat or until juices are thickened.

When ready to serve, uncover beef, sweet potatoes, and apples and generously ladle sauce over top.

Serves 6

ⓘ I have included a recipe for Hallee's Savory Stocky Crock Pot Beef Brothⓘ in this cookbook. If you don't have stock on hand, be sure to use a good organic stock with low or no salt.

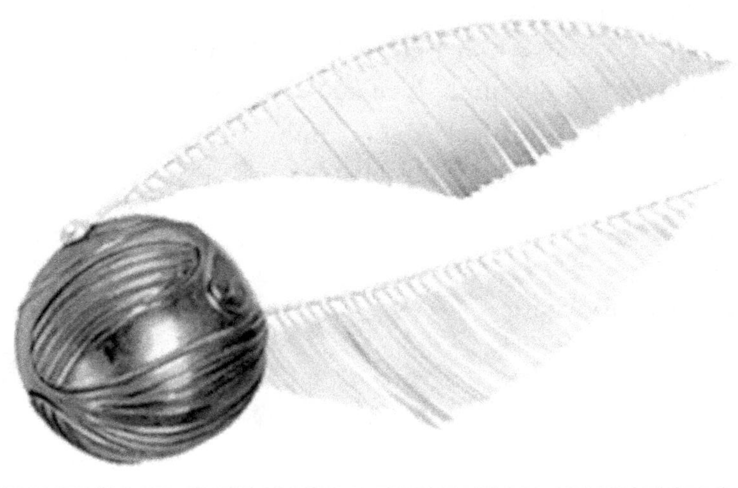

Chamber of Secrets Chipotle Chili

Chipotle Chili

I'm not a big fan of shortcuts in recipes—I tend to think that the final outcome will have a better quality of flavor if the ingredients going into it are fresh. That said, one of my few exceptions to that rule is salsa and chili. Tossing salsa into a slow cooker for chili is a perfect "easy ingredient". It has all of the vegetables you need, most of the spices, and, depending on your heat level, a spicy kick.

1 TBS extra virgin olive oil

2 pounds beef for stew, cut into 1/2 inch pieces

1.5 cup chunky salsaⓘ

2 cups Hallee's Savory Stocky Crock Pot Beef Brothⓘ (or filtered water)

2 TBS chili powder

1 large onion, chopped (about 1 cup)

1 can (about 16 ounces) red kidney beans, drained (or 1 cup dried kidney beans, soaked overnight then cooked until tender.)

1 can (about 16 ounces) black beans, drained (or 1 cup black beans, soaked overnight, then cooked until tender)

OPTIONAL:

Shredded Cheddar cheese

Sour cream

At least 3 1/2 to 4 qt slow cooker
Skillet
measuring cups/spoons
good sharp knife/cutting board
slotted spoon and wooden spoon
Tongs
Whisk

Nutrition Facts
Serving Size: (457g)
Servings Per Container: 6

Amount Per Serving	
Calories 390	Calories from Fat 70
	% Daily Value*
Total Fat 8g	**12%**
Saturated Fat 3.5g	**18%**
Trans Fat 0g	
Cholesterol 95mg	**32%**
Sodium 900mg	**38%**
Total Carbohydrate 37g	**12%**
Dietary Fiber 13g	**52%**
Sugars 7g	
Protein 44g	
Vitamin A 20% •	Vitamin C 8%
Calcium 8% •	Iron 35%

* Percent Daily Values are based on a 2,000 calorie diet. Your daily values may be higher or lower depending on your calorie needs:

	Calories:	2,000	2,500
Total Fat	Less than	65g	80g
Sat Fat	Less than	20g	25g
Cholesterol	Less than	300mg	300mg
Sodium	Less than	2,400mg	2,400mg
Total Carbohydrate		300g	375g
Dietary Fiber		25g	30g

Chop the onion.
If needed, prepare kidney beans.
Cut the beef into 1/2 inch pieces, trimming fat as needed.

Directions

Heat olive oil in skillet over medium-high heat until hot. Add the meat. Sear on every side for 30 seconds to 1 minute until nicely browned on all sides. Turn with kitchen tongs. Do not puncture the meat.

Whisk 1/2 cup Hallee's Savory Stocky Crock Pot Beef Broth🛈 into skillet. Use the whisk to scrape all the bits of caramelized meat from the skillet into the broth to make a flavorful sauce. Add to the slow cooker.

Mix salsa, broth, chili powder, onion, beef, and beans in slow cooker. Cover and cook until beef is fork-tender; on low heat for 8 to 9 hours or on high heat for 4 to 5 hours.

Serve with cheese and sour cream if desired.

About 6 servings

ⓘ For a good recipe to make your own homemade fresh salsa, follow this link:

http://www.halleethehomemaker.com/2009/09/spicy-tomato-jalapeno-salsa/

ⓘ I have included a recipe for Hallee's Savory Stocky Crock Pot Beef Brothⓘ in this cookbook. If you don't have stock on hand, be sure to use a good organic stock with low or no salt.

Here's a tip! Serve this smokey chipotle chili with savory corn muffins. When making regular corn muffins, substitute equal parts of Hallee's Savory Stocky Crock Pot Beef Brothⓘ for milk in the recipe.

Hallows Hearty Healthy Beef Stew

Hallee's Hearty Healthy Beef Stew

Beef stew makes almost a weekly appearance in our house during the winter months. Every one of my children love it, and it's such an easy meal to prepare in the morning and serve in the evening. I typically serve it with cheddar biscuits and a garden salad, but it would be just as good with a side of grilled cheese.

For the healthiest heart recipe, be sure to minimize the use of salt in this recipe. I have included a recipe for Hallee's Savory Stocky Crock Pot Beef Broth🛈 in this cookbook which includes instructions to make either a stock or a broth. This beef stew recipe calls for a stock, not a broth, the main difference being a stock will not have any salt. If you don't have stock on hand, be sure to use a good organic stock with low or no salt.

Nutrition Facts

Serving Size: (538g)
Servings Per Container: 6

Amount Per Serving	
Calories 410	Calories from Fat 70
	% Daily Value*
Total Fat 8g	**12%**
Saturated Fat 3g	**15%**
Trans Fat 0g	
Cholesterol 70mg	**23%**
Sodium 580mg	**24%**
Total Carbohydrate 52g	**17%**
Dietary Fiber 5g	**20%**
Sugars 7g	
Protein 33g	
Vitamin A 150% •	Vitamin C 35%
Calcium 8% •	Iron 30%

* Percent Daily Values are based on a 2,000 calorie diet. Your daily values may be higher or lower depending on your calorie needs:

	Calories:	2,000	2,500
Total Fat	Less than	65g	80g
Sat Fat	Less than	20g	25g
Cholesterol	Less than	300mg	300mg
Sodium	Less than	2,400mg	2,400mg
Total Carbohydrate		300g	375g
Dietary Fiber		25g	30g

At least 3 1/2 to 4 qt slow cooker

measuring cups/spoons

good sharp knife/cutting board

slotted spoon

wooden spoon

Skillet

Whisk

1 1/2 pounds beef for stew, cut into 1-inch pieces

About 1/4 cup flour (I use fresh ground, soft-white wheat)

3 cups Hallee's Savory Stocky Crock Pot Beef Brothⓘ (or filtered water)

1 TBS extra virgin olive oil

4-5 medium potatoes (about 2 1/2 cups), cubed

4 medium carrots, sliced (about 2 cups)

2 medium onions, cut into large chunks

4 cloves garlic, minced

1 TBS Worcestershire sauce

1 tsp dried thyme leaves, crushed

1 bay leaf

fresh ground black pepper

1 cup frozen peas

1/4 cup filtered water

1/4 cup flour (I use fresh ground, soft-white wheat)

Cube the potatoes.

Slice the carrots.

Cut the onion.

Mince the garlic.

Cut the beef into 1-inch pieces, trimming fat as needed. Toss the meat with the flour.

Heat olive oil in skillet over medium-high heat until hot. Add the meat coated in flour. Sear on every side for 30 seconds to 1 minute until nicely browned on all sides. Turn with kitchen tongs. Do not puncture the meat.

Whisk $1/2$ cup of the Hallee's Savory Stocky Crock Pot Beef Brothⓘ into skillet. Use the whisk to scrape all the bits of caramelized meat from the skillet into the stock to make a flavorful sauce. Add to the slow cooker.

Place remaining stock, potatoes, carrots, onions, and garlic in slow cooker. Top with beef. Add Worcestershire sauce, thyme, and bay leaf.

Cover and cook until beef is fork-tender; on low heat for 8 to 9 hours or on high heat for 5 to 6 hours.

Mix remaining flour and water until smooth. Add flour and water mixture and peas to cooker. Turn to high heat if necessary.

Cover and cook on high heat for 15 minutes or until slightly thickened.

About 6 servings

ⓘ I have included a recipe for Hallee's Savory Stocky Crock Pot Beef Brothⓘ in this cookbook. This recipe calls for a stock, not a broth, the main difference being a stock will not have any salt. If you don't have stock on hand, be sure to use a good organic stock with low or no salt.

Sirius Spaghetti & Meatballs

Spaghetti & Meatballs

Spaghetti and meatballs is such a fun dinner to serve anyone. It's one of those classic comfort foods from generations back. Being able to cook the meal all day long in the slow cooker makes actual meal time such a breeze.

1 lbs ground beef

extra virgin olive oil

2 white onions, finely chopped① and divided

2 cloves garlic, crushed and divided

1 tsp dried basil, divided

1 tsp dried oregano, divided

14 oz canned tomatoes, drained

2 tsp Worcestershire sauce

6 oz can tomato paste

1 cup water

1 bay leaf

1 tsp salt (Kosher or sea salt is best)

1/4 tsp fresh ground black pepper

1 lbs whole grain or whole wheat spaghetti

1 oz Parmigiano Reggiano (Parmesan) cheese, grated

Nutrition Facts

Serving Size: (448g)
Servings Per Container: 4

Amount Per Serving	
Calories 740	Calories from Fat 200
	% Daily Value*
Total Fat 22g	**34%**
Saturated Fat 8g	**40%**
Trans Fat 1g	
Cholesterol 75mg	**25%**
Sodium 870mg	**36%**
Total Carbohydrate 102g	**34%**
Dietary Fiber 17g	**68%**
Sugars 12g	
Protein 44g	
Vitamin A 15% •	Vitamin C 30%
Calcium 20% •	Iron 50%

* Percent Daily Values are based on a 2,000 calorie diet. Your daily values may be higher or lower depending on your calorie needs:

	Calories:	2,000	2,500
Total Fat	Less than	65g	80g
Sat Fat	Less than	20g	25g
Cholesterol	Less than	300mg	300mg
Sodium	Less than	2,400mg	2,400mg
Total Carbohydrate		300g	375g
Dietary Fiber		25g	30g

At least 3 1/2 to 4 qt slow cooker

measuring cups/spoons

good sharp knife/cutting board

Mixing bowl

Skillet

Saucepan

Colander

Finely dice the onion. Separate out 1/2 cup.

Mince the garlic. Divide in half.

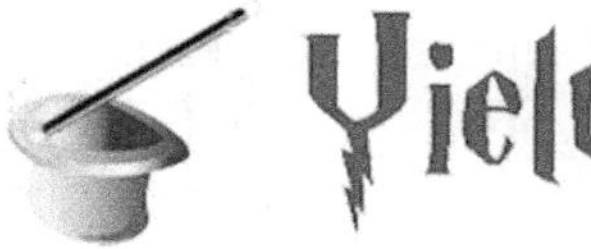

Serves 4

In a mixing bowl, combine ground beef, 1/2 cup onion, 1 clove of the garlic (minded), 1/2 tsp salt, 1/2 tsp basil, 1/2 tsp oregano. Roll into small balls (about 1 TBS mixture per ball). Heat the oil in the skillet over medium high heat and sauté the meatballs until slightly browned.

Place meatballs into slow cooker and add all remaining ingredients, except pasta and cheese. Cook on low for 4 hours.

Prepare the pasta according to the package directions. Use the colander to drain, then add to slow cooker and stir through sauce.

Serve sprinkled with grated Parmigiano Reggiano (Parmesan) cheese.

ⓘ For information about a tip for chopping vegetables, follow this link:

http://www.halleethehomemaker.com/2009/08/tips-chopping-onions/

Ravenclaw Red Beans Over Squib Spanish Rice

Red Beans Over Spanish Rice

Rice and beans seems like a really simple meal until you start packing in the flavors you can find in this recipe. Garlic, cumin, peppers, onions—this is a spicy, tangy wonderful dish that will please even the pickiest of eaters.

FOR THE RED BEANS:

3/4 lbs beef chuck roast, cut into 1-inch pieces

2 cups dry red beans or dry kidney beans (or 1 cup of each)

5 cups cold filtered water

1 TBS extra virgin olive oil

2 1/2 cups chopped onions

6 garlic cloves, chopped

1 TBS ground cumin

4 cups filtered water

FOR THE SPANISH RICE:

2 TBS extra virgin olive oil

1/2 onion, finely chopped

2 1/2 cups white rice

1 1/2 cup chunky salsa

4 cups Homemade Vegetable Broth🛈 (See NOTES)

OPTIONAL TOPPINGS:

extra virgin olive oil or unsalted butter according to personal taste

fresh jalapeño peppers, sliced

Cut the meat into 1-inch pieces, trimming any fat as needed.

Finely mince the onions for the rice.

Rinse the beans.

Chop the onions.

Chop the garlic

Nutrition Facts

Serving Size: (224g)
Servings Per Container: 8

Amount Per Serving	
Calories 510	Calories from Fat 60
	% Daily Value*
Total Fat 7g	**11%**
Saturated Fat 2g	**10%**
Trans Fat 0g	
Cholesterol 35mg	**12%**
Sodium 660mg	**28%**
Total Carbohydrate 85g	**28%**
Dietary Fiber 10g	**40%**
Sugars 8g	
Protein 27g	
Vitamin A 8% •	Vitamin C 10%
Calcium 8% •	Iron 25%

* Percent Daily Values are based on a 2,000 calorie diet. Your daily values may be higher or lower depending on your calorie needs:

	Calories:	2,000	2,500
Total Fat	Less than	65g	80g
Sat Fat	Less than	20g	25g
Cholesterol	Less than	300mg	300mg
Sodium	Less than	2,400mg	2,400mg
Total Carbohydrate		300g	375g
Dietary Fiber		25g	30g

3 1/2 or 4 qt slow cooker

measuring cups/spoons

good sharp knife

cutting board

mixing bowl

Whisk

Skillet with lid

In a large saucepan, combine the rinsed beans and the 5 cups water; bring to a boil. Reduce heat and simmer 10 minutes.

Remove from heat. Cover and let stand 1 hour. Rinse the beans with hot water and drain.

Heat olive oil in skillet over medium-high heat until hot. Add the meat coated in flour. Sear on every side for 30 seconds to 1 minute until nicely browned on all sides. Turn with kitchen tongs. Do not puncture the meat.

Lightly grease the inside of the slow cooker with either extra virgin olive oil or unsalted butter according to personal taste. Add beans, beef, onions, garlic, and cumin. Pour in the 4 cups water; stir.

Cover; cook on low heat 10 to 11 hours.

TO MAKE THE RICE:

Heat oil in skillet over medium heat. Stir in onion, and cook until tender, about 5 minutes.

Mix rice into skillet, stirring often. When rice begins to brown, stir in vegetable broth and salsa. Reduce heat, cover, and simmer 20 minutes, until liquid has been absorbed.

TO SERVE:

Using a slotted spoon, remove beans and beef. Serve beans over rice, and spoon liquid over the top.

Garnish with fresh sliced jalapeño.

6 to 8 servings

For this recipe, I prefer to use a combination of 1 cup of kidney beans and 1 cup of red beans because I really like the subtle differences in texture and flavor. I think it really adds to the dish. But you can use just about any variety of single bean or any combination of colored bean you like from black turtle beans to pinto beans although it wouldn't really qualify as "red beans" and rice. Regardless, any legume is going to be packed with flavor and nutrition. In the recipe directions, I have provided instructions for a quick soak as a timesaver. The best way to prepare your beans for just about any recipe is to soak your beans overnight, drain and rinse, then add them to the slow cooker to finish cooking.

ⓘ You can substitute Hallee's Heavenly Homemade Bird Brothⓘ for the water and reduce the amount of added salt by half. This will give the non-refried refried beans a richer flavor. I have included a recipe for Hallee's Heavenly Homemade Bird Brothⓘ in this cookbook. If you don't have stock on hand, be sure to use a good organic stock with low or no salt.

Leprechaun Lamb Tagine

Lamb, Apricot, & Olive Tagine

Lamb is always a nice break when you want red meat but just don't want beef. It's an extremely tender meat that just melts in your mouth when you eat it—especially when it's cooked low and slow in a slow cooker. The sweetness of the apricots combined with the zing of the green olives adds a fun kick to this tagine. Serve over couscous with a side of pita bread.

1 1/2 lbs lamb shoulder, trimmed and cut into 1 inch pieces

2 TBS flour (I use fresh ground, soft white wheat flour)

4 carrots, cut into 1-inch pieces

1 medium onion, choppedⓘ

2 cloves garlic, minced

1/2 cup dried apricots, halved

1/2 cup pitted green olives

1 tsp paprika

1 tsp ground cumin

1/2 tsp ground cinnamon

1/2 tsp ground ginger

1 tsp salt (Kosher or sea salt is best)

1/4 tsp fresh ground black pepper

1 cup couscous

chopped pistachios, fresh cilantro leaves, and lemon wedges, for serving

4 to 6 qt slow cooker

measuring cups/spoons

good sharp knife

cutting board

skillet

Nutrition Facts

Serving Size: (114g)
Servings Per Container: 6

Amount Per Serving	
Calories 200	Calories from Fat 35
	% Daily Value*
Total Fat 3.5g	**5%**
Saturated Fat 0.5g	**3%**
Trans Fat 0g	
Cholesterol <5mg	**2%**
Sodium 700mg	**29%**
Total Carbohydrate 37g	**12%**
Dietary Fiber 4g	**16%**
Sugars 8g	
Protein 6g	
Vitamin A 150% •	Vitamin C 6%
Calcium 4% •	Iron 6%

* Percent Daily Values are based on a 2,000 calorie diet. Your daily values may be higher or lower depending on your calorie needs:

	Calories:	2,000	2,500
Total Fat	Less than	65g	80g
Sat Fat	Less than	20g	25g
Cholesterol	Less than	300mg	300mg
Sodium	Less than	2,400mg	2,400mg
Total Carbohydrate		300g	375g
Dietary Fiber		25g	30g

Slice the carrots

Chop the onion

Mince the garlic

In slow cooker, mix together the lamb, carrots, onion, apricots, olives, garlic, flour, paprika, cumin, cinnamon, ginger, 1 tsp salt, 1/4 tsp pepper, and 1/2 cup water.

Cover and cook until the lamb and vegetables are tender, on low for 7 to 8 hours or on high for 4 to 5.

Ten minutes before serving, cook the couscous according to the package directions. Serve the lamb on the couscous with the pistachios, cilantro, and lemon wedges.

Serves 6

ⓘ For information about a tip for chopping vegetables, follow this link:

http://www.halleethehomemaker.com/2009/08/tips-chopping-onions/

No Need to Wave a Magic Wand.

Growing up in a family from the Pacific Northwest, fresh fish is one of my favorite proteins. I especially love Rainbow Trout and Salmon. There are just a few recipes in this cooking for fish—it isn't the cooking method I usually go for when preparing seafood—but they're amazing recipes that you don't want to pass up.

I would recommend using fresh fish. I have found that frozen fish tends to be very soggy when it thaws out, and recipes don't always turn out the way I like them.

When buying fish, there are two options: wild caught or farm raised.

Farm Raised Fish: Farmers raise fish commercially in tanks and/or enclosures in lakes, ponds, rivers and oceans. Due to the cramped space being taken up by so many fish, they tend to have more diseases and toxins. To combat the diseases and toxins, they're given antibiotics. And, because they can't move around like wild caught fish, they contain more fat.

Wild caught fish tend to be higher in Omega 3 fatty acids, protein and contain very low levels of disease. Because they're not controlled, they have no antibiotics, pesticides, or artificial dyes. Wild caught also have less fat than farm raised fish.

While you may pay more for wild caught fish, you're getting a much better, safer, and cleaner product for your dollar.

When you buy whole fish, make sure the eyes are not sunken or cloudy.

Don't be afraid to touch and inspect the fish. It should have a firm body that is springy to the touch and only a mild smell. A "fishy" smell is something to be avoided.

If you're buying fish that is already cut into fillets or steaks, it should have firm, elastic and moist-looking flesh. The skin should be shiny and bright.

Again, it should only have a mild smell—nothing "fishy".

When you purchase fish, you should prepare it within one or two days. It is highly perishable.

Transfiguration Tarragon Fish

Citrus & Tarragon Fish

I love white fish and citrus. It is one of my favorite ways to eat it. This recipe combines the sweetness of orange with the tartness of lemon and makes a delicious packet of fish.

4 white fish fillets (such as whitefish, tilapia, sole, flounder)

4 TBS dry white wine ⓘ (see NOTES for possible substitute)

2 oranges, each cut into four slices

2 lemons, each cut into four slices

8 large sprigs tarragon

4 TBS unsalted butter

Kosher or sea salt to taste

fresh ground black pepper to taste

At least 3 ½ to 4 qt slow cooker

measuring cups

measuring spoons

cutting board

good sharp knife

cutting board

aluminum foil

Nutrition Facts

Serving Size: (358g)
Servings Per Container: 4

Amount Per Serving	
Calories 430	Calories from Fat 210
	% Daily Value*
Total Fat 23g	**35%**
Saturated Fat 9g	**45%**
Trans Fat 0g	
Cholesterol 150mg	**50%**
Sodium 105mg	**4%**
Total Carbohydrate 16g	**5%**
Dietary Fiber 4g	**16%**
Sugars 6g	
Protein 39g	
Vitamin A 15% •	Vitamin C 140%
Calcium 10% •	Iron 6%

* Percent Daily Values are based on a 2,000 calorie diet. Your daily values may be higher or lower depending on your calorie needs:

	Calories:	2,000	2,500
Total Fat	Less than	65g	80g
Sat Fat	Less than	20g	25g
Cholesterol	Less than	300mg	300mg
Sodium	Less than	2,400mg	2,400mg
Total Carbohydrate		300g	375g
Dietary Fiber		25g	30g

Slice oranges

Slice lemons

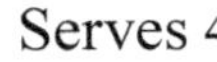

Cut four pieces of foil and lightly butter each. Place a fish fillet on each. Salt and pepper to taste.

Lay a tarragon sprig on each fillet, then a slice of orange and a slice of lemon side by side. Turn up the sides of the foil and spoon 1 TBS of wine over each fish fillet, then fold over the foil and seal the packets.

Place in the slow cooker and cook on high for 1 to $1\frac{1}{2}$ hours.

To serve, place parcels on serving places, open the top of each packet, and replace the cooked herb sprigs and citrus slices with fresh herb sprigs and citrus slices.

Alternately, carefully transfer the fillets to a serving platter or individual plates, then replace the herb sprigs and citrus slices with fresh herb sprigs and citrus slices.

With a spoon, drizzle the juices over the top.

ⓘ If you abstain from alcohol even in cooking, you can substitute a 100% pure grape juice (ensure there is no apple juice in it) and one teaspoon of distilled vinegar to approximate the same flavor and properties while cooking.

Weasley's Fish Stew

Fabulous Fish Stew

I lived in Florida for a number of years and fell in love with local seafood. One thing that I carried away from there was a deep and abiding affection for fish stew. It always brings to mind sitting on the deck of a friend's beach house, eating steaming bowls of fish stew while we watched a winter storm roll in. It quickly became one of those "comfort foods" for me.

Nutrition Facts

Serving Size: (455g)
Servings Per Container: 8

Amount Per Serving	
Calories 400	Calories from Fat 150
	% Daily Value*
Total Fat 16g	**25%**
Saturated Fat 8g	**40%**
Trans Fat 0g	
Cholesterol 70mg	**23%**
Sodium 980mg	**41%**
Total Carbohydrate 41g	**14%**
Dietary Fiber 6g	**24%**
Sugars 12g	
Protein 22g	
Vitamin A 20% •	Vitamin C 35%
Calcium 20% •	Iron 15%

* Percent Daily Values are based on a 2,000 calorie diet. Your daily values may be higher or lower depending on your calorie needs:

	Calories:	2,000	2,500
Total Fat	Less than	65g	80g
Sat Fat	Less than	20g	25g
Cholesterol	Less than	300mg	300mg
Sodium	Less than	2,400mg	2,400mg
Total Carbohydrate		300g	375g
Dietary Fiber		25g	30g

At least 3 1/2 to 4 qt slow cooker

measuring cups/spoons

good sharp knife and cutting board

Skillet

Wooden spoon

1 lb. White fish (like cod) cut into 1-inch pieces

1/2 cup white wineⓘ (see NOTES for possible substitute)

1 1/2 cups No Cans Cream of Celery Soupⓘ

1 1/2 cups Homemade Vegetable Brothⓘ

1 lb red potatoes

1 can (14 1/2 ounces) diced tomatoes, undrained

1 can (12-ounces) evaporated milk

1 package (10 oz.) frozen organic corn

1 1/2 cups cooked lima beans

1 large onion, finely choppedⓘ

1 celery stalk, finely choppedⓘ

4 cloves garlic, minced

zest of 1 lemon

1 bay leaf

2 tsp dried parsley flakes

1 tsp dried rosemary, crushed

1 tsp salt (Kosher or sea salt is best)

1 tsp fresh ground black pepper

If necessary, prepare dried lima beans. Soak overnight, then cover with water and cook until tender

Chop onion

Chop celery

Quarter the potatoes

Mince garlic

Zest lemon

In the slow cooker, combine everything except the fish, tomatoes, and evaporated milk. Cover and cook on low 6-8 hours or until the potatoes are tender.

Remove the bay leaf. Stir in the fish, tomatoes, and evaporated milk. Cook an additional 30 minutes or until fish flakes easily with a fork.

Yield

Serves 8

Notes

ⓘ If you abstain from alcohol even in cooking, you can substitute a 100% pure grape juice (ensure there is no apple juice in it) and one teaspoon of distilled vinegar to approximate the same flavor and properties while cooking.

ⓘ I have included a recipe for Hallee's Heavenly Homemade Bird Brothⓘ in this cookbook. To make a hearty homemade vegetable stock or broth, just leave out the bird and up the amount and variety of vegetables. The process is identical. If you don't have stock on hand, be sure to use a good organic stock with low or no salt.

Phoenix Poached Salmon

Poached Salmon

Although salmon isn't traditionally a protein that is slow cooked, poaching salmon in a slow cooker is easy and gives great results. Poaching is perfect for those not wanting any added fat and since the fish cooks in water and wine, it remains moist and flavorful. Vary the seasonings according to your own tastes if you'd like.

While you can certainly remove the skin prior to cooking if you like, I usually just go ahead and cook my salmon in a slow cooker with the skin still on it and remove it later. Poached salmon is tasty either hot or cold.

4 salmon steaks

1/4 cup dry white wine ⓘ (see NOTES for possible substitute)

1 cup water

1 onion, sliced

4 cloves garlic, minced

2 TBS lemon juice

2 TBS butter

1/2 tsp dried dill weed

1/2 tsp salt (Kosher or sea salt is best)

1/8 tsp fresh ground white pepper

Nutrition Facts

Serving Size: (455g)
Servings Per Container: 8

Amount Per Serving	
Calories 140	Calories from Fat 60
	% Daily Value*
Total Fat 7g	**11%**
Saturated Fat 2.5g	**13%**
Trans Fat 0g	
Cholesterol 45mg	**15%**
Sodium 220mg	**9%**
Total Carbohydrate 2g	**1%**
Dietary Fiber 0g	**0%**
Sugars <1g	
Protein 15g	
Vitamin A 4% •	Vitamin C 6%
Calcium 2% •	Iron 2%

* Percent Daily Values are based on a 2,000 calorie diet. Your daily values may be higher or lower depending on your calorie needs:

	Calories:	2,000	2,500
Total Fat	Less than	65g	80g
Sat Fat	Less than	20g	25g
Cholesterol	Less than	300mg	300mg
Sodium	Less than	2,400mg	2,400mg
Total Carbohydrate		300g	375g
Dietary Fiber		25g	30g

Supplies

3 1/2 to 4 quart slow cooker
saucepan
measuring cups/spoons
good sharp knife and cutting board
mixing bowl
Whisk

Preparation

Juice lemons if using fresh lemons.
Slice the lemon
Mince the garlic

Directions

In heavy saucepan, combine water and wine and bring to a boil. Reduce heat and simmer for 30 minutes.

Meanwhile, grease the bottom of slow cooker with butter or olive oil (depending on preference) and stack the salmon fillets inside.

Add the remaining ingredients to the saucepan and bring to a boil once more. Stir, then pour over salmon in slow cooker.

Cover, and cook on high heat for as little as 20 minutes and up to 3 1/2 hours—until salmon flakes when tested with a fork. Salmon should look opaque and be cooked through.

Yield

8 servings

ⓘ If you abstain from alcohol even in cooking, you can substitute a 100% pure grape juice (ensure there is no apple juice in it) and one teaspoon of distilled vinegar to approximate the same flavor and properties while cooking.

Squib Stone Salmon

Salmon with Caramelized Onions & Carrots

Salmon is one of my favorite meats, and this delicious recipe is perfect for entertaining or for the holidays. Serve this one dish meal with a rice pilaf or mashed potatoes to soak up all the wonderful juices.

1 1/2 lbs salmon filet

4 onions, thinly sliced

16 oz bag baby carrots

4 cloves garlic, minced

2 TBS olive oil

2 TBS butter

1/2 tsp dried dill weed

1/2 tsp salt (Kosher or sea salt is best)

1/8 tsp fresh ground black pepper

4-5 quart slow cooker

Needle nose pliers

measuring cups/spoons

good sharp knife and cutting board

mixing bowl

Whisk

Nutrition Facts

Serving Size: (606g)
Servings Per Container: 6

Amount Per Serving	
Calories 290	Calories from Fat 140
	% Daily Value*
Total Fat 15g	**23%**
Saturated Fat 4.5g	**23%**
Trans Fat 0g	
Cholesterol 70mg	**23%**
Sodium 380mg	**16%**
Total Carbohydrate 14g	**5%**
Dietary Fiber 4g	**16%**
Sugars 7g	
Protein 26g	
Vitamin A 220% •	Vitamin C 15%
Calcium 6% •	Iron 8%

* Percent Daily Values are based on a 2,000 calorie diet. Your daily values may be higher or lower depending on your calorie needs:

	Calories:	2,000	2,500
Total Fat	Less than	65g	80g
Sat Fat	Less than	20g	25g
Cholesterol	Less than	300mg	300mg
Sodium	Less than	2,400mg	2,400mg
Total Carbohydrate		300g	375g
Dietary Fiber		25g	30g

Slice the onions.

Mince the garlic

Using needle nose pliers, pull any bones out of the salmon filet

Place olive oil and butter in slow cooker. Add onions, baby carrots, and garlic, stir, cover, and cook on low for 6-7 hours, stirring once during cooking time, until vegetables begin to caramelize.

Lay salmon over vegetables in slow cooker and sprinkle with salt, pepper, and dill weed. Cover and cook on low for 1 to 2 hours until salmon flakes when tested with a fork (test at one hour time, if salmon is done, turn slow cooker off and keep covered until serving time). Place salmon on serving plate and top with onion mixture.

6 servings

To find the bones in the filet, run your finger along the flesh of the fish. You will be able to feel the bones, and easily pull them out with the pliers.

Vegetables

It Doesn't Take a Potion.

This section is full of meatless recipes. Some are side items, some are main dishes, and some can be used either way.

One of the things I love about cooking vegetables in the slow cooker is that it frees up space on the stove and in the oven. When I'm cooking a big meal, space can often be crucial. If I can set a slow cooker cooking away from the active busyness of my kitchen, it can be wonderful!

My family eats a vegetarian meal most nights during the week, so I'm always on the hunt for new recipes. Even when I do serve meat, with most dinners I serve a vegetable on the side. However, I often grow fatigued of coming up with side dishes that are different from the typical green beans or corn. It is always nice to have some other options, easy to make, on hand.

When cooking vegetables, I always try to start with fresh vegetables. If you can't get fresh, frozen is better than canned. These recipes all start with fresh or frozen. If you use canned, you may need to adjust cooking times or salt amounts.

On my Hallee the Homemaker website, I list the "Dirty Dozenⓘ"—that is, the vegetables that are most likely to retain remnants of pesticides even after washing. In that same article, I also list the top GMO foods and the foods you should always try to purchase as certified organic if you don't grow your own or have access to a trusted sustainable local farm.

The "Dirty Dozen" foods that are the most contaminated on average are:

1. **Peaches**
2. **Apples**
3. **Sweet Bell Peppers**
4. **Celery**
5. **Nectarines**
6. **Strawberries**
7. **Cherries**
8. **Lettuce**
9. **Grapes (imported)**
10. **Pears**
11. **Spinach**
12. **Potatoes**

If organic vegetables are too costly for you, try to at least purchase these ingredients organic.

Order of the Phoenix Fondue

Pizza Fondue

This is a dip that you'll have to double or triple if you have teenagers in the house. Serve it with crusty french bread and watch them go to town. It's amazing.

1/4 cup Parmigiano Reggiano (Parmesan) cheese, shredded

2 cups mozzarella cheese, shredded

2 1/2 cups water

1 6-ounce can tomato paste

1 15 1/2-ounce can tomato sauce

3/4 tsp garlic powder

2 1/4 tsp oregano,

1/4 tsp dried basil

1/4 tsp dried sage

1/4 tsp dried thyme

1/2 tsp Kosher or sea salt

1/4 tsp fresh ground black pepper

Nutrition Facts

Serving Size: (96g)
Servings Per Container: 15

Amount Per Serving	
Calories 70	Calories from Fat 35
	% Daily Value*
Total Fat 4g	**6%**
Saturated Fat 2g	**10%**
Trans Fat 0g	
Cholesterol 15mg	**5%**
Sodium 350mg	**15%**
Total Carbohydrate 4g	**1%**
Dietary Fiber 1g	**4%**
Sugars 3g	
Protein 5g	
Vitamin A 8% •	Vitamin C 8%
Calcium 10% •	Iron 4%

* Percent Daily Values are based on a 2,000 calorie diet. Your daily values may be higher or lower depending on your calorie needs:

	Calories:	2,000	2,500
Total Fat	Less than	65g	80g
Sat Fat	Less than	20g	25g
Cholesterol	Less than	300mg	300mg
Sodium	Less than	2,400mg	2,400mg
Total Carbohydrate		300g	375g
Dietary Fiber		25g	30g

1 1/2 quart slow cooker

Measuring cups/spoons

Cheese grater

Grate the cheese

Mix all ingredients in the slow cooker. Cover and cook 4-6 hours on low or 2-3 hours on high until heated through and cheese is melted.

Serve with chunks of French bread for dipping.

15 servings

Try to use block cheese instead of pre-grated cheeses. They are tossed with an agent to prevent the shreds from sticking together, and that will impede the way they melt.

Magic Wand Bean Dip

Non-Refried "Refried" Beans Black & Pinto Bean Dip

Flavorful, friendly refried bean dip seasoned with garlic, peppers, and cumin. You make these in your slow-cooker instead of frying and refrying so they are healthy and delicious. Serve with vegetables, pita triangles, chips—whatever you want to use as a medium to get the dip from the bowl into your mouth.

9 cups filtered water or Homemade Vegetable Broth🛈 (See NOTES)

$^1/_2$ fresh jalapeño pepper, seeded and chopped (or one small can of green chiles)

1 onion, peeled and halved

1 $^1/_2$ cups dried pinto beans

1 $^1/_2$ cups dried black beans

2 TBS minced garlic

1 TBS salt (Kosher or sea salt is best)

1 $^3/_4$ tsp fresh ground black pepper

$^1/_8$ tsp ground cumin (optional)

2 cups chunky salsa🛈

2 cups shredded Colby-Jack Cheese

8 oz cream cheese

16 oz plain yogurt (or sour cream)

2 TBS chili powder

$^1/_2$ tsp additional ground cumin

Nutrition Facts

Serving Size: (520g)
Servings Per Container: 15

Amount Per Serving	
Calories 430	Calories from Fat 170
	% Daily Value*
Total Fat 19g	**29%**
Saturated Fat 12g	**60%**
Trans Fat 0.5g	
Cholesterol 65mg	**22%**
Sodium 1330mg	**55%**
Total Carbohydrate 44g	**15%**
Dietary Fiber 7g	**28%**
Sugars 17g	
Protein 23g	
Vitamin A 30% •	Vitamin C 8%
Calcium 50% •	Iron 15%

* Percent Daily Values are based on a 2,000 calorie diet. Your daily values may be higher or lower depending on your calorie needs:

	Calories:	2,000	2,500
Total Fat	Less than	65g	80g
Sat Fat	Less than	20g	25g
Cholesterol	Less than	300mg	300mg
Sodium	Less than	2,400mg	2,400mg
Total Carbohydrate		300g	375g
Dietary Fiber		25g	30g

Slow cooker

good wooden spoon

potato masher or hand blender

measuring cups/spoons

Colander

Pick through the beans and rinse them.

Place the onion, rinsed beans, jalapeno (or chiles), garlic, salt, pepper, and cumin into a slow cooker. Pour in the water and stir to combine. Cook on High for 8 hours, adding more water as needed.

Once the beans have cooked, strain them, and reserve the liquid. Mash with a potato masher, or use a hand blender, slowly adding small amounts of the reserved liquid as needed to attain the desired consistency.

Mix in the remaining ingredients and let cook in the slow-cooker on low for a couple hours longer to allow the flavors to blend.

This makes a huge batch suitable for a party.

You can freeze the leftovers. It keeps just great.

15 servings

Notes

ⓘ Substituting a small can of green chiles for the jalapeños results in a milder flavor.

ⓘ You can substitute Hallee's Heavenly Homemade Bird Brothⓘ for the water and reduce the amount of added salt by half. This will give the non-refried refried beans a richer flavor. I have included a recipe for Hallee's Heavenly Homemade Bird Brothⓘ in this cookbook. If you don't have stock on hand, be sure to use a good organic stock with low or no salt.

ⓘ For a good recipe to make your own homemade fresh salsa, follow this link:

http://www.halleethehomemaker.com/2009/09/spicy-tomato-jalapeno-salsa/

Hufflepuff Eggplant Lasagna

Eggplant Lasagna

I never miss meat when I make an eggplant lasagna. The meaty vegetable provides exactly the consistency I'm looking for—and it always goes great with the Italian flavors in the dish.

1 jar (26 oz) organic pasta sauce (or 3 1/4 cup Hallee's Homemade Spaghetti Sauce ⓘ)

8 oz package whole wheat lasagna noodles, cooked and drained

1 cup grated Parmigiano Reggiano (Parmesan) cheese, divided

1 1/2 cup (6 oz) shredded Monterey Jack cheese

2 cups part-skim ricotta cheese

2 TBS extra virgin olive oil, divided

1 TBS unsalted butter

1 small eggplant, sliced into 1/2-inch rounds

1 medium zucchini, thinly sliced

8 ounces mushrooms, sliced

1 small onion, diced

1 tsp dried basil

1 tsp dried oregano

1/2 tsp salt (Kosher or sea salt is best)

Nutrition Facts

Serving Size: 500 grams (473g)
Servings Per Container: 6

Amount Per Serving	
Calories 590	Calories from Fat 280
	% Daily Value*
Total Fat 31g	**48%**
Saturated Fat 15g	**75%**
Trans Fat 0.5g	
Cholesterol 75mg	**25%**
Sodium 1240mg	**52%**
Total Carbohydrate 49g	**16%**
Dietary Fiber 9g	**36%**
Sugars 14g	
Protein 34g	
Vitamin A 35% •	Vitamin C 20%
Calcium 70% •	Iron 20%

* Percent Daily Values are based on a 2,000 calorie diet. Your daily values may be higher or lower depending on your calorie needs:

	Calories:	2,000	2,500
Total Fat	Less than	65g	80g
Sat Fat	Less than	20g	25g
Cholesterol	Less than	300mg	300mg
Sodium	Less than	2,400mg	2,400mg
Total Carbohydrate		300g	375g
Dietary Fiber		25g	30g

4-5 quart slow cooker

Skillet

Paper towels

Pastry brush

measuring cups/spoons

good sharp knife

cutting board

mixing bowl

Whisk

Cheese grater

If necessary, slice the mushrooms (I like to buy them pre-sliced because they're also washed)

Slice eggplant

Dice onion

Grate cheeses

Prepare the lasagna noodles according to package directions

Slice the zucchini

If necessary, prepare the spaghetti sauce

Sprinkle eggplant with salt; let sit 10 to 15 minutes (this will pull a lot of excess moisture out of the vegetable). Rinse and pat dry with paper towels. Brush with 1 TBS olive oil. Brown on both sides in medium skillet over medium heat. Set aside.

Heat remaining 1 TBS olive oil and butter in same skillet over medium heat; cook and stir mushrooms and onion until softened. Stir in pasta sauce, basil and oregano. Set aside.

Combine ricotta cheese, Monterey Jack cheese and 1/2 cup Parmigiano Reggiano (Parmesan) cheese in medium bowl. Set aside.

Spread 1/3 sauce mixture in bottom of slow cooker. Layer with 1/3 lasagna noodles, 1/2 eggplant, 1/2 cheese mixture. Repeat layers once. For last layer use remaining 1/3 lasagna noodles, zucchini, remaining of sauce mixture and top with remaining 1/2 cup Parmigiano Reggiano (Parmesan).

Cover; cook on low heat for 6 hours or 3 1/2 to 4 hours on high heat. Let sit 15 to 20 minutes before serving.

6 servings

ⓘ If you would like to make your own pasta sauce, with or without meat, you can look up Hallee's Homemade Spaghetti Sauce on the web at this link:

www.halleethehomemaker.com/2009/09/italian-turkey-sausage-spaghetti-sauce/

Every Flavour Baked Beans

Ambrosial Picnic-Perfect Baked Beans

I think I could live on baked beans and potato salad, if someone would let me. This is a simple baked bean dish that packs a ton of great flavor. It is the perfect side to any summer picnic you're attending.

1 lbs dried navy beans

$^{1}/_{4}$ cup Hallee's Homemade Organic Ketchupⓘ

$^{1}/_{4}$ cup unsulphured molasses

$^{1}/_{4}$ cup brown sugar

5 cups water

1 cup tomato juice

$^{1}/_{2}$ cup chopped onion

1 tsp chili powder

$^{1}/_{2}$ tsp dry mustard

$^{1}/_{4}$ tsp salt (Kosher or sea salt is best)

$^{1}/_{4}$ tsp fresh ground black pepper

measuring cups/spoons

good sharp knife and cutting board

mixing bowl

whisk

Nutrition Facts

Serving Size: 500 grams (272g)
Servings Per Container: 8

Amount Per Serving	
Calories 270	Calories from Fat 10
	% Daily Value*
Total Fat 1g	**2%**
Saturated Fat 0g	**0%**
Trans Fat 0g	
Cholesterol 0mg	**0%**
Sodium 210mg	**9%**
Total Carbohydrate 53g	**18%**
Dietary Fiber 14g	**56%**
Sugars 17g	
Protein 13g	
Vitamin A 6% •	Vitamin C 15%
Calcium 15% •	Iron 25%

* Percent Daily Values are based on a 2,000 calorie diet. Your daily values may be higher or lower depending on your calorie needs:

	Calories:	2,000	2,500
Total Fat	Less than	65g	80g
Sat Fat	Less than	20g	25g
Cholesterol	Less than	300mg	300mg
Sodium	Less than	2,400mg	2,400mg
Total Carbohydrate		300g	375g
Dietary Fiber		25g	30g

Soak beans overnight.

Chop onion

8 servings

Drain the beans you've had soaking overnight and rinse with hot tap water. Place in large pot and cover with 5 cups of fresh water. Bring to a boil, then simmer over medium-low heat for 1 hour.

Drain beans, reserving the liquid, and add to the slow cooker.

In bowl, combine tomato juice, onion, ketchup, molasses, brown sugar, dry mustard, salt, black pepper, and chili powder. Stir until mixed.

Add to beans and stir well. Add as much of the reserved liquid as needed to cover the beans by about an inch.

Cover and cook until beans are tender and flavorful; on low heat for 7 to 9 hours or on high heat for 4 to 5 hours. During cooking, try to leave covered as much as possible, but add more liquid as necessary.

ⓘ I cannot even explain how the flavors explode with incredible depth when these homemade items, and not store-bought factory substitutes, form the base. The only way to make this dish even better would be to start with a batch of your very own Hallee's Homemade Organic Ketchupⓘ. I have included recipe in this cookbook and strongly encourage you to try it out.

Hippogriff Veggie Lasagna

Slow Cooked Veggie Lasagna

This Veggie Lasagna is one of my biggest recent crock pot success stories and it only took me a few minutes to put the whole thing together. No sautéing or stove-watching required. Just chop your veggies, mix the cheeses and layer everything into the pot. By the time you get home from picking up the kids at school and an afternoon of errands, this delicious dinner will be waiting for you—just take the lid off and serve.

1 jar (26 oz) organic pasta sauce (or 3 1/4 cup Hallee's Homemade Spaghetti Sauce ⓘ)

1/2 cup Parmigiano Reggiano (Parmesan) cheese, grated

2 cups mozzarella cheese, grated

15 oz ricotta cheese

1 large egg

1 box lasagna noodles (uncooked)

1 TBS Hallee's Inviting Italian Seasoning ⓘ

1/2 cup sliced zucchini

1/2 cup chopped broccoli

1/2 cup chopped cauliflower

1/2 cup sliced mushrooms

1/2 cup baby spinach

1/2 tsp garlic powder

1 tsp salt (Kosher or sea salt is best)

measuring cups/spoons
good sharp knife
cutting board
mixing bowl
Food processor

Prepare sauce, if necessary.
Grate cheeses

Nutrition Facts
Serving Size: 500 grams (295g)
Servings Per Container: 6

Amount Per Serving	
Calories 310	Calories from Fat 130
	% Daily Value*
Total Fat 14g	**22%**
Saturated Fat 8g	**40%**
Trans Fat 0g	
Cholesterol 80mg	**27%**
Sodium 1320mg	**55%**
Total Carbohydrate 21g	**7%**
Dietary Fiber 4g	**16%**
Sugars 8g	
Protein 27g	
Vitamin A 35% •	Vitamin C 25%
Calcium 60% •	Iron 15%

* Percent Daily Values are based on a 2,000 calorie diet. Your daily values may be higher or lower depending on your calorie needs:

	Calories:	2,000	2,500
Total Fat	Less than	65g	80g
Sat Fat	Less than	20g	25g
Cholesterol	Less than	300mg	300mg
Sodium	Less than	2,400mg	2,400mg
Total Carbohydrate		300g	375g
Dietary Fiber		25g	30g

Place the vegetables in a food processor and pulse to roughly chop.

Place the ricotta, Parmigiano Reggiano (Parmesan) cheese, herbs, garlic powder, salt and egg in a bowl and stir to combine.

Pour half of the pasta sauce in the bottom of a crock pot.

Place a layer of noodles on top of the sauce, covering the entire surface, breaking the noodles to fit the pot.

Layer half of the ricotta mixture on top of the noodles, followed by 1 cup of the chopped vegetables and then one cup of mozzarella cheese.

Repeat with another layer of noodles, followed by the remaining ricotta mixture and the chopped vegetables.

Pour the remaining pasta sauce on top of the lasagna and top with the remaining cup of the grated cheese.

Cook on low for 4 hours. Serve.

Yield

6 servings

Notes

ⓘ If you would like to make your own pasta sauce, with or without meat, you can look up Hallee's Homemade Spaghetti Sauce on the web at this link:

www.halleethehomemaker.com/2009/09/italian-turkey-sausage-spaghetti-sauce/

ⓘ It's somewhat important to use homemade Hallee's Inviting Italian Seasoningⓘ in this recipe. Store-bought versions nearly always contain salt. I challenge you to try it without the added salt and then feel free to add salt when the dish is done.

Gryffindor Stew

Tuscan Lentil Stew

Lentils are one of my go-to items to add to soups and stews. I love their versatility and the punch of nutrition they provide. This stew is wonderfully full of flavorful Italian herbs and the simple flavors of vegetables.

1 1/2 cups Homemade Vegetable Brothⓘ (See NOTES)

2 tsp Hallee's Inviting Italian Seasoningⓘ

fresh Parmigiano Reggiano (Parmesan) cheese, shaved or shredded

extra virgin olive oil or unsalted butter

3/4 cup (1 bag) fresh baby spinach leaves, chopped

1 1/2 lbs russet potatoes (3 large), cut into 3/4 inch pieces

3 cloves garlic, finely minced

1 cup dried lentils, sorted, rinsed

2 large onions (about 2 cups), choppedⓘ

3 1/2 cups fresh (or 2 15-cans) tomatoes, diced

1/4 tsp crushed red pepper flakes

1 tsp salt (Kosher or sea salt is best)

Serves 6

4 to 6 quart slow cooker
measuring cups/spoons
good sharp knife and cutting board
kitchen tongs
2 forks

Nutrition Facts
Serving Size: 500 grams (406g)
Servings Per Container: 6

Amount Per Serving	
Calories 250	Calories from Fat 5
	% Daily Value*
Total Fat 0.5g	**1%**
Saturated Fat 0g	**0%**
Trans Fat 0g	
Cholesterol 0mg	**0%**
Sodium 710mg	**30%**
Total Carbohydrate 52g	**17%**
Dietary Fiber 14g	**56%**
Sugars 7g	
Protein 13g	
Vitamin A 20% •	Vitamin C 45%
Calcium 10% •	Iron 30%

* Percent Daily Values are based on a 2,000 calorie diet. Your daily values may be higher or lower depending on your calorie needs:

	Calories:	2,000	2,500
Total Fat	Less than	65g	80g
Sat Fat	Less than	20g	25g
Cholesterol	Less than	300mg	300mg
Sodium	Less than	2,400mg	2,400mg
Total Carbohydrate		300g	375g
Dietary Fiber		25g	30g

Cut potatoes
Mince garlic
Rinse lentils
Chop spinach
Shave cheese
Peel, seed, and chop tomatoes (if necessary)

Lightly grease the inside of the slow cooker with either extra virgin olive oil or unsalted butter according to personal taste. Put the potatoes into the slow cooker.

Add garlic, lintels, onions, tomatoes, salt, red pepper flakes, and Italian seasoning. Slowly pour in broth. (In other words, add all ingredients except spinach and cheese ensuring that you pour in the broth last.)

Cover and cook on low heat setting 8 to 10 hours or on high heat for 4 to 5 hours.

Stir in spinach.

Cover and cook until spinach is wilted; about 5 minutes longer.

Ladle into bowls or mugs to serve. Sprinkle each serving with Parmigiano Reggiano (Parmesan) cheese.

Serve with a mixed-greens salad and garlic toast.

ⓘ I have included recipes for both Hallee's Heavenly Homemade Bird Broth and Hallee's Savory Stocky Crock Pot Beef Broth in this cookbook. To make vegetable broth or stock, follow either recipe and just leave out the meat and bone but up the variety and amount of vegetables to produce a homemade all vegetable stock or broth. If you don't have stock on hand, be sure to use a good organic stock with low or no salt.

ⓘ If you don't have a good homemade broth on hand, be sure to use a good organic broth with low or no salt.

ⓘ It's somewhat important to use homemade Hallee's Inviting Italian Seasoningⓘ in this recipe. Store-bought versions nearly always contain salt and most contain MSG. I challenge you to try it without the added salt and then feel free to add salt when the dish is done.

ⓘ For information about a tip for chopping vegetables, follow this link:

http://www.halleethehomemaker.com/2009/08/tips-chopping-onions/

House-Elf Soup

White Bean with Fennel Soup

Fennel is such an underused vegetable! I love the slight licorice flavor and in fact keep candied fennel seeds near my desk to munch on when I'm looking for a quick sweet bite.

For this recipe, I prefer to use white kidney (cannelloni) beans as I feel they go best with the fennel. But you can use just about any variety of single bean or any combination of light colored bean you like from my preference of white kidney (cannelloni), to white beans, great northern, white navy, corona, or lupini. Any legume is going to be packed with flavor and nutrition. You could even use lighter colored beans like cranberry beans or pink beans. The best way to prepare your beans for this recipe is to soak your beans overnight then drain and rinse and add them to this chili to finish cooking.

2 cups favorite light color dried beans, rinsed & drained (I use white kidney which is also called cannellini)

4 1/2 cups Homemade Vegetable Broth🛈 (See NOTES)

4 cups water

1 small bulb fennel (about 1/2 pound), trimmed and sliced (about 2 cups)

1 medium onion (about 1/2 cup), chopped🛈

2 cloves garlic, minced

1 1/4 cup (10 oz frozen package) leaf spinach

2 cups (14 1/2 oz can) diced tomatoes

1 tsp salt (Kosher or sea salt is best)

1/8 tsp fresh ground black pepper

5 1/2 to 6 qt slow cooker

Trim and slice the fennel bulb.

Rinse and drain the beans

Chop the onion

Mince the garlic

Nutrition Facts

Serving Size: 500 grams (406g)
Servings Per Container: 6

Amount Per Serving	
Calories 240	Calories from Fat 0
	% Daily Value*
Total Fat 0g	**0%**
Saturated Fat 0g	**0%**
Trans Fat 0g	
Cholesterol 0mg	**0%**
Sodium 880mg	**37%**
Total Carbohydrate 45g	**15%**
Dietary Fiber 12g	**48%**
Sugars 7g	
Protein 16g	
Vitamin A 50% •	Vitamin C 30%
Calcium 20% •	Iron 40%

* Percent Daily Values are based on a 2,000 calorie diet. Your daily values may be higher or lower depending on your calorie needs:

	Calories:	2,000	2,500
Total Fat	Less than	65g	80g
Sat Fat	Less than	20g	25g
Cholesterol	Less than	300mg	300mg
Sodium	Less than	2,400mg	2,400mg
Total Carbohydrate		300g	375g
Dietary Fiber		25g	30g

Place the beans, water, Homemade Vegetable Broth①, pepper, onion, and garlic in slow cooker.

Cover and cook on high heat for 2-3 hours. Add the fennel and cook for another 2-3 hours, or until the beans are tender. Add spinach and tomatoes. Cook on high for an additional hour.

Serves 6

① I have included recipes for both Hallee's Heavenly Homemade Bird Broth and Hallee's Savory Stocky Crock Pot Beef Broth in this cookbook. To make vegetable broth or stock, follow either recipe and just leave out the meat and bone but up the variety and amount of vegetables to produce a homemade all vegetable stock or broth. If you don't have stock on hand, be sure to use a good organic stock with low or no salt.

ⓘ For information about a tip for chopping vegetables, follow this link:

http://www.halleethehomemaker.com/2009/08/tips-chopping-onions/

If you use pre-cooked beans, don't add the water and make the initial cooking time 3-4 hours on high heat. Then, add the beans with the spinach and tomatoes

Goblin Soup

Roasted Tomato, Red Pepper, & Bread Soup

This is one of those heavenly soups that everyone just pauses as they take the first bite. It is so rich, so comforting, and so wonderful to eat.

4 cups Hallee's Heavenly Homemade Bird Broth ⓘ
2 slices bread, crusts removed and torn into pieces
2 medium onions (about 1 cup), finely diced ⓘ
2 lbs Roma or plum tomatoes
2 red peppers
3 cloves garlic, crushed
2 tsp ground cumin
1 tsp ground coriander
1 TBS balsamic vinegar
2 TBS extra virgin olive oil
salt (Kosher or sea salt is best) to taste
fresh ground black pepper to taste

3 1/2 to 4 qt slow cooker
measuring cups/spoons
good sharp knife
cutting board
Cookie sheet

Nutrition Facts
Serving Size: 500 grams (609g)
Servings Per Container: 4

Amount Per Serving	
Calories 160	Calories from Fat 70
	% Daily Value*
Total Fat 8g	**12%**
Saturated Fat 1g	**5%**
Trans Fat 0g	
Cholesterol 0mg	**0%**
Sodium 640mg	**27%**
Total Carbohydrate 19g	**6%**
Dietary Fiber 4g	**16%**
Sugars 8g	
Protein 4g	

Vitamin A 45%	•	Vitamin C 140%
Calcium 4%	•	Iron 6%

* Percent Daily Values are based on a 2,000 calorie diet. Your daily values may be higher or lower depending on your calorie needs:

	Calories:	2,000	2,500
Total Fat	Less than	65g	80g
Sat Fat	Less than	20g	25g
Cholesterol	Less than	300mg	300mg
Sodium	Less than	2,400mg	2,400mg
Total Carbohydrate		300g	375g
Dietary Fiber		25g	30g

Preheat oven to 350° degrees F (180° degrees C).

On a cookie sheet, drizzle tomatoes and peppers with olive oil. Toss to coat. Arrange and roast for 20 minutes or until skins have blistered.

Add garlic, onion, cumin, and coriander and roast for five additional minutes.

Let cool. Remove skins from the tomatoes and peppers and roughly chop.

Set slow cooker to high heat. Put in the roasted vegetables and the broth. Cook for 2 hours.

Add bread, balsamic vinegar, and salt and pepper. Cook for an additional 50 minutes.

Serves 4

ⓘ I have included a recipe for Hallee's Heavenly Homemade Bird Brothⓘ in this cookbook. If you don't have stock on hand, be sure to use a good organic stock with low or no salt.

ⓘ For information about a tip for chopping vegetables, follow this link:

http://www.halleethehomemaker.com/2009/08/tips-chopping-onions/

Diagon Alley Chowder

Easy Corn Chowder

I never thought I'd like corn chowder—until I had it. Now, whenever I see it on a menu, I try to order it. It's creamy and crunchy, and beef (not turkey) bacon gives it a wonderful salty smoked meat flavor if you depart from vegetarian.

1 cup Hallee's Heavenly Homemade Bird Broth ⓘ

2 cups (16 oz bag frozen) corn kernels

1 red bell pepper, diced ⓘ

1 medium onion, diced ⓘ

1 celery stalk, sliced

1/4 tsp ground coriander

1/2 cup heavy cream

1/2 tsp salt (Kosher or sea salt is best)

1/2 tsp fresh ground black pepper

3 small potatoes, peeled and cut into 1/2 inch pieces

8 slices beef bacon, crisp cooked and crumbled (optional)

Nutrition Facts

Serving Size: 500 grams (141g)
Servings Per Container: 6

Amount Per Serving	
Calories 90	Calories from Fat 35
	% Daily Value*
Total Fat 4g	**6%**
Saturated Fat 2.5g	**13%**
Trans Fat 0g	
Cholesterol 15mg	**5%**
Sodium 290mg	**12%**
Total Carbohydrate 13g	**4%**
Dietary Fiber 2g	**8%**
Sugars 3g	
Protein 2g	
Vitamin A 20% •	Vitamin C 50%
Calcium 2% •	Iron 2%

* Percent Daily Values are based on a 2,000 calorie diet. Your daily values may be higher or lower depending on your calorie needs:

	Calories:	2,000	2,500
Total Fat	Less than	65g	80g
Sat Fat	Less than	20g	25g
Cholesterol	Less than	300mg	300mg
Sodium	Less than	2,400mg	2,400mg
Total Carbohydrate		300g	375g
Dietary Fiber		25g	30g

3 ½ to 4 qt slow cooker

measuring cups/spoons

good sharp knife

cutting board

Peel and cut potatoes

Dice pepper

Dice onion

Prepare beef bacon as needed

Place broth, corn, potatoes, bell pepper, onion, celery, salt, black pepper and coriander into slow cooker.

Cover and cook on low heat for 6 to 7 hours or on high heat for 3 to 3 ½ hours.

Partially mash soup mixture with potato masher to thicken. Stir in cream; cook on high heat, uncovered, until hot.

Adjust seasonings, if desired.

Garnish with beef bacon.

Serves 6

ⓘ I have included a recipe for Hallee's Heavenly Homemade Bird Brothⓘ in this cookbook. If you don't have stock on hand, be sure to use a good organic stock with low or no salt.

Half-Blood Corn Pudding

Sweet Corn Pudding

Whenever I'm at a church potluck, I always go for the corn pudding. There's something about the cheesy, creamy, salty crunch that I just love. This is perfect for potlucks—you can prepare it the night before and take with you as you leave for church the next morning. It's also great when you're cooking a holiday meal, because you can prepare it in the slow cooker, then get it out of your way in the kitchen while it cooks.

16 ounces frozen organic sweet corn kernels

1 cup Monterey jack cheese, shredded

8 ounces cream cheese, softened

1/2 cup milk

1/4 cup flour (I use fresh ground soft white wheat)

1/4 cup cornmeal

2 TBS honey (pure, raw, local honey is always best)

1/2 tsp aluminum-free baking powder

1/4 tsp Kosher salt (or sea salt)

3 1/2 or 4 quart slow cooker

measuring cups/spoons

Shred cheese

Serves 6

Place all ingredients in a slow cooker.

Mix well until combined.

Cover and cook on low for 2 hours and 45 minutes.

Remove the cover and cook uncovered for an additional 15 minutes.

Nutrition Facts

Serving Size: 500 grams (141g)
Servings Per Container: 6

Amount Per Serving	
Calories 340	Calories from Fat 180
	% Daily Value*
Total Fat 20g	**31**%
Saturated Fat 11g	**55**%
Trans Fat 0.5g	
Cholesterol 60mg	**20**%
Sodium 420mg	**18**%
Total Carbohydrate 32g	**11**%
Dietary Fiber 2g	**8**%
Sugars 10g	
Protein 11g	
Vitamin A 15% •	Vitamin C 8%
Calcium 20% •	Iron 6%

* Percent Daily Values are based on a 2,000 calorie diet. Your daily values may be higher or lower depending on your calorie needs:

	Calories:	2,000	2,500
Total Fat	Less than	65g	80g
Sat Fat	Less than	20g	25g
Cholesterol	Less than	300mg	300mg
Sodium	Less than	2,400mg	2,400mg
Total Carbohydrate		300g	375g
Dietary Fiber		25g	30g

Notes

Add a 7 ounce can of green chilis during prep and reduce the sugar to 1 tablespoon for a delicious Green Chili Corn Pudding.

Defense Against the Dark Arts Casserole

Cheesy Winter Vegetables Casserole

This is a nice cheesy side dish that you can leave cooking all day long. The kids will love the creamy cheesyness of it, and you'll love that they ate every bit of the vegetables!

3 TBS butter

3 TBS flour (I use fresh ground soft white wheat)

1 1/2 cup cheddar cheese, shredded

1 cup Colby Jack cheese, shredded

1 cup whole milk

1 cup frozen sweet peas, thawed

2 1/2 cup (20 oz) new potatoes, cut in wedges

2 cups carrots, cut into 1-inch pieces (or baby carrots)

1 medium stalk celery, cut into 1-inch pieces

2 tsp Worcestershire sauce

1/8 tsp ground red pepper (cayenne), if desired

3 1/2 to 4 qt slow cooker

measuring cups/spoons

good sharp knife and cutting board

Skillet

whisk

Quarter the new potatoes

Peel and slice the carrots

Cut the celery

Shred the cheeses

In a skillet over medium, melt the butter. Whisk in the flour and whisk until smooth. Slowly whisk in the milk and bring it to a soft boil. Boil and stir for 1 minute. Remove from heat and stir in the cheddar cheese. Add Worcestershire sauce and ground red pepper. Mix well.

In slow cooker, combine potatoes, carrots, and celery. Pour cheese mixture over vegetables; stir gently to coat.

Cover and cook on low heat for 6 to 7 hours or on high heat for 3 to 3 $^{1}/_{2}$ hours.

About 10 minutes before serving, gently stir thawed peas and shredded Colby Jack cheese into vegetable mixture.

Cover and cook on low heat for an additional 10 minutes or until carrots are tender.

Nutrition Facts

Serving Size: 500 grams (118g)
Servings Per Container: 12

Amount Per Serving	
Calories 180	Calories from Fat 100
	% Daily Value*
Total Fat 11g	**17%**
Saturated Fat 7g	**35%**
Trans Fat 0g	
Cholesterol 35mg	**12%**
Sodium 200mg	**8%**
Total Carbohydrate 12g	**4%**
Dietary Fiber 2g	**8%**
Sugars 3g	
Protein 8g	
Vitamin A 80% •	Vitamin C 10%
Calcium 20% •	Iron 4%

* Percent Daily Values are based on a 2,000 calorie diet. Your daily values may be higher or lower depending on your calorie needs:

	Calories:	2,000	2,500
Total Fat	Less than	65g	80g
Sat Fat	Less than	20g	25g
Cholesterol	Less than	300mg	300mg
Sodium	Less than	2,400mg	2,400mg
Total Carbohydrate		300g	375g
Dietary Fiber		25g	30g

12 ($^{1}/_{2}$ cup) servings

Serving suggestion: Serve this casserole with a beef roast.

For a crisp onion topping at your potluck, tote French fried onions along with your slow cooker and garnish the casserole with them just before serving.

Death Eater Onion Soup

Creamy Onion Soup

This rich soup is usually made with Hallee's Savory Stocky Crock Pot Beef Brothⓘ but Hallee's Heavenly Homemade Bird Brothⓘ makes for a lighter yet still savory flavor if you aren't going meat free with this soup. Using the beef broth will turn this into more of a hearty traditional French onion soup.

There is no way to really describe the depth and richness of the flavors when using a vegetable broth in place of a meat broth. It's something you have to taste for yourself. I prefer to use my own Homemade Vegetable Broth (see NOTES)ⓘ.

This particular crock pot dish requires a little more interaction on your part than others but believe me it is worth the tiny bit of extra effort. Carefully read the directions then set timers or reminders, stage ingredients (*Mise en Place*) for what comes next, and enjoy the amazing aromas as they fill our home along the way. This is a wonderful dish to let children help prepare as well.

You can serve this in wide mugs for guests to slowly sip as they mingle or with a side of French bread at the dinner table.

5 to 6 qt slow cooker

potato masher or immersion blender

measuring cups/spoons

good sharp knife

cutting board

4 cups Homemade Vegetable Broth① (See NOTES) (reserve 1/2 cup)
1/4 cup flour (I use fresh ground soft white wheat)
1 TBS pure or raw honey (local, raw honey is always best)
3 TBS unsalted butter
6 onions, chopped①
6 cloves garlic, minced
1 tsp Kosher or sea salt
1 tsp dried marjoram leaves
1 tsp dried thyme leaves
2 cups shredded Gruyere cheese
1 1/2 cups heavy cream

Nutrition Facts
Serving Size: 500 grams (393g)
Servings Per Container: 6

Amount Per Serving	
Calories 410	Calories from Fat 260
	% Daily Value*
Total Fat 29g	**45%**
Saturated Fat 17g	**85%**
Trans Fat 1g	
Cholesterol 95mg	**32%**
Sodium 1020mg	**43%**
Total Carbohydrate 25g	**8%**
Dietary Fiber 3g	**12%**
Sugars 12g	
Protein 14g	
Vitamin A 25% •	Vitamin C 20%
Calcium 45% •	Iron 6%

* Percent Daily Values are based on a 2,000 calorie diet. Your daily values may be higher or lower depending on your calorie needs:

	Calories:	2,000	2,500
Total Fat	Less than	65g	80g
Sat Fat	Less than	20g	25g
Cholesterol	Less than	300mg	300mg
Sodium	Less than	2,400mg	2,400mg
Total Carbohydrate		300g	375g
Dietary Fiber		25g	30g

chop onions
shred cheese

Place butter in slow cooker and turn to high heat. When butter melts, reduce to low heat.

Add onion and garlic then top with honey and salt.

Cover and cook until onions are golden brown; on low heat for 6 to 7 hours or on high heat for 3 to 4 1/2 hours.

NOTE: Stir only twice during cooking time at even intervals (On low heat after 1 hour and then again after 5 hours. On high heat after 1 hour and then again after 3 hours). Stir thoroughly but rapidly and cover again as quickly as possible. Your goal should be to keep the dish covered as much as possible during cooking time.

When onions are nice and golden brown and dish appears cooked through, uncover and use potato masher or immersion blender and purée onions. Mix the flour with the reserved broth and stir into the slow cooker.

Increase to high heat if needed then cover and cook on high heat for 30 minutes. Decrease to low heat.

Gradually stir in 2 cups of the broth and blend well into the thickened liquid in the pot. Add remaining broth along with marjoram and thyme. Cover and cook on low heat for 2 to 3 hours.

Uncover and stir in heavy cream and shredded cheese. Cook and stir on high until cheese melts and soup is creamy; about 10 to 15 minutes.

Serve immediately.

Serves 6 to 8

ⓘ I have included recipes for both Hallee's Heavenly Homemade Bird Broth and Hallee's Savory Stocky Crock Pot Beef Broth in this cookbook. To make vegetable broth or stock, follow either recipe and just leave out the meat and bone but up the variety and amount of vegetables to produce a homemade all vegetable stock or broth. If you don't have stock on hand, be sure to use a good organic stock with low or no salt.

ⓘ For information about a tip for chopping vegetables, follow this link:

http://www.halleethehomemaker.com/2009/08/tips-chopping-onions/

Seeker Spinach & Azkaban Artichoke Dip

This is my teenager's favorite dip. The best thing is, you don't have to fuss over appetizers at your next get-together when you make this dip. Literally throw everything needed in the slow cooker, step away, and let it do all of the hard work.

When this deliciously creamy and cheesy dip is finished, pour it into a serving bowl or keep it warm by serving it directly from the slow-cooker. Serve it with chips, crackers, or fresh bread for an appetizer everyone will love.

1 1/4 cup (10 oz bag) baby spinach, fresh or frozen

1 3/4 cup (14 oz can) artichoke hearts, drained and chopped

8 oz organic plain yogurt (or sour cream)

8 oz cream cheese

1 cup Parmigiano Reggiano (Parmesan) cheese, shredded

1/2 cup milk

1/2 cup feta cheese

1/2 cup Hallee's Homemade Mayonnaiseⓘ

1 TBS red wine vinegar

2 garlic cloves, peeled and minced

1/4 tsp Kosher salt (or sea salt)

1/4 tsp fresh ground black pepper

measuring cups/spoons
good sharp knife
cutting board
mixing bowl
whisk

Drain and chop artichokes.
Roughly chop spinach
Mince garlic
Shred cheese

Place all ingredients in a slow cooker. Mix well with a spoon until the ingredients are combined. Cook on high for 1 hour 30 minutes or on low for 2 hours and 30 minutes.

Stir and pour into a serving dish or set the slow-cooker to warm and serve out of the slow-cooker. Serve with tortilla chips, crackers, pita chips, or a sliced baguette.

Nutrition Facts

Serving Size: 500 grams (295g)
Servings Per Container: 8

Amount Per Serving	
Calories 320	Calories from Fat 190
	% Daily Value*
Total Fat 21g	**32%**
Saturated Fat 10g	**50%**
Trans Fat 0g	
Cholesterol 55mg	**18%**
Sodium 840mg	**35%**
Total Carbohydrate 17g	**6%**
Dietary Fiber 7g	**28%**
Sugars 4g	
Protein 16g	
Vitamin A 510% •	Vitamin C 130%
Calcium 50% •	Iron 50%

* Percent Daily Values are based on a 2,000 calorie diet. Your daily values may be higher or lower depending on your calorie needs:

	Calories:	2,000	2,500
Total Fat	Less than	65g	80g
Sat Fat	Less than	20g	25g
Cholesterol	Less than	300mg	300mg
Sodium	Less than	2,400mg	2,400mg
Total Carbohydrate		300g	375g
Dietary Fiber		25g	30g

Serves 8

ⓘ If you want to make your own mayonnaise, it is equally easy. Check out my recipe at this link:

http://www.halleethehomemaker.com/2009/09/mayonnaise/

Desserts

Preparation Not Prestidigitation

As I said in the intro to this book, I use fresh ground grains. I grind them myself in a grain mill. For cornmeal, I grind popcorn. For wheat, I grind either a combination of hard red and hard white wheats for yeast breads, and soft white wheat for desserts and quick breads. Fresh ground wheat is not the same as store-bought whole wheat flour. It has a finer texture and acts more like white flour in recipes. So, if you don' have fresh-ground flour, you might want to use an unbleached white flour instead of whole wheat. If you prefer whole wheat, then it may be necessary to adjust some of these recipes. Play around with them and see what you can come up with.

It's better to weigh flour versus measuring it, because the measurements can vary depending upon how firmly you pack the flour in the measuring cup, etc.

- Fresh ground flour weighs 4 ounces per cup.
- Unbleached all-purpose flour weighs 4 1/4 ounces per cup

I also don't ever use artificial sweeteners. In the following recipes, I use sugar; however, honey can always be substituted for sugar. Try to always use local, raw honey.

Here are the rules for the substitution:

- For every 1 cup of sugar, substitute 1/2 to 2/3 cup honey.
- For every 1 cup of honey you're using, subtract 1/4 cup of other liquids from the recipe.
- Add 1/4 teaspoon baking soda for every 1 cup honey used.

Padfoot Cobbler

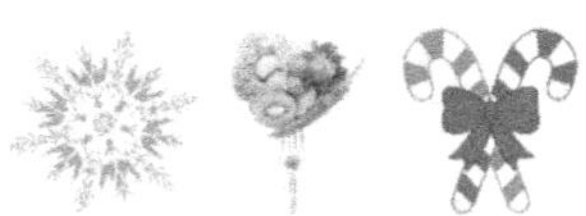

Peach cobbler is the bomb! The spice of cinnamon and nutmeg combined with the sweetness of the peaches—yum. I always try to convince myself that it's good for me—because, you know, it's fruit!

4 cups (32 ounces frozen) peaches, room temperature and drained

3/4 cup flour (I use fresh ground soft white wheat)

3/4 cup plus 1 TBS raw sugar, divided

2 tsp ground cinnamon, divided

1/2 tsp ground nutmeg

6 TBS unsalted butter, cut into bits

whipped cream (optional)

measuring cups/spoons

mixing bowl

4-6 quart slow cooker

Grind nutmeg, if needed (fresh ground nutmeg is the best way to utilize that spice)

Nutrition Facts

Serving Size: (107g)
Servings Per Container: 6

Amount Per Serving	
Calories 420	Calories from Fat 100
	% Daily Value*
Total Fat 11g	**17%**
Saturated Fat 7g	**35%**
Trans Fat 0g	
Cholesterol 30mg	**10%**
Sodium 10mg	**0%**
Total Carbohydrate 80g	**27%**
Dietary Fiber 4g	**16%**
Sugars 65g	
Protein 3g	
Vitamin A 20% •	Vitamin C 260%
Calcium 2% •	Iron 8%

* Percent Daily Values are based on a 2,000 calorie diet. Your daily values may be higher or lower depending on your calorie needs:

	Calories:	2,000	2,500
Total Fat	Less than	65g	80g
Sat Fat	Less than	20g	25g
Cholesterol	Less than	300mg	300mg
Sodium	Less than	2,400mg	2,400mg
Total Carbohydrate		300g	375g
Dietary Fiber		25g	30g

Directions

Combine peaches, $^3/_4$ cup sugar, 1 $^1/_2$ tsp ground cinnamon, and nutmeg in medium bowl. Place into slow cooker.

Combine flour, remaining 1 TBS sugar and remaining $^1/_2$ tsp ground cinnamon, in separate bowl. Cut in butter with pastry cutter or 2 knives until mixture resembles coarse crumbs. Sprinkle over peach mixture.

Cover and cook on high heat for 2 hours.

Serve with freshly whipped cream, if desired.

Yield

4 to 6 servings

Notes

This is one of my go-to company desserts. You can use fresh or frozen peaches. I wouldn't recommend canned peaches because of the syrup.

Chocolate Mudblood Cake

Chocolate Mud Cake

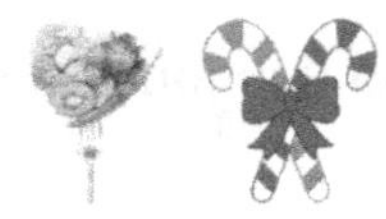

If I have two favorite things, they are chocolate, cake, and my slow cooker. Okay, three favorite things. This recipe combines the best of all of them.

Why bake in a slow cooker? Well, it's a fun novelty. The kids love the idea, but the real proof is in the taste of the chocolate cake.

Reminiscent of a hot-fudge-brownie cake, this dessert is so moist and chocolaty, "it's like getting to lick the batter from an entire cake."

1 cup flour (I use fresh ground soft white wheat)

1/3 cup brown sugar or honey (pure, raw, local honey is always best)

2/3 cup and 1/3 cup sugar, (divided, added separately)

2 tsp aluminum free baking powder

1/3 cup dark chocolate chips

3 TBS plus 1/3 cup Dutch-processed cocoa

1/4 tsp salt (Kosher or sea salt is best)

6 TBS unsalted butter, softened

1/3 cup whole milk

1 farm fresh egg yolk

1 1/2 cup hot black coffee (or hot water)

1 TBS pure vanilla extract

whipped cream or ice cream

2 ½ to 5-quart slow cooker (Note: the cake's cooking time and final appearance will vary depending on your crock's size.)

Double boiler (or glass bowl to use in microwave)

measuring cups/spoons

mixing bowl

sifter

whisk

Sift together flour and baking powder. Set aside.

Lightly coat the inside of the slow cooker with butter then lightly dust with flour (or powdered sugar).

In a large bowl, melt butter and chocolate in the microwave or over a pan of simmering water (double boiler) and mix well.

Whisk in ⅔ cup of sugar, 3 TBS of cocoa, vanilla extract, salt, milk, and egg yolk. Using a spatula, fold in the flour mixture then stir until thoroughly mixed.

Gently pour the batter into the slow cooker and spread it evenly. In a medium bowl, whisk together the remaining sugar, cocoa, and hot water until the sugar is dissolved.

Pour the mixture over the batter in the slow cooker. Cover and cook on high for 1 to 2 hours, depending on the size of the crock pot.

Nutrition Facts

Serving Size: (80g)
Servings Per Container: 8

Amount Per Serving	
Calories 330	Calories from Fat 120
	% Daily Value*
Total Fat 13g	**20%**
Saturated Fat 8g	**40%**
Trans Fat 0g	
Cholesterol 45mg	**15%**
Sodium 220mg	**9%**
Total Carbohydrate 54g	**18%**
Dietary Fiber 3g	**12%**
Sugars 39g	
Protein 4g	
Vitamin A 6% •	Vitamin C 2%
Calcium 4% •	Iron 10%

* Percent Daily Values are based on a 2,000 calorie diet. Your daily values may be higher or lower depending on your calorie needs:

	Calories:	2,000	2,500
Total Fat	Less than	65g	80g
Sat Fat	Less than	20g	25g
Cholesterol	Less than	300mg	300mg
Sodium	Less than	2,400mg	2,400mg
Total Carbohydrate		300g	375g
Dietary Fiber		25g	30g

You can't use the "toothpick test" to check when this cake is done, since it will be floating on a layer of molten chocolate. When the top layer is set and the edges start to pull away from the sides of the slow cooker, you'll know it's done.

Remove the lid and turn the power off. Let it cool for 25 minutes, then serve it in bowls topped with whipped cream or ice cream.

Makes 6 to 8 servings.

I use homemade vanilla extract—simply because it tastes way better and is MUCH MUCH cheaper than store-bought vanilla extract. For more information and the full scoop, read this article from my Hallee the Homemaker website at this link:

http://www.halleethehomemaker.com/2009/11/vanilla/

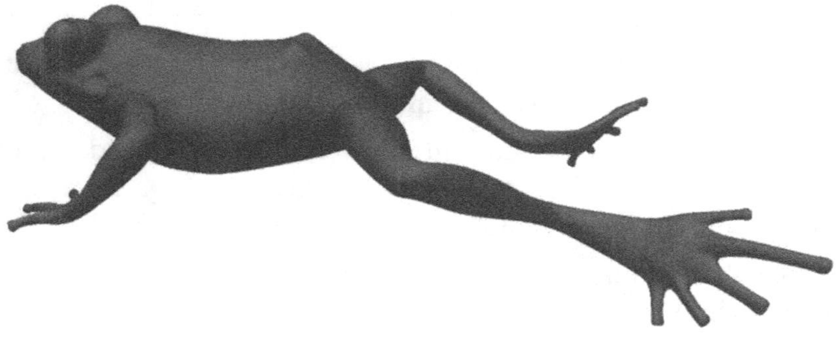

Portkey Pears with Remembrall Raspberry Sauce

Poached Pears with Raspberry Sauce

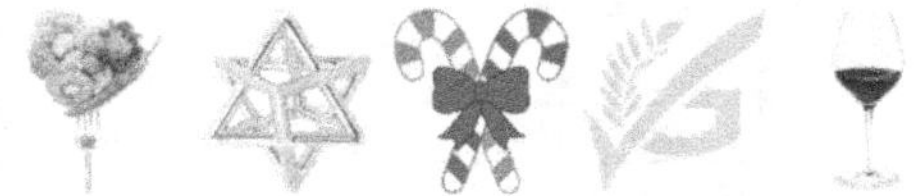

Poached pears are such a wonderful dessert to serve in the autumn. Adding the raspberry sauce just turns a deliciously simple dessert into something truly decadent.

4 cups organic cran-raspberry juice cocktail (make sure that the ingredients list sugar instead of high fructose corn syrup)

2 cups Rhine or Riesling wineⓘ (see NOTES for possible substitute)

1/4 cup sugar

2 cinnamon sticks, broken into halves

4 to 5 firm Bosc or Anjou pears, peeled and cored

1 1/4 cup (10 ounce frozen package) raspberries, room temperature

1/4 cup additional assorted fresh berries (optional)

4-6 quart slow cooker

measuring cups/spoons

good sharp knife and cutting board

Apple corer

blender

Nutrition Facts

Serving Size: (128g)
Servings Per Container: 5

Amount Per Serving	
Calories 1010	Calories from Fat 45
	% Daily Value*
Total Fat 5g	**8%**
Saturated Fat 0g	**0%**
Trans Fat 0g	
Cholesterol 0mg	**0%**
Sodium 95mg	**4%**
Total Carbohydrate 227g	**76%**
Dietary Fiber 19g	**76%**
Sugars 177g	
Protein 1g	
Vitamin A 2% •	Vitamin C 35%
Calcium 10% •	Iron 15%

* Percent Daily Values are based on a 2,000 calorie diet. Your daily values may be higher or lower depending on your calorie needs:

	Calories:	2,000	2,500
Total Fat	Less than	65g	80g
Sat Fat	Less than	20g	25g
Cholesterol	Less than	300mg	300mg
Sodium	Less than	2,400mg	2,400mg
Total Carbohydrate		300g	375g
Dietary Fiber		25g	30g

Peel and core pears, trying to keep them whole

Combine juice, wine, sugar, and cinnamon stick halves in slow cooker. Submerge pears in mixture.

Cover and cook on low heat until pears are tender, about 3 1/2 to 4 hours.

Remove and discard cinnamon stick halves.

Process raspberries in food processor or blender until smooth. Strain and discard seeds. Spoon raspberry sauce onto serving plates. Place pear on top of sauce. Garnish with fresh berries, if desired.

4 to 5 servings

ⓘ If you abstain from alcohol even in cooking, you can substitute a 100% pure grape juice (ensure there is no apple juice in it) and one teaspoon of distilled vinegar to approximate the same flavor and properties while cooking.

Broom Rider Spice Cake

Brown Sugar Spice Cake

This is a great dessert to make when you're entertaining and the oven is occupied with another dish.

1 can (10 $^{1}/_{2}$ oz) organic condensed tomato soupⓘ (see notes)

2 eggs

1 $^{1}/_{4}$ cups flour (I use fresh ground soft white wheat)

2 tablespoons cornstarch (non-gmo/organic is best)

2 teaspoons aluminum free baking powder

$^{1}/_{4}$ teaspoon salt (Kosher or sea salt is best)

extra virgin olive oil or unsalted butter according to personal taste

$^{1}/_{2}$ cup filtered water plus 1 $^{1}/_{4}$ cups hot filtered water (divided)

1 cup brown sugar plus $^{3}/_{4}$ cup packed brown sugar (divided)

$^{1}/_{2}$ tsp ground cinnamon plus 1 tsp ground cinnamon (divided)

$^{1}/_{2}$ tsp ground ginger

$^{1}/_{4}$ tsp ground nutmeg

$^{1}/_{4}$ tsp allspice

$^{1}/_{4}$ tsp ground cloves

Pure vanilla ice cream to taste

Nutrition Facts

Serving Size: (80g)
Servings Per Container: 8

Amount Per Serving	
Calories 310	Calories from Fat 15
	% Daily Value*
Total Fat 1.5g	**2%**
Saturated Fat 0.5g	**3%**
Trans Fat 0g	
Cholesterol 45mg	**15%**
Sodium 300mg	**13%**
Total Carbohydrate 69g	**23%**
Dietary Fiber 1g	**4%**
Sugars 50g	
Protein 4g	

Vitamin A 4%	•	Vitamin C 4%
Calcium 10%	•	Iron 4%

* Percent Daily Values are based on a 2,000 calorie diet. Your daily values may be higher or lower depending on your calorie needs:

	Calories:	2,000	2,500
Total Fat	Less than	65g	80g
Sat Fat	Less than	20g	25g
Cholesterol	Less than	300mg	300mg
Sodium	Less than	2,400mg	2,400mg
Total Carbohydrate		300g	375g
Dietary Fiber		25g	30g

3 1/2 to 4 qt slow cooker
measuring cups/spoons
good sharp knife
cutting board
Sifter
mixing bowl
whisk

Lightly grease the inside of the slow cooker with unsalted butter then lightly dust with flour (or powdered sugar).

In a large bowl, sift together the flour, corn starch, baking powder, salt, ginger, 1/2 tsp cinnamon, nutmeg, allspice, and cloves. Mix in 1 cup brown sugar. Add the soup, 1/2 cup water, and eggs. Pour batter into slow cooker.

Mix water the 1 1 / 4 cup hot water with the remaining brown sugar and cinnamon. Pour over batter.

Cover and cook on high heat for 2 to 2 1/2 hours or until toothpick inserted in center comes out clean.

Spoon warm cake into bowls, scooping sauce from bottom of cooker. Serve warm with ice cream.

Serves 8

I have included my recipe for organic condensed tomato soupⓘ in this cookbook.

If you don't make your own, try to use an organic condensed tomato soup, or at least a brand that doesn't have bad ingredients. Here is the ingredient list of a popular, non-organic condensed tomato soup:

Tomato Puree (Water, Tomato Paste), High Fructose Corn Syrup, Wheat Flour, Water, Contains Less Than 2% Of: Salt, Potassium Chloride, Flavoring, Citric Acid, Lower Sodium Natural Sea Salt, Ascorbic Acid (Vitamin C), Monopotassium Phosphate.

Here is the ingredient list for an organic condensed tomato soup:

Tomato puree, water, cane sugar, corn starch, sea salt, extra virgin olive oil, onion powder, garlic powder

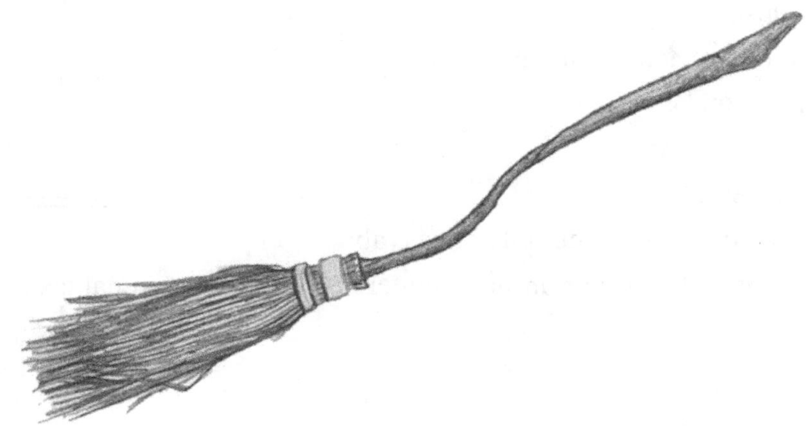

Chocolate Frogs Bread Pudding

Chocolate Almond Bread Pudding with Dried Cherries

I used to go to a restaurant in Florida that had THE BEST bread pudding. Seriously. That dish was worth every dime of the inflated lunch prices just to get to have some. I have loved this dessert since my first bite. And now, here's one with chocolate! Chocolate AND bread pudding? These are a few of my favorite things...

Nutrition Facts

Serving Size: (107g)
Servings Per Container: 6

Amount Per Serving	
Calories 510	Calories from Fat 210
	% Daily Value*
Total Fat 23g	**35%**
Saturated Fat 12g	**60%**
Trans Fat 0g	
Cholesterol 160mg	**53%**
Sodium 400mg	**17%**
Total Carbohydrate 54g	**18%**
Dietary Fiber 5g	**20%**
Sugars 29g	
Protein 21g	

Vitamin A 15% • Vitamin C 6%
Calcium 45% • Iron 20%

* Percent Daily Values are based on a 2,000 calorie diet. Your daily values may be higher or lower depending on your calorie needs:

	Calories:	2,000	2,500
Total Fat	Less than	65g	80g
Sat Fat	Less than	20g	25g
Cholesterol	Less than	300mg	300mg
Sodium	Less than	2,400mg	2,400mg
Total Carbohydrate		300g	375g
Dietary Fiber		25g	30g

sweetened whipped cream (optional)
toasted almonds (optional)
$^1/_2$ cup dried cherries, chopped
$^1/_2$ cup semi-sweet chocolate pieces
1 $^3/_4$ cups milk
$^1/_3$ cup unsweetened baking cocoa
$^1/_4$ tsp almond extract
$^1/_4$ tsp vanilla extract
4 eggs, beaten
10 slices fresh bread, cut into cubes (about 5 cups)
extra virgin olive oil or unsalted butter according to personal taste

4 $^1/_2$ to 5 qt slow cooker
measuring cups/spoons
good sharp knife / bread knife
cutting board
mixing bowl
whisk

Slice the bread
Chop the cherries

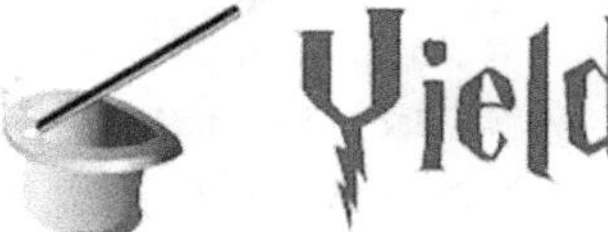

Serves 6

Lightly grease the inside of the slow cooker with either extra virgin olive oil or unsalted butter according to personal taste then lightly dust with flour (or powdered sugar).

Place bread cubes in slow cooker. Sprinkle with cherries and chocolate.

In a mixing bowl, use a whisk to mix milk, sugar, cocoa, almond extract, vanilla extract, and eggs. Pour over bread mixture. Stir and push bread cubes into milk mixture to coat.

Cover and cook on low heat for 2 $^1/_2$ to 3 hours or until set. Serve warm with whipped cream and almonds, if desired.

I use homemade vanilla extract—simply because it tastes way better and is MUCH MUCH cheaper than store-bought vanilla extract. For more information and the full scoop, read this article from my Hallee the Homemaker website at this link:

http://www.halleethehomemaker.com/2009/11/vanilla/

Doby's Rice Pudding

Creamy Rice Pudding

When I was growing up, I'd eat white rice, butter, sugar, and milk for breakfast as a treat. As I got older, I discovered a lot of those similar flavors could be found in rice pudding. It's a simple dessert, uses up leftover rice, and has wonderful, clean flavors.

zest of 1 orange, grated

2 1/2 cups cooked rice

1 cup milk

1 egg

2/3 cup sugar

4 TBS butter, softened

1/2 tsp vanilla extract

1/2 tsp ground cinnamon or nutmeg

1/3 cup golden raisins

Nutrition Facts

Serving Size: (107g)
Servings Per Container: 6

Amount Per Serving	
Calories 280	Calories from Fat 110
	% Daily Value*
Total Fat 12g	**18%**
Saturated Fat 7g	**35%**
Trans Fat 0g	
Cholesterol 150mg	**50%**
Sodium 65mg	**3%**
Total Carbohydrate 35g	**12%**
Dietary Fiber <1g	**3%**
Sugars 15g	
Protein 7g	

Vitamin A 10%	•	Vitamin C 2%
Calcium 8%	•	Iron 10%

* Percent Daily Values are based on a 2,000 calorie diet. Your daily values may be higher or lower depending on your calorie needs:

	Calories:	2,000	2,500
Total Fat	Less than	65g	80g
Sat Fat	Less than	20g	25g
Cholesterol	Less than	300mg	300mg
Sodium	Less than	2,400mg	2,400mg
Total Carbohydrate		300g	375g
Dietary Fiber		25g	30g

measuring cups/spoons

good sharp knife

cutting board

Mixing bowl

Zest the orange

Prepare rice, if necessary.

Beat the egg

Directions

Reserve a little orange zest to garnish, then, in a mixing bowl, mix the rice with all other ingredients. Lightly grease the inside of the slow cooker with either extra virgin olive oil or unsalted butter according to personal taste. Add the rice mixture.

Cook on low for 4 to 6 hours or on high for approximately 1 to 2 hours.

Stir occasionally during the first hour of cooking. Serve with a little cream and a pinch of grated orange zest.

Yield

Serves 6

Notes

To make the perfect white rice, go for the 2-1-1 ratio: 2 cups water (or broth) to 1 cup rice to 1 tsp salt. Mix together, bring to a boil, reduce heat to low, cover, and boil for 20 minutes. Perfect, fluffy, yummy rice. For more information, find the recipe at Hallee the Homemaker:

http://www.halleethehomemaker.com/2009/11/perfect-white-rice/

This recipe is made with white rice, but it can easily be made with brown rice. For information how to make brown rice, here is the complete recipe on Hallee the Homemaker:

http://www.halleethehomemaker.com/2009/11/perfect-brown-rice/

I use homemade vanilla extract—simply because it tastes way better and is MUCH MUCH cheaper than store-bought vanilla extract. For more information and the full scoop, read this article from my Hallee the Homemaker website at this link:

http://www.halleethehomemaker.com/2009/11/vanilla/

Quaffle Berry Cake

Mixed Berry Cake

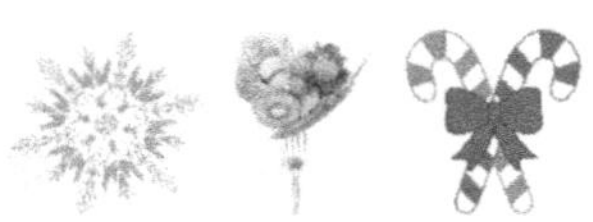

It's kind of neat to place a pan into a slow cooker and use the slow cooker as an oven. That's how this recipe is prepared, and it's so good. The sweet berries mixed with the pumpkin pie spices makes an amazing flavor.

3/4 cup mixed berries, (strawberries, blueberries, raspberries, or blackberries)

8 TBS (4 oz) unsalted butter

1/4 cup sugar

1 1/2 teaspoon vanilla extract

2 eggs, lightly beaten

2 cup flour (I use fresh ground soft white wheat)

2 tsp aluminum free baking powder

1 tsp salt (Kosher or sea salt is best)

1/4 tsp ground ginger

1/4 tsp cinnamon

1/8 tsp nutmeg

1/8 tsp allspice

1/8 tsp ground cloves

1/2 cup milk

1/2 tsp ground cinnamon

1 1/2 tsp powdered sugar

Nutrition Facts

Serving Size: (80g)
Servings Per Container: 8

Amount Per Serving	
Calories 340	Calories from Fat 110
	% Daily Value*
Total Fat 13g	**20%**
Saturated Fat 8g	**40%**
Trans Fat 0g	
Cholesterol 75mg	**25%**
Sodium 380mg	**16%**
Total Carbohydrate 50g	**17%**
Dietary Fiber 2g	**8%**
Sugars 27g	
Protein 5g	
Vitamin A 10% •	Vitamin C 4%
Calcium 6% •	Iron 4%

* Percent Daily Values are based on a 2,000 calorie diet. Your daily values may be higher or lower depending on your calorie needs:

	Calories:	2,000	2,500
Total Fat	Less than	65g	80g
Sat Fat	Less than	20g	25g
Cholesterol	Less than	300mg	300mg
Sodium	Less than	2,400mg	2,400mg
Total Carbohydrate		300g	375g
Dietary Fiber		25g	30g

Supplies

measuring cups/spoons
good sharp knife
cutting board
mixing bowl
Whisk
Sifter
9-inch springform pan

Preparation

Lightly beat the eggs

Directions

Cream the butter, sugar, and vanilla, then fold eggs into mixture.

Sift flour, baking powder, and salt together and stir in spices. Fold $^{1}/_{3}$ of flour mixture into the cream, butter, and egg mixture. Add half of the milk, then another third of flour mixture, rest of milk, and rest of flour mixture, gently folding each time to combine.

Spoon into a greased and floured 9 inch springform pan, and arrange berries on top.

Cover tightly with foil and place in slow cooker. Cook on high setting for approximately 3 hours, taking care not to remove the foil or slow cooker lid until the last hour of cooking.

Combine cinnamon and sugar. Dust cake with cinnamon sugar before serving. Serve with whipped cream if desired.

Serves 8

I use homemade vanilla extract—simply because it tastes way better and is MUCH MUCH cheaper than store-bought vanilla extract. For more information and the full scoop, read this article from my Hallee the Homemaker website at this link:

http://www.halleethehomemaker.com/2009/11/vanilla/

Sauces, Spices, Gravies, Rubs, and Soups

Presto! Change-O! Voila!

This section is all about flavor and convenience. In coming up with so many of my favorite slow cooker recipes for this cookbook, I discovered that I rely on a lot of whole food, real food, clean food seasoning mixes, spice blends, sauces, gravies, and soups to bring these meals to life.

The seasoning mixes you'll find here are especially useful in all kinds of recipes. I make these seasoning mixes fresh and keep them on hand in my spice cabinet year-round. Try adding just a dash more or less of certain spices in your own personalized combinations to create your own signature flavors.

It is so easy and economical to make these yourself, and such a money saver, you may never buy overpriced store-bought blends again. Best of all, there is nothing better than knowing 100% of the ingredients you are using in your cooking and knowing for certain that you are only using real food. You control the amount of salt, and you can purposefully exclude potentially harmful ingredients like GMOs or MSG.

Hallee's Pre-Made Poultry Rub Recipes

There are a few different poultry seasonings that I really like and I decided to share them both. There is no salt in these recipes. Salt wicks moisture (water) from your bird and that is almost never what you want. You want a bird that is juicy and moist, not dry. It's best to season your bird dishes with salt to your personal taste after your bird is fully cooked.

The absence of salt means that these seasonings can also safely act as rubs for red meats or fish if you like.

The first recipe is probably what most people in North America think of as the most traditional kind of poultry seasoning we grew up with. It is a sage based seasoning but the main flavor kick comes from the marjoram. This seasoning mix is light in color and goes well in traditional soups, stews, and especially in stuffings. In fact, if you are making a savory corn bread, you should be sure not to leave this out. I have included some optional ingredients that I have found fill out the flavor of this seasoning especially if you are making a bird for a holiday meal.

The second recipe is paprika based and, while it is a traditional continental poultry seasoning, Americans will relate it more with southwestern or southern dishes. It is especially good as a rub if you are roasting, broiling, or popping an entire bird in the rotisserie oven.

Combine them in a 2:1 ratio and as the seasoning base for your southern fried chicken before you apply a thick buttermilk batter and you are in for flavors the Colonel himself would have envied.

POULTRY SEASONING MIX 1

Nutrition Facts

Serving Size: 500 grams (1.4g)
Servings Per Container: 30

Amount Per Serving	
Calories 0	Calories from Fat 0
	% Daily Value*
Total Fat 0g	**0%**
Saturated Fat 0g	**0%**
Trans Fat 0g	
Cholesterol 0mg	**0%**
Sodium 0mg	**0%**
Total Carbohydrate <1g	**0%**
Dietary Fiber 0g	**0%**
Sugars 0g	
Protein 0g	
Vitamin A 0% •	Vitamin C 2%
Calcium 2% •	Iron 2%

* Percent Daily Values are based on a 2,000 calorie diet. Your daily values may be higher or lower depending on your calorie needs:

	Calories:	2,000	2,500
Total Fat	Less than	65g	80g
Sat Fat	Less than	20g	25g
Cholesterol	Less than	300mg	300mg
Sodium	Less than	2,400mg	2,400mg
Total Carbohydrate		300g	375g
Dietary Fiber		25g	30g

Ingredients: Celery Flakes, Dried, White Pepper, Oregano, Ground Ginger, Thyme, Rosemary, Parsley, Nutmeg, Sage, Marjoram

POULTRY SEASONING MIX 1:

1 TBS sage

1 TBS marjoram

2 TBS parsley flakes

1 TBS oregano

1 TBS thyme

1 TBS rosemary

1 TBS celery leaves

1 TBS fresh ground white pepper

OPTIONAL (for holiday meals)

1 TBS ginger

1 tsp fresh ground nutmeg

POULTRY SEASONING MIX 2:

1 TBS paprika

1 TBS dry mustard

1 TBS onion powder

1 tsp garlic powder

1 tsp thyme

½ tsp basil

1 ½ tsp fresh ground white pepper

POULTRY SEASONING MIX 2

Nutrition Facts

Serving Size: 500 grams (2.5g)
Servings Per Container: 15

Amount Per Serving	
Calories 10	Calories from Fat 0
	% Daily Value*
Total Fat 0g	**0%**
Saturated Fat 0g	**0%**
Trans Fat 0g	
Cholesterol 0mg	**0%**
Sodium 0mg	**0%**
Total Carbohydrate 1g	**0%**
Dietary Fiber 0g	**0%**
Sugars 0g	
Protein 0g	
Vitamin A 4% •	Vitamin C 0%
Calcium 0% •	Iron 2%

* Percent Daily Values are based on a 2,000 calorie diet. Your daily values may be higher or lower depending on your calorie needs:

	Calories:	2,000	2,500
Total Fat	Less than	65g	80g
Sat Fat	Less than	20g	25g
Cholesterol	Less than	300mg	300mg
Sodium	Less than	2,400mg	2,400mg
Total Carbohydrate		300g	375g
Dietary Fiber		25g	30g

Ingredients: Garlic Powder, Onion Powder, Paprika, Mustard Seed, White Pepper, Thyme, Basil

Supplies

measuring cups/spoons

shaker, clean empty spice jar, or other small airtight container like a small Mason jar for finished mixes

MAY NEED:

mortar & pestle OR coffee grinder OR food processor OR blender

MAY NEED:

zester or very fine grater if grating fresh nutmeg

Preparation

You may need some means to crush and combine the seasoning once mixed depending on the coarseness or fineness you desire to personally achieve.

If you have a mortar and pestle you can prepare these seasoning mixes in a very artisan fashion. An electric coffee grinder works great and a food processor or a sturdy blender will also suffice.

Directions

For each recipe, mix all ingredients well. If desired, briefly grind with a mortar and pestle or use a coffee grinder, a food processor, or a blender and just pulse a few times until your personally desired consistency has been achieved.

Store at room temperature in an airtight container away from light. Keeps well for up to three months.

Yield

Poultry mix 1 yields 10 Tablespoons of mix. Use about 2-3 Tablespoons per recipe, according to your taste.

Poultry mix 2 yields 4 Tablespoons. Use 2-3 Tablespoons per recipe, according to your taste.

Notes

As a timesaver, I keep some pre-made seasoning mixes on-hand for various recipes. These poultry seasoning mixes keep well in airtight containers and it is nearly always a welcome surprise how good and fresh they smell when opening them to use in a recipe here and there.

These size well so feel free to double, triple, or quadruple the ingredients.

Referenced Recipes

Hallee's Signature Crock Pot Hot Brown

Hallee's Herbed Turkey Breast

Hallee's Inviting Italian Seasoning (or Rub)

When reading the first four ingredients to this mix, if the old song that goes, "Parsley, sage, rosemary, and thyme" doesn't get stuck in your head, then you probably think I am REALLY old. These four herbs in various ratios are the foundation for any Italian seasoning and this recipe is no exception.

Nutrition Facts

Serving Size: 500 grams (1.3g)
Servings Per Container: 20

Amount Per Serving	
Calories 0	Calories from Fat 0
	% Daily Value*
Total Fat 0g	**0%**
Saturated Fat 0g	**0%**
Trans Fat 0g	
Cholesterol 0mg	**0%**
Sodium 0mg	**0%**
Total Carbohydrate <1g	**0%**
Dietary Fiber 0g	**0%**
Sugars 0g	
Protein 0g	
Vitamin A 0% •	Vitamin C 0%
Calcium 2% •	Iron 4%

* Percent Daily Values are based on a 2,000 calorie diet. Your daily values may be higher or lower depending on your calorie needs:

	Calories:	2,000	2,500
Total Fat	Less than	65g	80g
Sat Fat	Less than	20g	25g
Cholesterol	Less than	300mg	300mg
Sodium	Less than	2,400mg	2,400mg
Total Carbohydrate		300g	375g
Dietary Fiber		25g	30g

I typically make my seasoning mixes in the summertime when my fresh herbs are taking over the world and I always have more than I can possibly use. I just lay my herbs out on a baking sheet lined with parchment and low bake them in the oven or, if it isn't otherwise in use, I'll put them in the dehydrator. In a few hours I have fresh dried herbs. I usually pulse them in the food processor or coffee grinder until they reach the desired consistency. A blender works also, just not as well.

If you aren't using fresh herbs, you can just mix store-bought dried herbs together. No need to grind them. But store-bought herbs seem to have a better flavor when you grind them right before using them. Likely it releases some of the remaining essential oils.

This mix is a perfect rub. It's great on chicken, pasta, or even as a dipping sauce when mixed with a little extra virgin olive oil for crusty bread.

measuring spoons

air tight shaker, spice jar, or other air tight container like a small Mason jar for finished mix

possibly mortar with pestle OR a coffee grinder OR a food processor OR a blender

4 REQUIRED INGREDIENTS	**OPTIONAL** (or to taste)
1 TBS dried flat leaf Italian parsley	1 TBS dried basil
1 TBS dried sage	1 TBS dried oregano
1 TBS dried rosemary	1 TBS dried marjoram
1 TBS dried thyme	1 TBS fresh ground white pepper

OPTIONAL (only if making a seasoning mix)

1/2 TBS salt (Kosher salt is best)

If you have a mortar and pestle you can prepare this seasoning in a very artisan fashion. You may need some means to crush the ingredients once combined.

An electric coffee grinder works great and a food processor or a blender will also suffice.

If making an **ITALIAN SEASONING**:

Start with 1/2 TBS salt. Otherwise, skip this. Then:

If making an **ITALIAN RUB**:

Combine 1 TBS each of dried basil, marjoram, oregano, rosemary, sage, thyme, flat leaf Italian parsley, and 1 TBS fresh ground white pepper. Mix all ingredients well.

If using fresh dried herbs, grind with a mortar and pestle or use a coffee grinder, food processor, or blender and pulse a few times.

Store at room temperature in an airtight container away from light. Use within three months.

1/2 cup (8 Tablespoons)—use 2 to 3 Tablespoons per recipe per taste.

As a timesaver, I keep some premade spice mixes on-hand for various recipes. This one keeps well in an airtight container for up to 3 months in a cool dry cabinet.

If there is a particular flavor you don't care for, simply leave it out. Don't like basil? Don't add it. Oregano not your thing? Leave it out or substitute a different fresh herb that is to your liking. Personally, I almost always leave out the pepper. If I want or need pepper, I prefer to just add fresh ground black pepper right on the spot.

I really recommend leaving off the salt in this mix. When you leave out the salt, you still have a tasty and delicious seasoning and an always ready dry rub.

Greek Chicken Stew

Meatball Stew

Slow Cooked Veggie Lasagna

Tuscan Lentil Stew

Speechless Oriental Seasoning

The ingredients that come in a packet of Oriental Seasoning mix with Ramen noodles or the shakers you buy off the shelf are often packed with things no human being should eat. Things like monosodium glutamate and hydrogenated oils.

This seasoning mix not only serves as a great marinade but also uses good ingredients that will make your normally over salty and somewhat hum-drum Ramen noodles sing a happy tune.

1 cup gluten-free soy sauce (Tamari or fermented soy sauce strongly preferred)

1/3 cup light unsulfured molasses

2 TBS ground ginger

2 TBS dry mustard

1 tsp garlic powder

1/2 tsp onion powder

Nutrition Facts

Serving Size: (53g)
Servings Per Container: 8

Amount Per Serving	
Calories 70	Calories from Fat 5
	% Daily Value*
Total Fat 0.5g	**1%**
Saturated Fat 0g	**0%**
Trans Fat 0g	
Cholesterol 0mg	**0%**
Sodium 2010mg	**84%**
Total Carbohydrate 13g	**4%**
Dietary Fiber <1g	**3%**
Sugars 7g	
Protein 4g	
Vitamin A 0% •	Vitamin C 0%
Calcium 8% •	Iron 15%

* Percent Daily Values are based on a 2,000 calorie diet. Your daily values may be higher or lower depending on your calorie needs:

	Calories:	2,000	2,500
Total Fat	Less than	65g	80g
Sat Fat	Less than	20g	25g
Cholesterol	Less than	300mg	300mg
Sodium	Less than	2,400mg	2,400mg
Total Carbohydrate		300g	375g
Dietary Fiber		25g	30g

measuring cups/spoons

small mason jar with lid

(or other air tight container)

A small mason jar is ideal for both mixing and storing this seasoning.

Directions

In a jar with a screw top lid combine soy sauce, molasses, ginger, mustard, garlic powder, and onion powder. Shake vigorously to mix.

Store, covered, in the refrigerator for up to six weeks.

Use this seasoning in place of Oriental Seasoning packets that come with Ramen noodles or as a marinade for burgers, steak or chops.

Yield

About 1 $^{1}/_{3}$ cup

Notes

As a timesaver, I keep some pre-made spice mixes on-hand for various recipes. This one keeps well in an airtight container for up to six months.

Referenced Recipes

Chicken & Ramen Noodle Soup

Cajun-Creole Seasoning

This Cajun-Creole seasoning blend is MSG-free and can be made salt free simply by leaving off the optional salt. It is excellent for seasoning rice, meats, soups and stews, or anything that needs a flavor boost. It also makes a thoughtful gift when placed in a decorative jar with recipes attached.

5 TBS paprika

2 TBS onion powder

2 TBS garlic powder

2 TBS dried oregano

2 TBS dried basil

1 TBS dried thyme

1 TBS cayenne pepper

1 TBS fresh ground white pepper

1 TBS fresh ground black pepper

OPTIONAL

3 TBS salt (Kosher salt is best)

Nutrition Facts

Serving Size: (3.5g)
Servings Per Container: 40

Amount Per Serving	
Calories 10	Calories from Fat 0
	% Daily Value*
Total Fat 0g	**0%**
Saturated Fat 0g	**0%**
Trans Fat 0g	
Cholesterol 0mg	**0%**
Sodium 340mg	**14%**
Total Carbohydrate 2g	**1%**
Dietary Fiber <1g	**3%**
Sugars 0g	
Protein 0g	
Vitamin A 10% •	Vitamin C 0%
Calcium 2% •	Iron 4%

* Percent Daily Values are based on a 2,000 calorie diet. Your daily values may be higher or lower depending on your calorie needs:

	Calories:	2,000	2,500
Total Fat	Less than	65g	80g
Sat Fat	Less than	20g	25g
Cholesterol	Less than	300mg	300mg
Sodium	Less than	2,400mg	2,400mg
Total Carbohydrate		300g	375g
Dietary Fiber		25g	30g

measuring spoons

air tight shaker, spice jar, or other air tight container like a small Mason jar for finished mix

mortar with pestle OR a coffee grinder OR a food processor OR a blender

You will need some means to crush the ingredients once combined.

If you have a mortar and pestle you can prepare this seasoning in a very artisan fashion.

An electric coffee grinder works great and a food processor or a blender will also suffice.

If making a **CAJUN/CREOLE SEASONING:**

Add 3 tablespoon Kosher salt to the above.

If not, skip. Then:

If making a **CAJUN/CREOLE RUB**:

Combine 5 tablespoons paprika, 2 tablespoons onion powder, 2 tablespoons garlic powder, 2 tablespoons dried oregano, 2 tablespoons dried basil, 1 tablespoon dried thyme, 1 tablespoon cayenne pepper, 1 tablespoon fresh ground white pepper, 1 tablespoon fresh ground black pepper. Then:

Mix all ingredients well. Briefly grind with a mortar and pestle or use a coffee grinder, a food processor, or a blender and just pulse a few times.

Store at room temperature in an airtight container away from light. Use within three months.

About 1 1/4 cup—use 2-3 Tablespoons per recipe to taste.

I really recommend leaving off the salt in this mix. When you leave out the salt, you still have a tasty and delicious seasoning and an always ready dry rub.

As a timesaver, I keep some premade spice mixes on-hand for various recipes. This one keeps well in an airtight container and I have never found a more authentic tasting essence for Cajun or Creole inspired dishes.

This mix may be stored for up to 3 months in a cool dry cabinet.

Montreal Steak Seasoning

According to multiple sources, Schwartz's Montreal Hebrew Delicatessen is credited with the creation of Montreal steak seasoning. The story goes that a Schwartz's broilerman by the name of Morris "The Shadow" Sherman, during the 1940s and 1950s began adding the deli's smoked meat pickling spices to his own rib and liver steaks. It didn't take long before customers began asking for the seasoning as well. Due to its popularity, it eventually became a norm in most Montreal delis and steakhouses.

Montreal steak seasoning is a true North American invention that combines the British love of beefsteaks with the French flair for seasoning. It's excellent on red meats like steaks as well as on sides like baked potatoes.

Nutrition Facts

Serving Size: (5g)
Servings Per Container: 15

Amount Per Serving	
Calories 10	Calories from Fat 0
	% Daily Value*
Total Fat 0g	**0%**
Saturated Fat 0g	**0%**
Trans Fat 0g	
Cholesterol 0mg	**0%**
Sodium 450mg	**19%**
Total Carbohydrate 2g	**1%**
Dietary Fiber <1g	**3%**
Sugars 0g	
Protein 0g	
Vitamin A 10% •	Vitamin C 2%
Calcium 2% •	Iron 2%

* Percent Daily Values are based on a 2,000 calorie diet. Your daily values may be higher or lower depending on your calorie needs:

	Calories:	2,000	2,500
Total Fat	Less than	65g	80g
Sat Fat	Less than	20g	25g
Cholesterol	Less than	300mg	300mg
Sodium	Less than	2,400mg	2,400mg
Total Carbohydrate		300g	375g
Dietary Fiber		25g	30g

2 TBS paprika

1 TBS crushed coriander

1 TBS garlic powder (not garlic salt)

1 TBS onion powder

1 TBS dill

1 TBS crushed red pepper flakes

2 TBS freshly ground black pepper

OPTIONAL

1 TBS salt (Kosher salt is best)

shaker, spice jar, or other container like a small Mason jar for finished mix

mortar with pestle OR a coffee grinder OR a food processor OR a blender

You will need some means to crush and combine the seasoning once mixed.

If you have a mortar and pestle you can prepare this seasoning in a very artisan fashion. An electric coffee grinder works great and a food processor or a blender will also suffice.

If making a **MONTREAL STEAK SEASONING:**

Start with 1 tablespoon Kosher salt. Otherwise, skip. Then:

If making a **MONTREAL STEAK RUB:**

Combine 2 tablespoons paprika, 2 tablespoons crushed black pepper, 1 tablespoon granulated garlic, 1 tablespoon granulated onion, 1 tablespoon crushed coriander, 1 tablespoon dill, and 1 tablespoon crushed red pepper flakes.

Mix all ingredients well. Briefly grind with a mortar and pestle or use a coffee grinder, a food processor, or a blender and just pulse a few times.

Store at room temperature in an airtight container away from light. Use within three months.

Yield

About ³/₄ cup

Notes

As a timesaver, I keep some pre-made spice mixes on-hand for various recipes. This one keeps well in an airtight container and I have never found a more tasty rub for red meat dishes.

I really recommend leaving off the salt in this mix. When you leave out the salt, you still have a tasty and delicious seasoning and an always ready dry rub.

Referenced Recipes

Ale-Braised Corned Beef, Brussels Sprouts, & Carrots

Weekday Pot Roast

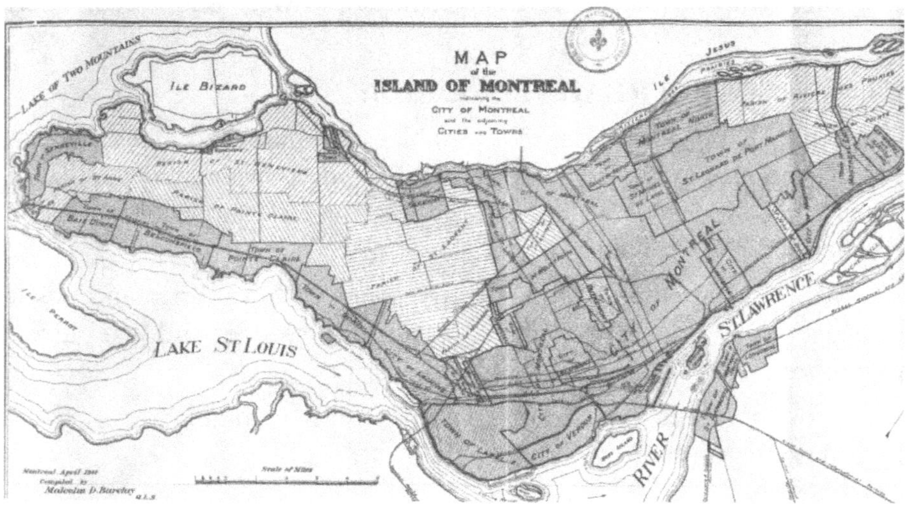

Taco Seasoning

I started making my own taco seasoning when we removed MSG from our diet. This recipe makes the equivalent of one packet of taco seasoning. You honestly will find that it has a better flavor than any seasoning packet you will find.

1 TBS chili powder

2 tsp onion powder

1 tsp garlic powder

1 tsp ground cumin

1 tsp paprika

1 tsp oregano

1 tsp sugar

½ tsp salt (Kosher or sea salt is best)

Nutrition Facts

Serving Size: (507g)
Servings Per Container: 6

Amount Per Serving	
Calories 10	Calories from Fat 0
	% Daily Value*
Total Fat 0g	**0%**
Saturated Fat 0g	**0%**
Trans Fat 0g	
Cholesterol 0mg	**0%**
Sodium 240mg	**10%**
Total Carbohydrate 3g	**1%**
Dietary Fiber <1g	**3%**
Sugars <1g	
Protein 0g	
Vitamin A 10% •	Vitamin C 0%
Calcium 2% •	Iron 2%

* Percent Daily Values are based on a 2,000 calorie diet. Your daily values may be higher or lower depending on your calorie needs:

	Calories:	2,000	2,500
Total Fat	Less than	65g	80g
Sat Fat	Less than	20g	25g
Cholesterol	Less than	300mg	300mg
Sodium	Less than	2,400mg	2,400mg
Total Carbohydrate		300g	375g
Dietary Fiber		25g	30g

No special preparation is needed

shaker, spice jar, or other container like a small Mason jar for finished mix

mortar with pestle OR a coffee grinder OR a food processor OR a blender

Mix all of the spices together.

About 1/4 cup

As a timesaver, I keep some pre-made spice mixes on-hand for various recipes. This one keeps well in an airtight container and I have never found a more tasty rub for red meat dishes.

I personally find the sugar in the recipe makes the spice blend too sweet, so I usually leave it out.

Referenced Recipes

Wonderful White Chicken Chili with Hominy

Shredded Chicken Nachos

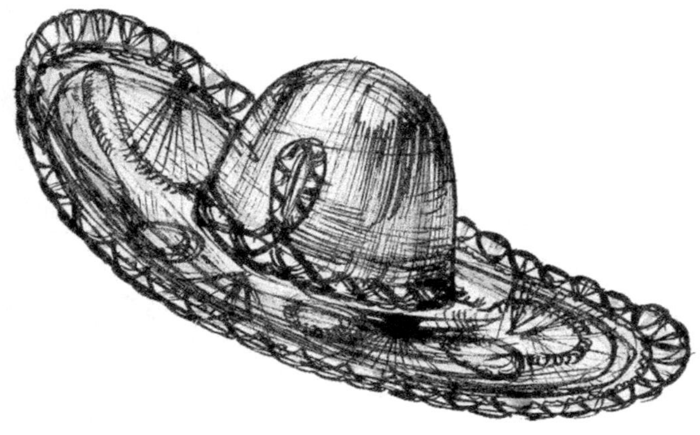

Red Meat Marinade

On "low" red meat cuts like plate, flank, skirt, shank, and even some rounds, you might want to tenderize the meat with a mallet or hammer or use a meat tenderizer that punctures the meat with dozens of sharp needles, then place it in a really good marinate to baste and soak for a day or two prior to cooking.

The marinade will further tenderize and deeply infuse the otherwise often plain cuts with delightful and unique flavor.

1/3 cup gluten-free soy sauce (Tamari or fermented soy sauce strongly preferred)

3 TBS dried basil

1 1/2 TBS dried parsley flakes

1 1/2 TBS garlic powder

1/2 cup extra virgin olive oil

1/3 cup fresh lemon juice

1/4 cup Worcestershire sauce

1 tsp minced garlic

1 tsp fresh ground white pepper

Optional:

1/4 tsp your favorite hot pepper sauce

Nutrition Facts

Serving Size: (50g)
Servings Per Container: 8

Amount Per Serving	
Calories 150	Calories from Fat 130
	% Daily Value*
Total Fat 14g	**22%**
Saturated Fat 2g	**10%**
Trans Fat 0g	
Cholesterol 0mg	**0%**
Sodium 850mg	**35%**
Total Carbohydrate 5g	**2%**
Dietary Fiber <1g	**3%**
Sugars 1g	
Protein 2g	
Vitamin A 0% •	Vitamin C 10%
Calcium 4% •	Iron 10%

* Percent Daily Values are based on a 2,000 calorie diet. Your daily values may be higher or lower depending on your calorie needs:

	Calories:	2,000	2,500
Total Fat	Less than	65g	80g
Sat Fat	Less than	20g	25g
Cholesterol	Less than	300mg	300mg
Sodium	Less than	2,400mg	2,400mg
Total Carbohydrate		300g	375g
Dietary Fiber		25g	30g

food processor OR a blender

Airtight container to store the marinating meat

No special preparation is needed

Place the minced garlic, soy sauce, extra virgin olive oil, lemon juice, Worcestershire sauce, garlic powder, basil, parsley, and white pepper in a food processor or blender. Add your favorite hot pepper sauce if desired.

In a food processor pulse several times. In a blender, blend on high speed for 30 seconds until thoroughly mixed.

Pour marinade over desired type of meat. Cover, and refrigerate for at least 8 hours and up to 2 days.

Cook meat as desired.

1 3/4 cup

If you don't abstain, you can add 1/2 cup of dry red wine to this marinate when intended for red meats and 1/2 cup of dry white wine when marinating any kind of bird.

I prefer to prepare this in my blender though I have done it both ways. From a blender, it pours easier when mixed and seems like an easier cleanup afterward.

Hallee's Homemade Organic Ketchup

Ketchup, Catsup—however you spell it, this is an incredibly flavorful condiment. I will forever use it for our homemade catsup (or ketchup, as my spell check prefers!).

It is the perfect base for homemade sauces, like Kelly's BBQ Sauce. It's easy, perfectly flavored, and keeps well.

If you're set on making your own steak sauce, this is also the recipe you will need! See the optional ingredients and NOTES section for details.

Nutrition Facts

Serving Size: 1 TBS (31g)
Servings Per Container: 320

Amount Per Serving	
Calories 10	Calories from Fat 0
	% Daily Value*
Total Fat 0g	**0%**
Saturated Fat 0g	**0%**
Trans Fat 0g	
Cholesterol 0mg	**0%**
Sodium 45mg	**2%**
Total Carbohydrate 2g	**1%**
Dietary Fiber 0g	**0%**
Sugars 2g	
Protein 0g	
Vitamin A 4% •	Vitamin C 8%
Calcium 0% •	Iron 0%

* Percent Daily Values are based on a 2,000 calorie diet. Your daily values may be higher or lower depending on your calorie needs:

	Calories:	2,000	2,500
Total Fat	Less than	65g	80g
Sat Fat	Less than	20g	25g
Cholesterol	Less than	300mg	300mg
Sodium	Less than	2,400mg	2,400mg
Total Carbohydrate		300g	375g
Dietary Fiber		25g	30g

large stock pot (or sauce pan) with lid
ladle
sharp knife/cutting board
measuring cups/spoons
mesh strainer or food mill
water bath canner
mason jars/lids
canning funnel for ladling sauce into jars
cheesecloth or muslin for a spice bag, string to tie bag
miniature grater or zester for the nutmeg

12 to 13 pounds of garden fresh ripe tomatoes (about 8 quarts)

10 medium apples

10 medium onions

3/4 cup brown sugar, packed

2 inch stick cinnamon

1 TBS paprika

1 TBS whole allspice

1 TBS mace

1 TBS black peppercorns

1/2 tsp dry mustard

2 long red peppers

2 cups apple cider vinegar

1 whole nutmeg

2 TBS Kosher or pickling salt

1 TBS whole celery seed

1 TBS cloves

1 clove garlic

2 small bay leaves

OPTIONAL:

1/2 cup dark raisins (see NOTES)

3/4 cup apple cider vinegar

Wash tomatoes and cut into small pieces.

Peel, core, and slice apples.

Slice onions.

Grate the nutmeg.

Chop the garlic.

Remove seeds and membranes of peppers (you may want to wear rubber gloves when handling peppers and remember not to rub your eyes)

Tie in cheesecloth or muslin bag: allspice, celery seed, cloves, mace, and peppercorns.

Directions

Simmer tomatoes, onions, peppers, and apples in large stock pot until soft.

Strain through a mesh strainer or food mill and return to the pot.

Add the spice bag, paprika, cinnamon, nutmeg, dry mustard, garlic, and bay leaves.

Boil rapidly without scorching, stirring often, about 1 1/2 hours or until thick and reduced to half.

In the meantime, bring water in your water bath canner to a boil, and sterilize your jars and lids in the boiling water, boiling for 20 minutes. Remove just prior to filling with the sauce so that the jars are hot when you fill them.

Remove spice bag and cinnamon.

Add vinegar and salt.

Simmer and adjust salt to taste. Boil 10 minutes longer until thick.

Wash your hands thoroughly. Carefully ladle into sterilized hot jars. Wipe the rims with a clean towel or clean paper towels. Seal. Place in the water bath canner and boil for 20 minutes. Remove. When cool, check to make sure all lids have sealed properly before storing.

About 5 to 6 quarts

This recipe makes a lot of Ketchup! But it also sizes well. Cut the ingredients exactly in half or by a quarter to evenly yield less product.

Try this! Reconstitute $^{1}/_{2}$ cup dark raisins in $^{3}/_{4}$ cup apple cider vinegar. The ideal way to do this is to combine them in a small crock pot and cook on low for 6 to 8 hours. Once the raisins are reconstituted, blend them into a raisin paste in a blender or foor processor. Add this raisin paste to the remainder of 1 quart of this Ketchup recipe and mix very well before canning. Congratulations! You just made "traditional steak sauce" with the most rich body and flavor you can imagine.

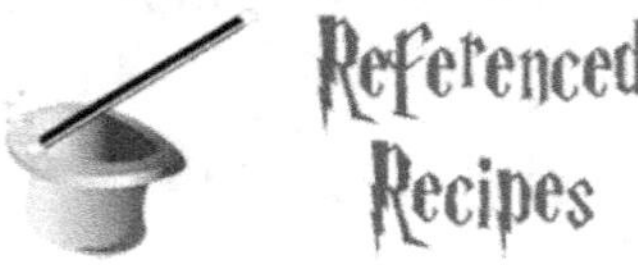

Wonderful White Chicken Chili With Hominy

Root Beer Barbecued Beef Sandwiches

Ambrosial Picnic-Perfect Baked Beans

Kelly The Kitchenkop's Incredible Organic BBQ Sauce

Kelly Moeggenborg a.k.a. Kelly the Kitchen Kop has been a "politically incorrect" voice for Real Food in the spirit of the Weston A. Price foundation since launching her popular website in 2008.

Kelly's recipe for homemade barbecue sauce is absolutely the best, hands down, that I have ever tried. I have never had any store-bought or restaurant barbecue sauce come even close to beating it. It's easy, perfectly flavored, and keeps well.

Visit her amazing website for even more Real Food ideas.

1/4 cup honey (pure, raw, local honey is always best) or brown sugar

24 oz (1 standard size bottle) organic ketchup (or Hallee's Homemade Organic Ketchupⓘ)

3 TBS gluten-free soy sauce (Tamari or fermented soy sauce strongly preferred)

2 TBS raw apple cider vinegar

2 TBS stone ground mustard (not Dijon)

Juice from 2 organic lemons

1/2 tsp onion powder

1/2 tsp paprika

1/4 tsp Kosher or sea salt—do not use iodized salt!

OPTIONAL:

about 1/4 cup to 1/2 cup purple raisins (see NOTES)

Use a really big mixing bowl. A stand mixer makes short work of this recipe.

Use glass jars to store the leftover sauce if possible. Plastic generally does not keep the sauce well since it is porous.

This makes a lot of sauce, you may want to halve the recipe. Mix it up well, do lots of taste testing and play around with it until you like it.

Nutrition Facts

Serving Size: 1 TBS (488g)
Servings Per Container: 20

Amount Per Serving	
Calories 70	Calories from Fat 0
	% Daily Value*
Total Fat 0g	**0%**
Saturated Fat 0g	**0%**
Trans Fat 0g	
Cholesterol 0mg	**0%**
Sodium 500mg	**21%**
Total Carbohydrate 18g	**6%**
Dietary Fiber 0g	**0%**
Sugars 14g	
Protein 1g	

Vitamin A 8%	•	Vitamin C 6%
Calcium 2%	•	Iron 2%

* Percent Daily Values are based on a 2,000 calorie diet. Your daily values may be higher or lower depending on your calorie needs:

	Calories:	2,000	2,500
Total Fat	Less than	65g	80g
Sat Fat	Less than	20g	25g
Cholesterol	Less than	300mg	300mg
Sodium	Less than	2,400mg	2,400mg
Total Carbohydrate		300g	375g
Dietary Fiber		25g	30g

Mix all the ingredients and taste. Add small amounts of whatever is needed until the taste suits you.

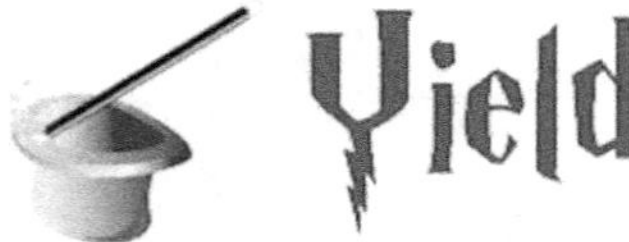

About 30 liquid ounces.

Root Beer Barbecued Beef Sandwiches

This is great on hot-wings. It's perfect for any barbecue flavor dish.

Try this! Reconstitute about $1/4$ cup to $1/2$ cup raisins in some of the vinegar. Once they are reconstituted, blend into a raisin paste and add to this recipe. This will give the sauce a much more "traditional steak sauce" type flavor and add some rich body to the sauce.

Enticing Enchilada Sauce

This sauce is so easy to make that there's absolutely no reason to buy canned or jarred. One of my children will pour this sauce on top of anything taco flavored. I think he would eat it with a spoon if I gave him a bowl-full.

2 cups Homemade Vegetable Broth🛈 (See NOTES)
3 TBS flour (I use fresh ground soft white wheat)
1 tsp white vinegar (you can use apple cider)
3 TBS extra virgin olive oil
1 TBS chili powder
1 tsp ground cumin
½ tsp garlic powder
¼ tsp dried oregano
2 TBS tomato paste
¼ tsp salt (Kosher or sea salt is best)
Freshly ground black pepper, to taste

Measuring cups/spoons
Small bowl
Skillet
Whisk

Nutrition Facts
Serving Size: (74g)
Servings Per Container: 8

Amount Per Serving	
Calories 70	Calories from Fat 50
	% Daily Value*
Total Fat 5g	**8%**
Saturated Fat 1g	**5%**
Trans Fat 0g	
Cholesterol 0mg	**0%**
Sodium 250mg	**10%**
Total Carbohydrate 5g	**2%**
Dietary Fiber <1g	**3%**
Sugars 1g	
Protein 1g	
Vitamin A 10% •	Vitamin C 2%
Calcium 0% •	Iron 2%

* Percent Daily Values are based on a 2,000 calorie diet. Your daily values may be higher or lower depending on your calorie needs:

	Calories:	2,000	2,500
Total Fat	Less than	65g	80g
Sat Fat	Less than	20g	25g
Cholesterol	Less than	300mg	300mg
Sodium	Less than	2,400mg	2,400mg
Total Carbohydrate		300g	375g
Dietary Fiber		25g	30g

This is going to come together fast. Measure all of your flour and spices and combine them in a small bowl.

Heat the olive oil in the skillet over medium heat until hot. Using the whisk, whisk in the flour and spice mixture. Cook until bubbly. Whisk in the tomato paste. Cook until bubbly (whisking the whole time). Gradually whisk in the vegetable broth.

Increase the heat to medium-high and bring up to a simmer. Cook, stirring regularly, for about 5 minutes or until mixture thickens. Remove from heat. Stir in vinegar.

2 cups

Layered Enchilada Dinner

ⓘ I've included recipes for beef broth and bird broth in this cookbook. To make your own homeade vegetable broth, follow either recipe and just leave out the meat and bones and up the amount of vegetables. If you don't have a good homemade vegetable broth on hand, use an organic (no MSG) broth with low to no salt.

Awesome Alfredo Sauce

This is rich and creamy with a kick of garlic and the tang of Parmigiano Reggiano (Parmesan) cheese. You'll never again want to open a pre-made jar after making this incredibly easy recipe.

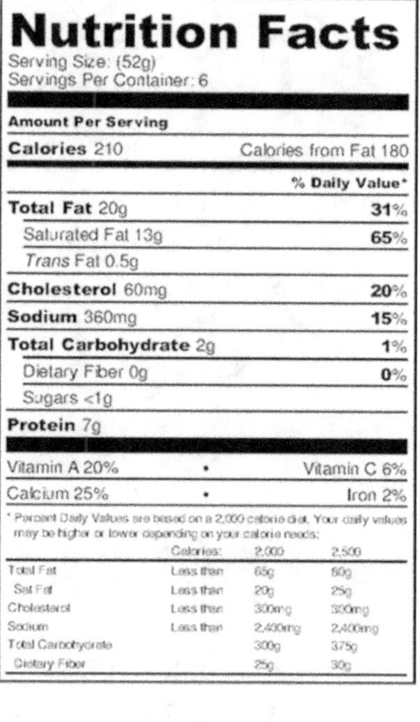

Nutrition Facts

Serving Size: (52g)
Servings Per Container: 6

Amount Per Serving	
Calories 210	Calories from Fat 180
	% Daily Value*
Total Fat 20g	**31%**
Saturated Fat 13g	**65%**
Trans Fat 0.5g	
Cholesterol 60mg	**20%**
Sodium 360mg	**15%**
Total Carbohydrate 2g	**1%**
Dietary Fiber 0g	**0%**
Sugars <1g	
Protein 7g	
Vitamin A 20% •	Vitamin C 6%
Calcium 25% •	Iron 2%

* Percent Daily Values are based on a 2,000 calorie diet. Your daily values may be higher or lower depending on your calorie needs:

	Calories:	2,000	2,500
Total Fat	Less than	65g	80g
Sat Fat	Less than	20g	25g
Cholesterol	Less than	300mg	300mg
Sodium	Less than	2,400mg	2,400mg
Total Carbohydrate		300g	375g
Dietary Fiber		25g	30g

1 1/2 cups grated Parmigiano Reggiano (Parmesan) cheese (don't use the green cannister—grate your own)

1 cup heavy whipping cream

1/4 cup unsalted butter

1 clove garlic, crushed

1/4 cup chopped fresh parsley

1/4 tsp salt (Kosher or sea salt is best)

1/4 tsp fresh ground black pepper

Measuring cups/spoons

Cheese grater

Sharp knife/cutting board

Sauce pan

Whisk

Crush the garlic

Grate the cheese

Chop the parsley

Melt the butter in the saucepan over medium low heat. Stir in the cream and let cook for 5 minutes. Stir in the garlic and Parmigiano Reggiano (Parmesan) cheese and whisk until cheese is melted. Heat through. Stir in parsley.

2 cups

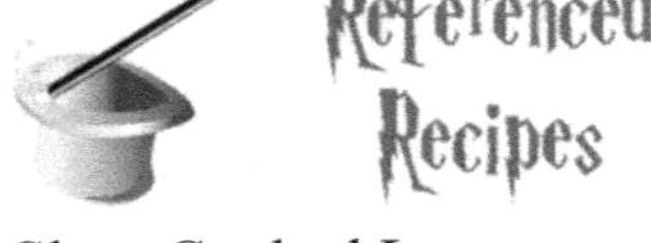

Slow-Cooked Lasagna

You can add some cooked chicken or salmon to this sauce and serve it over cooked pasta for an amazing meal.

If you use salted butter, make sure you taste it before adding any salt. Every little bit of salt will be tasted in this simple recipe.

You can use Romano cheese for a stronger flavor.

"Can-Do" No Cans Cream of Mushroom Soup

I don't know why it took me so long to start making my own cream of mushroom soup. I use it in many different casserole dishes. I was out of the canned soup one day while making a family favorite recipe and decided, rather than run to the store, to make my own. The recipe came out perfectly—the flavors were spot-on.

Using fresh mushrooms and your own broth, you can make it without using a can-opener even once.

2 cups broth (chicken, turkey, or vegetable broth, I use Hallee's Heavenly Homemade Bird Broth ⓘ)

3 TBS unsalted butter (if using fresh mushrooms, add 1 more TBS butter)

2 TBS flour (I used fresh ground whole wheat)

1 cup chopped mushrooms (fresh or 2 4-ounce cans)

1 1/2 cups whole milk

1/2 cup heavy cream

1 tsp grated onion

1 tsp paprika

1 tsp Kosher or sea salt

1/8 tsp fresh ground black pepper

Nutrition Facts

Serving Size: (107g)
Servings Per Container: 6

Amount Per Serving	
Calories 170	Calories from Fat 130
	% Daily Value*
Total Fat 14g	**22%**
Saturated Fat 9g	**45%**
Trans Fat 0g	
Cholesterol 50mg	**17%**
Sodium 600mg	**25%**
Total Carbohydrate 6g	**2%**
Dietary Fiber 0g	**0%**
Sugars 4g	
Protein 3g	
Vitamin A 15% •	Vitamin C 0%
Calcium 8% •	Iron 2%

* Percent Daily Values are based on a 2,000 calorie diet. Your daily values may be higher or lower depending on your calorie needs:

	Calories:	2,000	2,500
Total Fat	Less than	65g	80g
Sat Fat	Less than	20g	25g
Cholesterol	Less than	300mg	300mg
Sodium	Less than	2,400mg	2,400mg
Total Carbohydrate		300g	375g
Dietary Fiber		25g	30g

heavy saucepan

food processor or sharp knife/cutting board

cheese grater

wooden spoon/whisk

measuring cups/spoon

If you're using fresh mushrooms, chop them. In a skillet, sauté them in 1 TBS butter over medium heat until soft.

If you're using canned mushrooms, drain them and process them in the food processor.

Grate the onion

Melt butter over medium heat in saucepan. Whisk in the flour, salt, and pepper.

When it gets bubbly, whisk in the milk, cream, and broth.

Bring to a boil. Boil for 1 minute.

Stir in mushrooms and onion. Stir in paprika.

Cook, stirring regularly, for 10 minutes.

Remove from heat.

6 Servings

This is listed as Kosher and vegetarian. Please note that is only the case when vegetable broth is used.

Use this recipe as a single can of "condensed cream of mushroom soup" in your favorite recipe. I often substitute the milk with non-diluted evaporated milk when I'm making it for the purpose of a recipe.

Referenced Recipes

Wonderful White Chicken Chili with Hominy

Spinach, Chicken, & Wild Rice Soup

Hallee's Herbed Turkey Breast

Layered Enchilada Dinner

Condensed Tomato Soup

Here is the ingredient list of a popular, non-organic condensed tomato soup:

Tomato Puree (Water, Tomato Paste), High Fructose Corn Syrup, Wheat Flour, Water, Contains Less Than 2% Of: Salt, Potassium Chloride, Flavoring, Citric Acid, Lower Sodium Natural Sea Salt, Ascorbic Acid (Vitamin C), Monopotassium Phosphate.

It is much better to make your own. To serve, add 1 cup of water, vegetable broth, or milk to this recipe. Or, you can use it like it is for recipes that call for condensed tomato soup.

15 ounces tomato sauce

6 ounces tomato paste

1 cup vegetable broth

1/2 teaspoon garlic salt

2 1/2 tablespoons honey

1/4 teaspoon salt, plus more to taste

Whisk

Small bowl / saucepan

Measuring cups and spoons

Nutrition Facts

Serving Size: (221g)
Servings Per Container: 4

Amount Per Serving	
Calories 100	Calories from Fat 0
	% Daily Value*
Total Fat 0g	**0%**
Saturated Fat 0g	**0%**
Trans Fat 0g	
Cholesterol 0mg	**0%**
Sodium 860mg	**36%**
Total Carbohydrate 26g	**9%**
Dietary Fiber 3g	**12%**
Sugars 21g	
Protein 3g	
Vitamin A 25% •	Vitamin C 30%
Calcium 4% •	Iron 15%

* Percent Daily Values are based on a 2,000 calorie diet. Your daily values may be higher or lower depending on your calorie needs:

	Calories:	2,000	2,500
Total Fat	Less than	65g	80g
Sat Fat	Less than	20g	25g
Cholesterol	Less than	300mg	300mg
Sodium	Less than	2,400mg	2,400mg
Total Carbohydrate		300g	375g
Dietary Fiber		25g	30g

Directions

Mix together with a whisk.

Can be stored in the refrigerator for 4 days in an airtight container, or stored in the freezer for several weeks.

Yield

4 servings

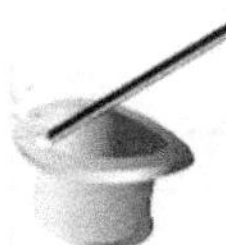

Notes

Add a cup of milk and serve with grilled cheese sandwiches for the best rainy-day comfort meal ever.

Referenced Recipes

Brown Sugar Spice Cake

No Cans Cream of Celery Soup

Cream of celery soup is often a go-to in casserole recipes. It's a favorite of mine. It's simple to make your own and allows you full control of the ingredients.

1/3 cup flour (I use fresh ground, soft white wheat)

3/4 cups Hallee's Heavenly Homemade Bird Broth ⓘ

2 cups very finely chopped celery (about 5 large stalks)

1 small yellow onion, finely chopped (about 1 cup)

1 clove garlic, minced

3/4 cups half-and-half

1/4 cup unsalted butter

1 tsp salt (Kosher or sea salt is best)

1/4 tsp freshly ground pepper

Nutrition Facts

Serving Size: (909g)
Servings Per Container: 4

Amount Per Serving	
Calories 220	Calories from Fat 160
	% Daily Value*
Total Fat 17g	**26%**
Saturated Fat 11g	**55%**
Trans Fat 0.5g	
Cholesterol 50mg	**17%**
Sodium 680mg	**28%**
Total Carbohydrate 13g	**4%**
Dietary Fiber 1g	**4%**
Sugars 4g	
Protein 4g	
Vitamin A 15% •	Vitamin C 6%
Calcium 8% •	Iron 4%

* Percent Daily Values are based on a 2,000 calorie diet. Your daily values may be higher or lower depending on your calorie needs:

	Calories:	2,000	2,500
Total Fat	Less than	65g	80g
Sat Fat	Less than	20g	25g
Cholesterol	Less than	300mg	300mg
Sodium	Less than	2,400mg	2,400mg
Total Carbohydrate		300g	375g
Dietary Fiber		25g	30g

Wisk

Small bowl / saucepan

Measuring cups and spoons

In a skillet over medium heat, melt butter. Stir in the yellow onion, 2 cups celery, and 1 clove minced garlic. Cook and stir for about 5 minutes, or until onion is translucent.

Using the whisk, stir in the flour, salt, and pepper. Stir in the Hallee's Heavenly Homemade Bird Broth ⓘ and half-and-half. Bring to a low boil, then reduce heat to low, simmering for 15 minutes.

4 servings

ⓘ If you don't have a good homemade broth on hand, be sure to use a good organic broth with low or no salt.

ⓘ You can use vegetable broth instead of bird broth if you'd like.

Referenced Recipes

Fabulous Fish Stew

Hallee's Savory Stocky Crock Pot Beef Broth

The health benefits of bone stocks and broths are really not in question among whole food, real food enthusiasts. Making your own stocks and broths ensures that you control all of the ingredients which is a very good thing since store-bought stocks and broths often contain MSG and other industrial grade chemicals.

Nutrition Facts

Serving Size: (242g)
Servings Per Container: 12

Amount Per Serving	
Calories 140	Calories from Fat 40
	% Daily Value*
Total Fat 4.5g	**7%**
Saturated Fat 2g	**10%**
Trans Fat 0g	
Cholesterol 40mg	**13%**
Sodium 115mg	**5%**
Total Carbohydrate 4g	**1%**
Dietary Fiber <1g	**3%**
Sugars 1g	
Protein 14g	

Vitamin A 50%	•	Vitamin C 4%
Calcium 2%	•	Iron 10%

* Percent Daily Values are based on a 2,000 calorie diet. Your daily values may be higher or lower depending on your calorie needs:

	Calories:	2,000	2,500
Total Fat	Less than	65g	80g
Sat Fat	Less than	20g	25g
Cholesterol	Less than	300mg	300mg
Sodium	Less than	2,400mg	2,400mg
Total Carbohydrate		300g	375g
Dietary Fiber		25g	30g

The vegetables needed to make a good stock or broth need not be absolutely fresh. In fact, making stocks regularly is a great way to clean out the pantry shelves and crisper drawers to use up all your supplies without waste. Slightly wilted celery or carrots and somewhat dry onions or garlic cloves, or those barely wrinkled potatoes that are just starting to sprout may not be something you would proudly serve up at a Sunday potluck—but all of them make a perfectly fine stock provided they aren't actually spoiled.

Make this beef broth and freeze it in 1 cup increments. I use breast milk storage bagsⓘ to freeze my broth. They are sterile, freezer safe, the perfect size, and have measurement marks right on them like a measuring cup. Whenever you need beef broth or beef stock, just pull it out of the freezer and defrost it.

6 cups

For a stock, you will only need:

1 large beef soup bone -AND/OR- 1 pound beef trimmings (whatever is on hand)

6 cups filtered water

1 TBS gluten-free soy sauce (Tamari or fermented soy sauce strongly preferred)

3 carrots

2 celery ribs (with leaves)

1 small onion

4 medium fresh white mushrooms

2 small bay leaves

1 tsp dried parsley

1/2 tsp garlic powder

1/4 tsp paprika

1 pinch ground thyme

2 cups dry red wineⓘ

If you are making a broth, add:

salt and pepper to taste (Kosher or sea salt is best/fresh ground pepper is best) and other herbs and seasonings of choice to taste

crock pot (or saucepan with lid)

sharp knife/cutting board

measuring cups/spoons

mesh strainer

Peel then roughly chop the carrots.

Roughly chop the celery.

Quarter the onion

Halve the mushrooms

Place all of the ingredients in crock pot and cook on low for 6 hours, skimming occasionally.

-OR-

Place all of the ingredients in the saucepan. Bring to a boil. Reduce heat. Cover and simmer on low for several hours, skimming occasionally.

Strain the solids from the stock with the mesh strainer.

Freeze.

If making a stock, do not salt at all. If making a broth, each time you skim, sample the liquid and add salt, pepper, and any other herbs and spices you like to taste. Remember that Kosher or sea salt is best. Iodized salt can add too much iodine to the mixture. Fresh ground pepper is always best.

To make a hearty vegetable stock or broth, just leave out the meat and bone and up the amount and variety of vegetables. The process is identical.

ⓘ For information about freezing in breast milk bags, check out this link:

http://www.halleethehomemaker.com/2010/05/the-perfect-solution-for-freezing-broth/

ⓘ If you abstain from alcohol even in cooking, you can substitute a 100% pure grape juice (ensure there is no apple juice in it) and one teaspoon of distilled vinegar to approximate the same flavor and properties while cooking.

Referenced Recipes

Philly Cheese Steak Sandwiches

Corned Beef & Cabbage

Weekday Pot Roast

Slow Cooker Cuban Braised Beef & Peppers

Beef & Barley Stew

Spiced Braised Beef with Sweet Potatoes

Beef with Apples & Sweet Potatoes

Chipotle Chili

Hallee's Hearty Healthy Beef Stew

Tuscan Lentil Stew

Hallee's Heavenly Homemade Crock Pot Bird Broth

Are you in that place where you never know what to do with the leftover bird carcass after a holiday meal? Hearty bone stocks and bone broths are the perfect solution. You can also freeze your chicken, duck, goose, squab, or other game bird carcasses until you have enough on hand to make a broth.

The vegetables need not be absolutely fresh. In fact, making stocks regularly is a great way to clean out the pantry shelves and crisper drawers to use up all your supplies without waste. Slightly wilted celery or carrots and somewhat dry onions or garlic cloves, or those barely wrinkled potatoes that are just starting to sprout may not be something you would proudly serve up at a Sunday potluck—but all of them make a perfectly fine stock provided they aren't actually spoiled.

Make stock or broth and freeze it in 1-cup increments. I use breast milk storage bagsⓘ to freeze my broth. They are sterile, freezer safe, the perfect size, and have measurement marks right on them like a measuring cup. Then, when you need a cup of stock or broth, just pull it out of the freezer, defrost, and use it.

crock pot (or saucepan with lid)
sharp knife/cutting board
measuring cups/spoons
mesh strainer

Peel then roughly chop the carrots.
Roughly chop the celery.
Quarter the onion
Halve the garlic

For a stock, you will only need:

1 turkey carcass, (or a few smaller bird carcasses) need not be intact

skin and any remaining giblets (in other words, the bones, meat bits, skin, any part of the bird you don't care to eat)

2 cups dry white wine (see NOTES for possible substitution)

6 cloves garlic

4 stalks of celery, with leaves

4 carrots

3 onions

1 TBS whole black peppercorns

$^1/_2$ tsp basil

$^1/_2$ tsp parsley

water to cover

If you are making a broth, add:

3 tsp each of Kosher or sea salt

1 tsp fresh ground black pepper

Add any other herbs, spices, or seasonings of your choice to taste.

Nutrition Facts

Serving Size: (194g)
Servings Per Container: 24

Amount Per Serving	
Calories 70	Calories from Fat 20
	% Daily Value*
Total Fat 2g	**3%**
Saturated Fat 0.5g	**3%**
Trans Fat 0g	
Cholesterol 25mg	**8%**
Sodium 40mg	**2%**
Total Carbohydrate 3g	**1%**
Dietary Fiber <1g	**3%**
Sugars 1g	
Protein 6g	

Vitamin A 35%	•	Vitamin C 2%
Calcium 2%	•	Iron 2%

* Percent Daily Values are based on a 2,000 calorie diet. Your daily values may be higher or lower depending on your calorie needs:

	Calories:	2,000	2,500
Total Fat	Less than	65g	80g
Sat Fat	Less than	20g	25g
Cholesterol	Less than	300mg	300mg
Sodium	Less than	2,400mg	2,400mg
Total Carbohydrate		300g	375g
Dietary Fiber		25g	30g

Place all of the ingredients in the crock pot and cook on low for 6 hours. -OR-

Place all of the ingredients in the saucepan. Bring to a boil. Cover and simmer on low for several hours.

Strain the broth with the mesh strainer.

Freeze.

Use in any recipe that calls for turkey broth or turkey stock.

Yield

6 quarts

Notes

If you are making a broth, each time you skim, sample the liquid and add salt, pepper, and any other herbs and spices you like to taste. Fresh ground pepper is always best. Kosher or sea salt is best. Iodized salt can add too much iodine to the mixture.

To make a hearty vegetable stock or broth, just leave out the bird and up the amount and variety of vegetables. The process is identical.

ⓘ For information about freezing in breast milk bags, check out this link:

http://www.halleethehomemaker.com/2010/05/the-perfect-solution-for-freezing-broth/

ⓘ If you abstain from alcohol even in cooking, you can substitute a 100% pure grape juice (ensure there is no apple juice in it) and one teaspoon of distilled vinegar to approximate the same flavor and properties while cooking.

Referenced Recipes

How to Break Down a Chicken
Chicken Tortellini Vegetable Stew
Orange Chicken with Green Onions & Walnuts
Spinach, Chicken, & Wild Rice Soup
Chicken & Ramen Noodle Soup
Southwestern Chicken & White Bean Soup
Buffalo Chicken Chili
Red & White Turkey Chili
Slow-Simmered Chicken Rice Soup
Beef Bratwurst with Sauerkraut
Red Beans Over Spanish Rice
Fabulous Fish Stew
Non-Refried "Refried" Beans Black & Pinto Bean Dip
Tuscan Lentil Stew
Roasted Tomato, Red Pepper, & Bread Soup
Easy Corn Chowder

Hallee's Revitalizing Roast Beef Gravy

A roast beef dinner is not complete without roast beef gravy. I pour it over everything on my plate. I think the gravy is the best part of the meal.

Nutrition Facts

Serving Size: (71g)
Servings Per Container: 8

Amount Per Serving	
Calories 90	Calories from Fat 60
	% Daily Value*
Total Fat 7g	**11%**
Saturated Fat 3g	**15%**
Trans Fat 0g	
Cholesterol 5mg	**2%**
Sodium 300mg	**13%**
Total Carbohydrate 4g	**1%**
Dietary Fiber 0g	**0%**
Sugars 0g	
Protein 2g	

Vitamin A 0% • Vitamin C 0%
Calcium 0% • Iron 2%

* Percent Daily Values are based on a 2,000 calorie diet. Your daily values may be higher or lower depending on your calorie needs:

	Calories:	2,000	2,500
Total Fat	Less than	65g	80g
Sat Fat	Less than	20g	25g
Cholesterol	Less than	300mg	300mg
Sodium	Less than	2,400mg	2,400mg
Total Carbohydrate		300g	375g
Dietary Fiber		25g	30g

whisk

measuring cups

jar (like a Mason type jar) with lid

drippings; (all the remnants in the pan or skillet after cooking any kind of beef)

beef stock (about 1 to almost 2 cups—you want to end up with a total of 2 cups when you combine the stock with the drippings)

1/2 cup flour (I use fresh ground soft white wheat)

salt to taste (Kosher or sea salt is best)

fresh ground black pepper to taste

8 servings

Meatball Stew

Meatball & Gravy Sandwiches

Directions

While this gravy can be made purely with beef broth, it is best when you reserve the drippings after preparing a roast beef or searing a steak or meatballs or frying up a batch of beef bacon. So, if necessary, prepare the beef and reserve the drippings to prepare to make this gravy.

If your roasting pan can be used to cook on the top of the stove, you can use it. Otherwise, you need to transfer your drippings to a sauce pan. Combine broth and drippings until you have about 1 cup in the pan.

Place the pan on the stove over medium high heat and bring the juices and drippings in the pan to a boil.

Put the flour and about a cup of beef broth into a jar, cover, and shake until smooth.

TIP: A sports cup with a blender ball works amazingly well for this task.

Using the whisk, whisk the flour mixture into the drippings in the pan. Add any remaining broth until there are about two cups in the pan. Return to a boil. Boil and whisk for 2 minutes.

Salt and pepper to taste.

Notes

You may need to add or take out some broth, depending on how much liquid is in the drippings in the pan. You want a total of 2 cups of liquid.

Hallee's Toothsome Traditional Turkey Gravy

Turkey gravy is so vital to a turkey dinner. It is the final touch, and what could make or break the meal. It's also amazing poured over open faced turkey sandwiches. Don't be afraid of the seasonings—let the gravy be wonderful and full of flavor.

Ingredients

2 cups plus 1/2 cup Hallee's Heavenly Homemade Bird Broth ⓘ, divided (See NOTES for variations)

1/2 to 2 tsp dried parsley

1/2 to 1 tsp ground sage

1/4 to 1/2 tsp rosemary (to taste)

1/4 to 1/2 tsp thyme (to taste)

OR

substitute Hallee's Inviting Italian Seasoning ⓘ for the parsley, sage, rosemary, and thyme

1/4 to 1/2 tsp garlic powder (NOT garlic salt) (to taste)

1/4 to 1/2 tsp onion powder (to taste)

1/2 tsp fresh ground black pepper

Kosher or sea salt to taste

3 TBS organic cornstarch

Nutrition Facts

Serving Size: (80g)
Servings Per Container: 8

Amount Per Serving	
Calories 45	Calories from Fat 10
	% Daily Value*
Total Fat 1g	**2%**
Saturated Fat 0g	**0%**
Trans Fat 0g	
Cholesterol <5mg	**1%**
Sodium 250mg	**10%**
Total Carbohydrate 7g	**2%**
Dietary Fiber 0g	**0%**
Sugars 1g	
Protein 2g	
Vitamin A 0% •	Vitamin C 0%
Calcium 0% •	Iron 2%

* Percent Daily Values are based on a 2,000 calorie diet. Your daily values may be higher or lower depending on your calorie needs:

	Calories:	2,000	2,500
Total Fat	Less than	65g	80g
Sat Fat	Less than	20g	25g
Cholesterol	Less than	300mg	300mg
Sodium	Less than	2,400mg	2,400mg
Total Carbohydrate		300g	375g
Dietary Fiber		25g	30g

Preparation

No special preparation is required

saucepan or large skillet
measuring cups/spoons
small and medium bowls
whisk

Bring 2 cups of broth, pepper, sage, parsley, onion powder, and garlic powder to a boil. (Note: depending on the flavor of your broth, you may not need all of these seasonings—taste it and use your best judgment.)

In a small bowl, whisk 1/2 cup cold broth (or water) with the cornstarch until smooth.

Using a whisk, slowly pour the cornstarch mixture into the broth whisking as you pour until completely integrated.

As soon as it thickens, remove from heat (overcooking cornstarch will make it lose its thickening power.)

Salt to taste.

About 2 cups—or 8 servings

Taste as you season. So many variables make broths and gravies have different levels of seasoning. Sometimes you need more spices, sometimes you need less. Don't be wary of spicing up a bland gravy—your family will thank you for it.

ⓘ I have included the recipe for Hallee's Heavenly Homemade Bird Broth in this cookbook. If you don't have stock on hand, but you are roasting a bird, you can use the juices you recover from your roasting bird in place of a broth. If neither is an option, use a good organic stock with low or no salt.

ⓘ You can find Hallee the Homemaker's instructions on how to roast the perfect turkey here:

http://www.halleethehomemaker.com/2010/11/roasting-the-perfect-turkey/

Hallee's Signature Crock Pot Hot Brown

Afterword

It Really Isn't Magic

Years ago, I had a neighbor with whom I used to enjoy chatting as I came home from work every day. That was the time she usually had her kids outside playing. We lived at the end of a cul-de-sac in a quiet neighborhood and had a somewhat close-knit community and we'd stand in our shared front yard and talk about our days, our kids, and matters of faith.

As late October loomed, she and I found ourselves discussing Halloween. I told her that we waffled about whether to celebrate the "holiday" and she said that they absolutely did not, in any way, celebrate, acknowledge, or otherwise have anything to do with Halloween. Because Gregg and I were so on the fence, I asked her why. She confessed that in her teens and twenties, she'd been actively part of a witch coven and engaged in the occult. She told me emphatically that there is true evil in the world, and the imagery and traditional costumes of Halloween did nothing but glorify that evil. Having experienced the darkness, she knew in her heart that it was wrong to pretend otherwise.

I've never forgotten that conversation. As I set about writing this cookbook, it has stayed in the back of my mind. Where do Christians draw the line between good, harmless fun and actual evil?

Much like the plots of the literature and entertainment mentioned in the Foreword of this book, all around us there is an unseen spiritual battle waging between good and evil. In the tenth chapter of the book of Daniel, the angel Michael talks about being detained trying to come to the prophet with a message from God, and it took other angels to rescue him from the clutches of an evil kingdom. Because we are mortal humans on this earthly plane, we simply cannot see it happening.

However, that doesn't change the fact that we are definitely part of this battle.

> Be sober, be vigilant; because your adversary the devil walks about like a roaring lion, seeking whom he may devour.
>
> 1 Peter 5:8

The fact is, there is true evil in the world, in **this** world, this earthly plane. The Bible is infinitely clear about the fact that once we become followers of Christ and believers in the One-True-Jehovah-God, we become targets for the adversary in an ongoing spiritual battle.

> Yes, and all who desire to live godly in Christ Jesus will suffer persecution.
>
> 2 Timothy 3:12

We need to be diligent and faithful to God, protecting ourselves in word and prayer, arming ourselves with the Word of God, so that we can withstand the attacks rained down on us by this roaring lion.

In fact, the Apostle Paul gives us everything we need in order to withstand the attacks. In Ephesians 6 he says:

Finally, my brethren, **be strong in the Lord** and in the power of His might. Put on the whole armor of God, **that you may be able to stand against the wiles of the devil. For we do not wrestle against flesh and blood, but against principalities, against powers, against the rulers of the darkness of this age, against spiritual hosts of wickedness in the heavenly places**. Therefore take up the whole armor of God, that you may be able to withstand in the evil day, and having done all, to stand.

Stand therefore, having **girded your waist with truth, having put on the breastplate of righteousness, and having shod your feet with the preparation of the gospel of peace; above all, taking the**

shield of faith with which you will be able to quench all the fiery darts of the wicked one. And take the helmet of salvation, and the sword of the Spirit, which is the word of God; praying always with all prayer and supplication in the Spirit, being watchful to this end with all perseverance and supplication for all the saints—and for me, that utterance may be given to me, that I may open my mouth boldly to make known the mystery of the gospel, for which I am an ambassador in chains; that in it I may speak boldly, as I ought to speak.

The beginning of this section says “Be strong in the Lord ... for we do not wrestle against flesh and blood but against principalities, against powers, against the rulers of the darkness of this age, against spiritual hosts of wickedness in the heavenly places...” That sounds like the plot of a fantastical story that will culminate in an amazing climax of the battle between good and evil. But, it’s not a story. It’s what is actually happening around us. **Be strong in the Lord** is the important piece of this instruction, because our power in this battle comes from a relationship with Jehovah God, Yahweh. To have a relationship with the one true God, we must go through the son, Christ Jesus, Yeshua.

Colossians 2:13-15 says: And you, being dead in your trespasses and the uncircumcision of your flesh, He has made alive together with Him, having forgiven you all trespasses, having wiped out the handwriting of requirements that was against us, which was contrary to us. And He has taken it out of the way, **having nailed it to the cross. Having disarmed principalities and powers, He made a public spectacle of them, triumphing over them in it.**

Basically, Christ disarmed these spiritual principalities and powers on the cross! Through His sacrifice, He has given us the power to triumph over evil. We just have to follow Him.

Maybe you think you don’t need the disarming power of the Son of God. Maybe you think you’re a good person and that’s “good enough” so why do you need the real supernatural protection that comes with accepting Christ? Is sin really that big of a deal? But in your heart of hearts, you feel that ache and you know there is more.

If you want to accept more, say this simple prayer.

Dear God in heaven, I come to you in the name of Jesus. I acknowledge to You that I am a sinner, and I am sorry for my sins and the life that I have lived; I need your forgiveness.

I believe that your only begotten Son Jesus Christ shed His precious blood on the cross at Calvary and died for my sins, and I am now willing to turn from my sin.

You said in Your Holy Word, Romans 10:9 that if we confess the Lord our God and believe in our hearts that God raised Jesus from the dead, we shall be saved.

Right now I confess Jesus as the Lord of my soul. With my heart, I believe that God raised Jesus from the dead. This very moment I accept Jesus Christ as my own personal Savior and according to His Word, right now I am saved.

Thank you Jesus for your unlimited grace which has saved me from my sins. I thank you Jesus that your grace never leads to license, but rather it always leads to repentance. Therefore Lord Jesus transform my life so that I may bring glory and honor to you alone and not to myself.

Thank you, Jesus, for dying for me and giving me eternal life.

Amen.

Reading and watching such entertaining fictional accounts of the battle against forces of good and evil is fun, exciting, and can lead to fantastic teachable moments for your children to help them understand the concept of the unseen battle waging around us. But, don't mistake those fictional accounts for real life. Make sure you protect yourself with the full armor of God, and let Christ lead the charge of battle for you.

Measurements and Conversions

[illegible]				
1/3 TBS	1/6 fl oz	1 tsp	5 cc	5 ml
1 TBS	1/2 fl oz	3 tsp	15 cc	15 ml
2 TBS	1 fl oz	1/8 cup	6 tsp	30 ml
1/4 cup	2 fl oz	4 TBS	12 tsp	59 ml
1/3 cup	2 2/3 fl oz	5 TBS & 1 tsp	16 tsp	79 ml
1/2 cup	4 fl oz	8 TBS	24 tsp	118 ml
2/3 cup	5 1/3 fl oz	10 TBS & 2 tsp	32 tsp	158 ml
3/4 cup	6 fl oz	12 TBS	36 tsp	177 ml
7/8 cup	7 fl oz	14 TBS	42 tsp	207 ml
1 cup	8 fl oz	1/2 pt	16 TBS	237 ml
1 pt	16 fl oz	1 pt	32 TBS	473 ml
2 cups	16 fl oz	1 pt	32 TBS	473 ml
2 pts	32 fl oz	1 qt	1/4 gal	946 ml 0.946 l
4 cups	32 fl oz	1 qt	1/4 gal	946 ml
8 pts	1 gal/ 128 fl oz	4 qts	1 gal	3785 ml 3.78 l
4 qts	1 gal/128 fl oz	8 pts	1 gal	3785 ml 3.78 l
1 l	1.057 qts			1000 ml
1 gal	qts	128 fl oz		3785 ml 3.78 l

[illegible]		
1 oz		30 g (28.35 g)
2 oz		55 g
3 oz		85 g
4 oz	1/4 lbs	125 g
8 oz	1/2 lbs	240 g
12 oz	3/4 lbs	375 g
16 oz	1 lbs	454 g
32 oz	2 lbs	907 g
1/4 lbs	4 oz	125 g
1/2 lbs	8 oz	240 g
3/4 lbs	12 oz	375 g
1 lbs	16 oz	454 g
2 lbs	32 oz	907 g
1 k	2.2 lbs/ 35.2 oz	1000 g

(DRY)	1 pt	0.551 l
	1 qt	1.101 l
	1 peck	8.81 l
	1 bushel	35.25 l

(WEIGHT)	1 oz	28.35 g
	1 lbs	453.59 g
	1 lbs	0.454 kg

(LENGTH)	1 in	25.4 ml
	1 in	2.54 cm
	1 ft	304.8 ml
	1 ft	30.48 cm
	1 yd	914.4 ml
	1 yd	91.44 cm

About Hallee

www.halleebridgeman.com

With more than half a million sales, Hallee Bridgeman is a best-selling Christian author who writes action-packed romantic suspense focusing on realistic characters who face real world problems. Her work has been described as everything from refreshing to heart-stopping exciting and edgy.

An Army brat turned Floridian, Hallee finally settled in central Kentucky with her family so that she could enjoy the beautiful changing of the seasons. She enjoys the roller-coaster ride thrills that life with a National Guard husband, a teenaged daughter, and two elementary aged sons delivers.

A prolific writer, when she's not penning novels, you will find her in the kitchen, which she considers the 'heart of the home'. Her passion for cooking spurred her to launch a whole food, real food "Parody" cookbook series. In addition to nutritious, Biblically grounded recipes, readers will find that each cookbook also confronts some controversial aspect of secular pop culture.

Hallee is a member of the Published Author Network (PAN) of the Romance Writers of America (RWA) where she serves as a long time board member in the Faith, Hope, & Love chapter. She is a member of the American Christian Fiction Writers (ACFW) and the American Christian Writers (ACW) as well as being a member of Novelists, Inc. (NINC).

Hallee loves coffee, campy action movies, and regular date nights with her husband. Above all else, she loves God with all of her heart, soul, mind, and strength; has been redeemed by the blood of

Christ; and relies on the presence of the Holy Spirit to guide her. She prays her work here on earth is a blessing to you and would love to hear from you. You can reach Hallee via email by writing to her at hallee@halleebridgeman.com.

Sign up for Hallee's monthly newsletter! When you sign up, you will get a link to download Hallee's romantic suspense novella, On The Ropes. In addition, every newsletter recipient is automatically entered into a monthly giveaway! The real prize is you will never miss updates about upcoming releases, book signings, appearances, or other events.

Newsletter Sign Up:

tinyurl.com/HalleeNews/

Author Site:

www.halleebridgeman.com/

Facebook:

www.facebook.com/pages/Hallee-Bridgeman/192799110825012

Twitter:

twitter.com/halleeb

Google+:

/plus.google.com/105383805410764959843

Goodreads:

www.goodreads.com/author/show/5815249.Hallee_Bridgeman

Homemaking Blog:

www.halleethehomemaker.com/

by Hallee Bridgeman

Find the latest information and connect with Hallee at her website:
www.halleebridgeman.com

PARODY COOKBOOKS BY HALLEE

Vol 1: Fifty Shades of Gravy, a Christian gets Saucy!
Vol 2: The Walking Bread, the Bread Will Rise
Vol 3: Iron Skillet Man, the Stark Truth about Pepper and Pots
Vol 4: Hallee Crockpotter & the Chamber of Sacred Ingredients

FICTION BOOKS BY HALLEE

The Jewel Series:
Book 1: Sapphire Ice
Book 2: Greater Than Rubies
Book 3: Emerald Fire
Book 4: Topaz Heat
Book 5: Christmas Diamond
Book 6: Christmas Star Sapphire
Book 7: Jade's Match

The Dixon Brothers Series (Coming Soon):

Book 1: Courting Calla
Book 2: Valerie's Verdict
Book 3: Alexandra's Appeal
Book 4: Daisy's Decision

The Song of Suspense Series:

Book 1: A Melody for James
Book 2: An Aria for Nick
Book 3: A Carol for Kent
Book 4: A Harmony for Steve

Standalone Suspense:

On The Ropes

Virtues and Valor series:

Book 1: Temperance's Trial
Book 2: Homeland's Hope
Book 3: Charity's Code
Book 4: A Parcel for Prudence
Book 5: Grace's Ground War
Book 6: Mission of Mercy
Book 7: Flight of Faith
Book 8: Valor's Vigil

Better known as Bethlehem of Judea, the old Hebrew name *bêth lehem*, meaning "House of Bread," is known as the birthplace of King David and, above all, of Our Lord, Yeshua, known as Jesus of Nazareth. Thus, the "House of Bread" that is Bethlehem brought forth the Bread of Life that is our Savior.

The House of Bread imprint is pleased to publish healthy nutritious information in the form of cookbooks or informational pamphlets in order to better serve our community—the human race. We publish to reach every tribe and every nation for God has made of one blood all nations of men.

We pray that you enjoyed this fun attempt to redeem a recent secular phenomenon. Mostly, we pray that you come to know the joy and peace that is in serving Our Lord and Savior who is the King of kings, Lord of lords, and the Bread of Life.

Send inquiries to:

HOUSE OF BREAD BOOKS™

an imprint of: **Olivia Kimbrell Press™**

P.O. Box 470

Fort Knox, KY 40121-0470

Or email admin@oliviakimbrellpress.com

Index

C

D

E

F

G

H

I

J

K

L

M

N

O

P

R

S

T

V

W

Z

Table of Contents

www.ingramcontent.com/pod-product-compliance
Lightning Source LLC
Chambersburg PA
CBHW071538030726
47598CB00001B/148